Data Analytics
with
Google Cloud Platform

Build Real Time Data Analytics on
Google Cloud Platform

by

Murari Ramuka

FIRST EDITION 2020

Copyright © BPB Publications, India

ISBN: 978-93-89423-631

LIMITS OF LIABILITY AND DISCLAIMER OF WARRANTY

Distributors:

BPB PUBLICATIONS
20, Ansari Road, Darya Ganj
New Delhi-110002
Ph: 23254990/23254991

DECCAN AGENCIES
4-3-329, Bank Street,
Hyderabad-500195
Ph: 24756967/24756400

MICRO MEDIA
Shop No. 5, Mahendra Chambers,
150 DN Rd. Next to Capital Cinema,
V.T. (C.S.T.) Station, MUMBAI-400 001
Ph: 22078296/22078297

BPB BOOK CENTRE
376 Old Lajpat Rai Market,
Delhi-110006
Ph: 23861747

Published by Manish Jain for BPB Publications, 20 Ansari Road, Darya Ganj, New Delhi-110002 and Printed by him at Repro India Ltd, Mumbai

Disclaimer

This book is neither endorsed nor affiliated with Google.
Some of the images have been taken from Google

Dedicated to

My Lady Luck
Smt Kusum Ramuka, Smt Sunita Ramuka , Miss Sukriti Ramuka

About the Author

Murari Ramuka is a seasoned Data Analytics professional, with 12+ years of experience in enabling data analytics platform using traditional DW/BI and Cloud Technologies (Azure, Google Cloud Platform) to uncover hidden insights and maximize revenue, profitability and ensure efficient operations management. He has worked with several multinational IT giants like Capgemini, Cognizant, Syntel and Icertis.

He is a self-motivated and committed data enthusiast, with expertise in banking and healthcare domains. He has worked for various customers across the world. He has helped them in setting up their end-to-end Data platform, which enabled them to progress to the next level of analytics, which include Real-time Analytics, recommendation engine, sentiment analytics, with his expertise in data analytics, especially the Cloud platform.

His keen interest lies in Cloud data analytics, machine learning and applications of natural language processing in various industry sectors. In his leisure time, he enjoys reading about the latest trends in data space and sharing the knowledge about the same through his LinkedIn page.

He believes in sharing and spreading knowledge and has conducted several meetups and technical events across India in the past. He is also part of AIM Mentor of Change program, a Govt of India Initiative by Niti Ayog.

About the Reviewer

Saurabh Saraff has 6 plus years of experience in data engineering, data modeling and architecture. He has more than 3 Years of experience working on Google cloud platform and is a Google Cloud certified Cloud Architect, Cloud engineer, and a Data engineer. He pursued his B.E. in Information Technology from Pune University. He is a data enthusiast and is working on AI and ML projects.

Acknowledgement

First and foremost, I would like to thank God for giving me the courage to write this book. I would like to thank everyone at BPB Publications for giving me this opportunity to publish my book.

I would also like to thank my loving and caring wife, Mrs. Sunita Ramuka, and my family for their endless support and help in numerous ways.

I would like to thank my mentors, Mr. Sanjay Raj, Mr. Monish Darda, Mr. Chetan Manjrekar, Mr. Ashish Arora, Mrs. Hema Chandrasekhar, all the other seniors, and my friends, Mr. Sunil Upadhyay, Mr. Rakesh Sahay, Mr. Shrish Tripathi for their useful discussions and suggestions-right from deciding the topics, writing the concepts, framing exercises, etc.

Lastly, I would like to thank my critics and reviewers. Without their inputs, I would not have been able to write this book.

—*Murari Ramuka*

Preface

In the last few years, Cloud Computing has been very popular and has become the first choice for organizations. It is being used across different industries due to its unmatched features and benefits.

This book will help in learning and applying sophisticated knowledge on Cloud Computing. It also explains different types of data services/technology and machine learning algorithm/Pre-Trained API to real-business problems, which are built on the Google Cloud Platform (GCP). With some of the latest business examples and hands-on guide, this book will enable the developers entering the data analytics fields to implement an end-to-end data pipeline, using the GCP Data services. Through the course of the book, you'll come across multiple industries wise use cases, like Building Datawarehouse using Big Query, a sample real-time data analytics solution on machine learning, and Artificial Intelligence, which helped business decisions by employing a variety of data science approaches on the Google Cloud environment. Whether your business is at an early stage of cloud implementation in its journey or well on its way to digital transformation, Google Cloud's solutions and technologies will help chart a path to success. This book can be used to develop the GCP concepts in an easy way. It contains many examples showcasing the implementation of a GCP service. It also aids in learning the basic and advanced concepts of Google Cloud Data Platform. This book is divided into 7 chapters and provides a detailed description of the core concepts of each of the Data services offered by Google Cloud.

Through this book you will learn how to:

- Make different Services available in the Google cloud Platform and when to use what for an application.
- Build a real-time streaming data pipeline to carry out real-time analytics using Cloud Dataflow, Pub/Sub, and Big Query.
- Conduct interactive data exploration and discovery with Google BigQuery.
- Auto Scaling and high availability to run the business.
- Performing Data Transformation, Data Cleansing, Data Wrangling, and Data Visualization Activities using different Google Cloud Platform Services.

- Create a high-performing Machine learning prediction model with TensorFlow.
- Taking advantage of fully trained ML models from Google Cloud Platform.

Errata

We take immense pride in our work at BPB Publications and follow best practices to ensure the accuracy of our content to provide with an indulging reading experience to our subscribers. Our readers are our mirrors, and we use their inputs to reflect and improve upon human errors if any, occurred during the publishing processes involved. To let us maintain the quality and help us reach out to any readers who might be having difficulties due to any unforeseen errors, please write to us at :

errata@bpbonline.com

Your support, suggestions and feedbacks are highly appreciated by the BPB Publications' Family.

Table of Contents

CHAPTER 1
GCP Overview and Architecture

Introduction

Cloud computing is a buzz word in the market these days. Every organization wants to go for cloud first strategy where they can get the power of cloud computing. In this chapter, we will start with basic cloud computing concepts and discuss on Google Cloud Platforms (GCP), including their different cloud service offerings.

Structure

- Cloud computing
- Cloud models
- Major Cloud Vendors
- Google Cloud Platform
- Region and zone
- Important service in Google Cloud Platform

Objectives

The objective of this chapter is to explain the different cloud computing models and major vendors. You will get well versed with the GCP architecture, region, zone, billing, roles, and features along with different types of GCP services and can select appropriate services based on specific requirements.

In the earlier days, organizations were directly responsible for managing their own infrastructure. These infrastructures include servers, storages, and computing powers. Maintenance of these infrastructures was a tedious task and incurred enormous expenses to the companies. These drawbacks and unexpected initial cost of setting up an infrastructure triggered the need for cloud computing models.

Cloud computing helps organizations cater to on-demand availability of all the computer resources (that is, data storage, computing power, networks, and applications) without taking the ownership of their management. It is widely distributed over multiple network which supports huge data storage and computing power. In today's time, there is a central server for most of the large clouds, which have functions distributed over various locations. Basically, it is using someone else's server to host, run, and process any application along with storing the data. Hence, cloud computing enables enterprises to avoid or minimize different IT services costs upfront (that is, infrastructure, application deployment, and more). Not only just cost, but it helps organizations to set up and run their applications faster with improved insight and maintenance. The IT team can well handle the fluctuation of application demands during peak and off-peak hours via cloud, which is one of the very important features of cloud. Autoscaling, which is one of important features, helps in this type of scenario. Pay-as-you-go helps enterprises to select a proper costing model to support their infra and other services requirements. The following features led to foundation and growth of cloud computing:

- Availability of high-capacity networks
- Low-cost computers and storage devices
- Common adoption of hardware virtualization
- Service-oriented architecture
- Autonomic and utility computing
- Pay-as-you-go
- Autoscaling

Cloud computing history

Cloud computing has been in existence from early 2000. Amazon created subsidiary organization called **Amazon Web Services** in August 2006 and introduced its main service which is **Elastic Compute Cloud (EC2)**. In April 2008, Google also came in to cloud space and released Google App Engine with their beta release. In February 2010, Microsoft released Microsoft Azure, which was announced in October 2008. On March 1, 2011, IBM followed cloud race and announced the **IBM SmartCloud** framework to support Smarter Planet. Google Compute Engine, which is one of the services under GCP, was released in preview in May 2012, before being rolled out into general availability in December 2013.

On-premise versus cloud computing

It has been always a debate on pros and cons of on-premise and cloud infrastructure. Both have some advantages and disadvantages, which are listed as follows:

Factors	On-premise	Cloud computing
Deployment	Deployment of the resources is within the infrastructure. The organization will be responsible for maintaining and handling the deployment related process. Since the application is hosted within, the access is limited to the organization only.	In cloud computing, resources are deployed at the service provider's end and accessed by the public. In private cloud, resources and application are deployed according to the customer's need and can be accessed by them only.
Cost	The initial cost includes servers, hardware, storage devices, software, power consumption and space where architecture is built. Hence, the initial cost is high.	In cloud computing, the users only need to pay for the resources they use. There are no maintenance charge, no upfront charge, and no upkeep costs associated.
Security	Organizations having sensitive data, for example, agencies must use a certain level of security. The security is taken care by either a third party or by a group of staff using an external tool.	The secure environment is provided by the cloud service providers. There is a broad set of policies and technologies provided by the CSPs. These take care of the security of enterprise data.
Flexibility	When any infrastructure upgrade/ changes need to be applied, the cost incurred will be by the organization.	Enterprise can quickly upgrade their infrastructure to their requirements without having to make large investments in costly hardware every time.
Maintenance	The user/enterprises are responsible for maintaining the server hardware and software, the data backups, storage devices, and disaster recovery.	Cloud computing provides greater flexibility as the user/ organization only pay for what they use and can easily scale to meet the peak demand.

Considering the preceding highlighted differences, anyone can easily differentiate the advantages of using cloud over on-prem. As per **National Institute of Standards and Technology (NIST),** the definition of cloud computing identifies five essential characteristics, which are as follows:

- **On-demand self-service:** A consumer can unilaterally provision computing capabilities such as server time and network storage, as needed automatically without needing human interaction with each service provider.

- **Broad network access:** Capabilities are available over the network and accessed via standard mechanisms that promote use of heterogeneous thin or thick client platforms (for example, mobile phones, tablets, laptops, and workstations).

- **Resource pooling:** The provider's computing resources are pooled to serve multiple consumers using a multi-tenant model, with different physical and virtual resources dynamically assigned and reassigned according to consumer demand. There is a sense of location independence in that the customer generally has no control or knowledge over the exact location of the provided resources but may be able to specify a location at a higher level of abstraction (for example, country, state, or datacenter). Examples of resources include storage, processing, memory, and network bandwidth.

- **Rapid elasticity:** Capabilities can be elastically provisioned and released, and even automatically, to scale rapidly outward and inward commensurate with demand. To the consumer, the capabilities available for provisioning often appear to be unlimited and can be appropriated in any quantity at any time.

- **Measured service:** Cloud systems automatically control and optimize resource use by leveraging a metering capability at some level of abstraction appropriate to the type of service (for example, storage, processing, bandwidth, and active user accounts). Resource usage can be monitored, controlled, and reported, providing transparency for both the provider and consumer of the utilized service.

Benefits of cloud computing

Globally cloud computing has created a deep impact on innovation, and therefore, the political economy of any business and country. It permits business and organization with innovative concept to add an additional chance not solely to enhance flexibility, scale back prices, and specialize in core competencies, however, conjointly to completely rework no matter how they operate. For instance, by re-designing internal system workflows or client interactions that permits digital experiences from mobile devices to any or all the thanks to the cloud information centers.

Specifically, the business benefits of cloud computing includes:

- Various cloud services that incorporates storage, compute, network, and more is purchased and consumed on a *pay-as-you-go* basis and redoubled or diminished as required for optimum utilization.

- Cloud computing helps to convert capital expenses into operation expenses and therefore up the potency.
- Since there's no software system is put in, configured, or upgraded on personal devices, services are accessed from any place, and end-user productivity is probably getting increased.
- In order to enhance Infrastructure practicality, performance, dependableness and security area. As a result customers will like *vertically integrated* stacks that area unit be spoken at each level—which might be out of reach for on-premises deployments designed from off-the-peg parts.
- Cloud customers will specialize in speedy innovation while not the expense and complexities of hardware acquisition and infrastructure management.

Most of the cloud service providers offer their cloud services generally under three standard buckets/models:

- **Infrastructure as a service (IaaS)**
- **Platform as a service (PaaS)**
- **Software as a service (SaaS)**

The following diagram shows the key difference highlighted between on-premise, IaaS, PaaS, and the SaaS cloud model:

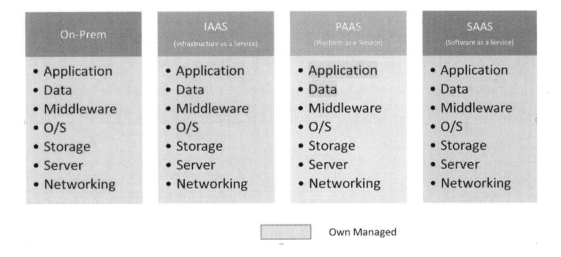

Figure 1.1: The cloud service model

Infrastructure as a Service (IaaS)

Cloud infrastructure services, called **Infrastructure as a Service (IaaS)**, are fabricated from extremely ascendable and automatic cipher resources. IaaS is absolutely self-service for accessing and watching things like computers, networking, storage, and alternative services. It permits businesses to get resources on-demand and as-needed rather than having to shop for hardware outright.

There are several advantages of selecting IaaS, such as:

- It's the foremost versatile cloud computing model and supports all the infrastructure want of any enterprises such as virtual machine and more.
- Easily permits machine-controlled readying of storage, networking, servers, and process power.
- Hardware will be purchased considering supported consumption.
- Gives shoppers complete management of their infrastructure.
- It is straightforward to scale the system as required and therefore is extremely ascendable.

Some vital characteristics of IAAS model are listed as follows:

- As the name recommends, resources are out there as a service.
- The total value is driven by consumption of resources.
- Multiple totally different services provided by cloud supplier are extremely ascendable.
- Provides complete management of the infrastructure to organizations.
- Typically includes multiple users on one piece of hardware.

Platform as a Service (PaaS)

Cloud platform services or **Platform as a Service (PaaS)** give cloud elements to bound code whereas getting used primarily for applications. PaaS delivers a framework for developers that they will devolve on and use to form custom-built applications. This platform can be used as a service, all servers, storage, and networking will be managed by the enterprise or a third-party supplier whereas the developers and organizations have to be compelled to maintain management of the applications solely.

PaaS advantage might not smite by the size of an associate degree organization company; there are various benefits for victimization PaaS:

- Cost effective, it makes the event and readying of any web / mobile apps easy, additionally as value optimized.
- The PaaS model is extremely simple to proportion whenever needed.
- As far as availability is concerned, it's extremely offered.

- Gives developers the flexibility to form custom-built apps while not the headache of maintaining the code.
- One of the vital benefits is it helps in reduction of the quantity of cryptography to an excellent extent.
- It helps enterprises to automate business policy that is extremely vital for any enterprise.
- It conjointly permits simple migration to the hybrid cloud model.

PaaS has several characteristics that outline it as a cloud service, including:

- It is constructed on virtualization technology, which means resources will simply be scaled up or down as per business changes.
- Provides a range of services to help with the event, testing, and readying of apps.
- Any range of users will access constant development application.
- Web services and databases square measure integrated.

Software as a Service (SaaS)

Software as a Service (SaaS) additionally referred to as cloud application services. The user will access the appliance hosted on this service directly through the net browser and therefore doesn't want any download or consumer tool installation. It additionally allows to represent the ordinarily used possibility for businesses within the cloud market. SaaS utilizes the Web to deliver applications that are managed by a third-party marketer, to their users.

SaaS provides many benefits to staff yet as organization by providing them:

- Great reduction in time to promote time.
- Money spent on tasks such as putting in, managing, and upgrading code.
- Availability of technical workers to pay on a lot of pressing matters and problems among the organization.

Once SaaS is being utilized it helps organization to measures and assist via multiple ways:

- Managed from a central location.
- Hosted on a distant server.
- Users/enterprises aren't liable for hardware or code updates.
- Application square measure accessible over the web.

The following table shows the common examples of SaaS, PaaS, and IaaS:

Service models	Some examples
IaaS	DigitalOcean, Rackspace, AWS, Cisco Metapod, Microsoft Azure, **Google Compute Engine (GCE)**
PaaS	AWS Elastic Beanstalk, Windows Azure, Force.com, Google App Engine, Apache Stratos, OpenShift, Google Big Query
SaaS	Google Apps, Dropbox, Salesforce, Cisco WebEx, Concur, GoToMeeting

The cloud computing architecture

There are many cloud components comprises in cloud computing architecture, each of them is loosely coupled. The cloud architecture is broadly divided into two parts:

- **Frontend:** Client part of cloud computing system is referred as frontend. It consists of interfaces and applications that are required to access the cloud computing platforms, for example, web browser.

- **Backend:** Cloud itself is referred as backend. It contains of all the resources required to provide cloud computing services. The backend includes huge data storage, virtual machines, services, security mechanism, deployment models, servers, and more.

Each of the components is associated via a network, usually via the internet. The following diagram shows the graphical view of cloud computing architecture:

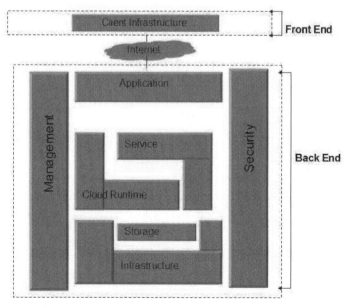

Figure 1.2: Cloud computing architecture

The popular cloud service providers in market are as follows:

- **Amazon Web Services (AWS):** AWS is one of the most popular and currently used cloud service providers. The service offered by AWS is mostly safe and it provides infrastructure services such as database storage, network, computing power which is fully managed. AWS can be used to host static website. There is free credit provided by AWS so that anyone can easily learn the AWS technology.

- **Microsoft Azure:** Microsoft Azure was known as Windows Azure in earlier days. It is widely used for application deployment, application designing and managing all the security and infrastructure-related stuff. There is a free trail available in the market that helps to understand and explore Microsoft Azure.

- **Google Cloud Platform:** The entire Google infrastructure which is supported by GCP, that is, virtual machines and hard disk, are present in the Google data centers. GCP has some services that inherit from their existing system, which has been used in the organization since a long time. GCP offers a free tier account and works on *pay-as-you-go* concept such as other cloud provider but with the flexible payment plans.

- **IBM Cloud:** IBM Cloud helps enterprises, business and large organization to gain the values by building different pioneering ways to adopt cloud strategy. Like other cloud service providers, IBM Cloud also support different model like IaaS, PaaS, and SaaS:
  o Salesforce
  o Oracle Cloud
  o SAP

  SAP HANA is the main umbrella under which all the SAP cloud offering is being offered. With it features like enhanced IT security, powerful business network and cloud collaboration, SAP is considered as one of the best cloud service providers.

Google Cloud Platform

Google Cloud Platform (GCP) hosts all the cloud services on its own Google infrastructure, which is used for Google search, photos, Gmail, and YouTube. This cloud suite provides a variety of services from computing to storage, data analytics to machine learning, and many more. The GCP API can be easily integrated with any application and project that distinguish Google cloud from other players in the market. Google cloud services can be accessed via public cloud or through a dedicated network connection by software developers and other cloud users. Unlike other cloud service provider such as AWS and Microsoft Azure, Google offers integrated, easy-to-use, expert-supported with state-of-the-art documentation,

GPU-enabled services at the operation scale of Google, can easily support the launch of any application.

Why Google Cloud Platform?

Some of the features of GCP what really gives it an upper hand over other vendor is as follows:

- Highly scalable
- Advance Big Data and machine learning analytics
- Serverless
- Cost effective

The following diagram shows important features:

Figure 1.3: Google Cloud Platform Features

Google Cloud Platform regions and zones

Google Cloud Platform (GCP) resources are spread in various locations worldwide. These locations comprises of regions and zones within those regions. In case when resources located in different zones in a region provides isolation from different types of infrastructure, hardware, and software failures. And vice versa, if resources in different regions provides an even higher degree of failure independence. This allows enterprise to design robust systems with resources spread across different failure domains.

While describing region and zone, the first part is the region and the second part of the name describes the zone in the region:

- **Region:** Grouping of zones is called as *regions*. Zones have high-bandwidth, low-latency network connections to other zones in the same region. In order to make high availability deploy fault-tolerant application, Google recommends deploying applications across multiple zones and multiple regions. This helps guard against unexpected failures of components, up to and including a single zone or region.

   Choose regions that make sense for your scenario. For example, if an enterprise only has customers in the US, or if they have specific needs that require their data to live in the US, it makes sense to store their resources in zones in the *us-central1* region or zones in the *us-east1* region.

- **Zone:** A zone is an isolated location within a region. The fully qualified name for a zone is made up of *<region>-<zone>*. For example, the fully qualified name for zone a in the region us-central1 is *us-central1-a*. Depending on how widely companies want to distribute your resources, create instances across multiple zones in multiple regions for redundancy.

The following diagram shows segregation of regions and zones and how GCP services are hosted on zones:

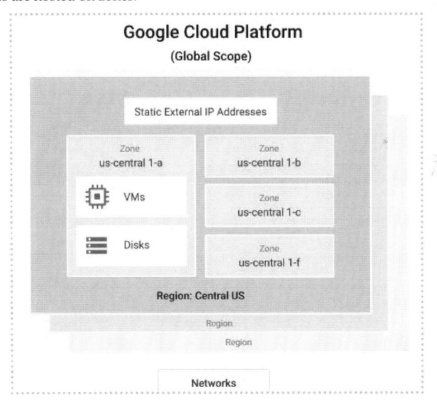

Figure 1.4: Region and Zones Segregation

The following picture shows the current GCP regions present across the globes:

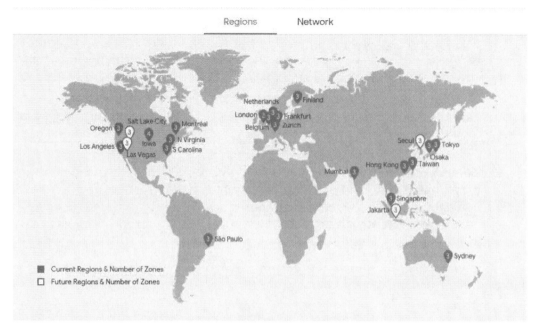

Figure 1.5: Current available GCP region

Google Cloud Platform Console

The GCP Console provides a web-based, graphical user interface that you can use to manage your GCP projects and resources. GCP Console enables users to create a new project, or choose an existing project, and use the resources that users want to create in the context of that project. A user can create multiple projects, so they can use projects to separate their work as per their requirement. For example, a user creates a new project if they want that only certain team members can access the resources in that project, while all team members can continue to access other resources in another project. The following screenshot shows the dashboard of a GCP Console:

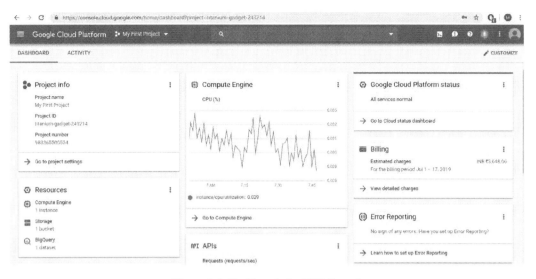

Figure 1.6: Dashboard of a GCP Console

Billing

GCP offers a free tier account that can be used by any individual with $300 credit. A billing account is ready up in GCP and is working to outline who pays for a given set of GCP resources. Access management to a billing account is established by Cloud **Identity and Access Management (IAM)** roles. A billing account is associated to a Google payments profile that has a payment instrument to that prices square measure charged:

Billing account	Payments profile
• A cloud-level resource managed in the GCP Console.	• Payment profile is a Google-level resource managed at payments.google.com.
• Tracks all of the costs (charges and usage credits) incurred by your GCP usage.	• Connects to all of your Google services (such as Google Ads, Google Cloud, and Fi phone service).
• A billing account can be linked to one or more projects.	• Processes payments for all Google services (not just Google Cloud).
• Project usage is charged to the linked billing account.	• Stores information like name, address, and tax ID (when required legally) of the one responsible for the profile.
• Results in a single invoice per billing account.	• Stores your various payment instruments (credit cards, debit cards, bank accounts, and other payment methods you've used to buy through Google in the past.)
• Operates in a single currency.	
• Defines who pays for a given set of resources.	

• Is connected to a Google payments profile, which includes a payment instrument, defining how you pay for your charges	• Functions as a document center, where you can view invoices, payment history, and so on.
• Have billing-specific roles and permissions to control accessing and modifying billing-related functions (established by Cloud IAM roles).	• Controls who can view and receive invoices for your various billing accounts and products.

Projects must be linked to a billing account; otherwise, they account cannot use GCP services that aren't free. The below diagram shows how the billing account and payment profile is linked to each other and with a project.

There are two types of billing accounts:

- **Self-serve:** The payment instrument is a credit or debit card or ACH direct debit, depending on availability in each country or region. Costs are charged automatically. The user can sign up for self-serve accounts online.

- **Invoiced:** The payment instrument can be cheque or wire transfer. Invoices are sent by mail or electronically. User must be eligible for invoiced billing. The following diagram shows the billing services within the GCP:

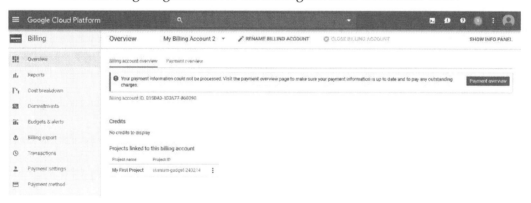

Figure 1.7: Billing services in GCP

Resource hierarchy

This section of book describes about the GCP resource hierarchy and also their sources that may be managed by resource manager. The purpose of the GCP resource hierarchy is two-fold:

- Provide a hierarchy of possession that binds the life cycle of a resource to its immediate parent within the hierarchy.

- Provide attach points and inheritance for access management and organization policies.

The following diagram shows the resource hierarchy of an organization:

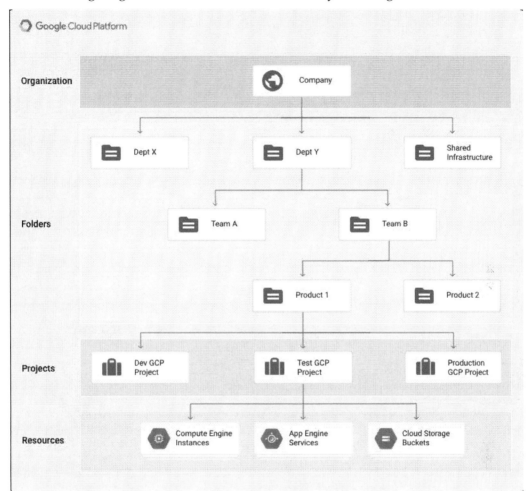

Figure 1.8: Resource hierarchy

Projects

Any GCP resources that any user simply allocates and uses should belong to a project. Users will be able to think about a project as an organizing entity on which all the services are building. A project is created of the settings, permissions, and alternative data that describe their applications. Resources at intervals one project will work along simply, for instance, by human action through an interior network, subject to the regions-and-zones rules. The resources that every project contains stay separate across project boundaries; the user will be able to solely interconnect them through associate degree external network affiliation. Each GCP project has:

- A project name, which user provide.

- A project ID, which an end user can provide or GCP can provide for them.
- A project number, which GCP provides.
- As user works with GCP, they will use these identifiers in certain command lines and API calls.

The following screenshot shows a project name, its ID, and number:

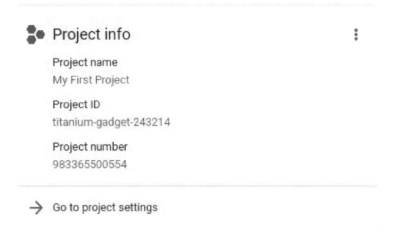

Figure 1.9: Project name and Project ID

In this example, `Project` is the **Project Name**, `example-id` is the **Project ID** and `983365500554` is the **Project Number**.

Each project ID is exclusive across GCP and unique. Once admin has created a project, they will be able to delete the project; however, its project ID cannot be deleted and re-used.

When asking is enabled, every project is related to one masking account. Multiple comes will have their resource usage beaked to a similar account.

A project is a namespace. This also suggests each resource among every project should have a novel name; however user typically use resource names if they're in separate comes. Some resource names should be globally distinctive.

- Projects are needed to use GCP service-level resources (such as reason Engine virtual machines (VMs), Cloud Pub/Sub topics, cloud storage buckets, and so on).
- All service-level resources are fostered by comes, the base-level organizing entity in GCP.
- The user will use comes to represent logical comes; teams, environments, or different collections that map to a business operate or structure.
- Projects make the premise for facultative services, APIs, and Cloud IAM permissions.

- Any given resource will solely exist in one project.

Here's the screenshot for selecting one of the projects if there are multiple projects under one account:

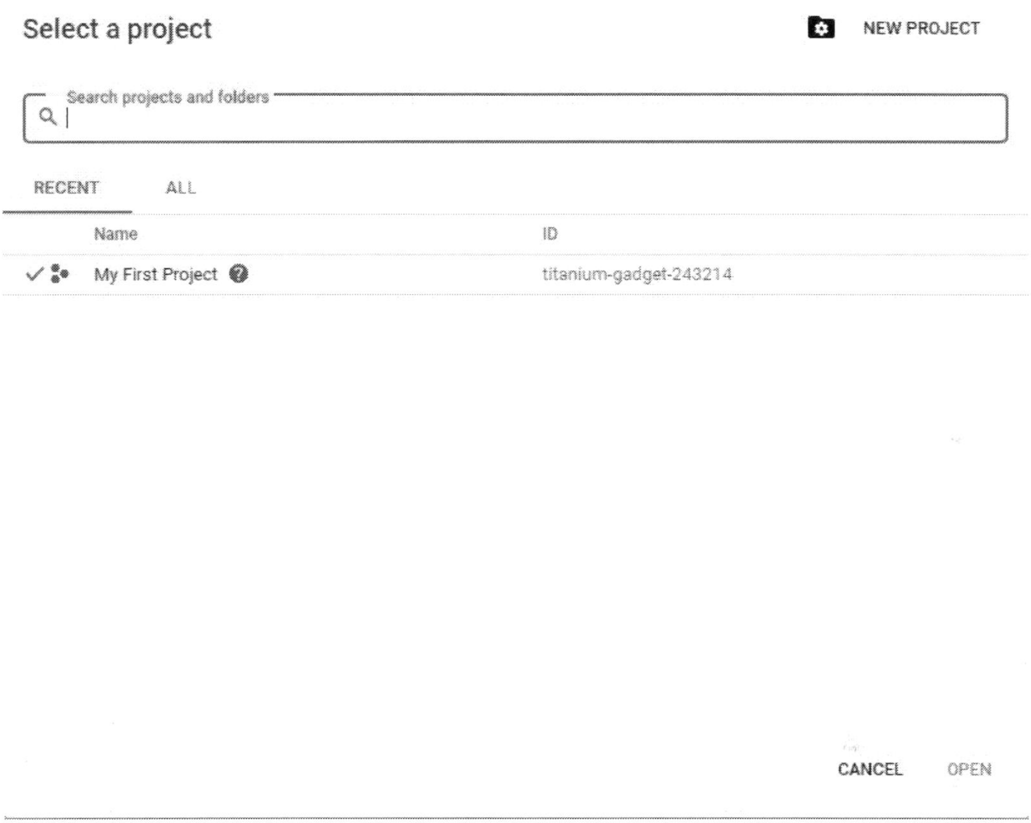

Select a project   ⚙ NEW PROJECT

Search projects and folders
🔍 |

RECENT   ALL

Name	ID
✓ 👥 My First Project ❔	titanium-gadget-243214

CANCEL   OPEN

Figure 1.10: Selecting a project from the list of projects

Command-line interface

Google Cloud SDK provides the gcloud command-line tool to a user who prefers to work in a terminal window, which gives users access to the commands they need. The gcloud tool can be used to manage both development workflow and GCP resources.

GCP also provides Cloud Shell, a browser-based, interactive shell environment for GCP. The user can access Cloud Shell from the GCP Console.

Cloud Shell offers:

- A temporary compute engine virtual machine instance.
- Command-line access to the instance from a web browser.

- Persistent disk storage of 5 GB.
- A built-in code editor.
- Pre-installed Google Cloud SDK and other tools.
- Multiple Language support that includes Java, Go, Python, Node.js, PHP, Ruby and .NET.
- Functionality of web preview.
- In-built authorization for access to GCP Console projects and resources.

The following screenshot shows how to access the gcloud command line:

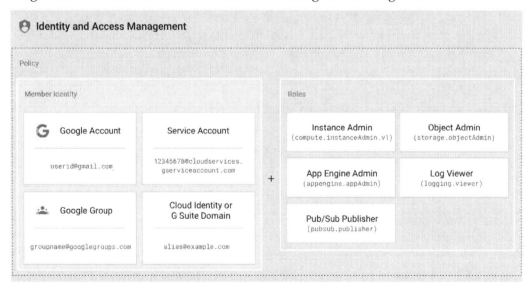

Figure 1.11: gcloud CLI

Roles and services in GCP

GCP offers Cloud IAM, which permits organizations to manage access management by allowing who (identity) has what access (role) of the resources. The following diagram shows how the IAM role has been managed and assigned:

Figure 1.12: Identity and Access Management

With Cloud IAM enterprises grants granular access to specific GCP resources and forestall unwanted access to alternative resources. Cloud IAM permits enterprises to adopt the protection principle of least privilege, thus they grant solely the mandatory access to their resources.

In Cloud IAM, companies grant access to their members. Members to whom the access needs to be granted should be of the subsequent types:

- **Google account:** A Google account helps a developer, administrator, or the any other user that interacts with GCP. An email address that is associated with a Google account is to be identity, in addition as gmail.com or various domains. New users can set up a Google account by reaching the Google account signup page.

- **Service account:** A service account is a special account configured within GCP that belongs to user application and virtual machine, instead of an individual and private user. Whenever any application gets executed for which the code is hosted at GCP, it uses the service account. It makes sure the end user is not involved directly. For example, a compute engine VM may run as a service account, and that account can be given all the required permissions to access the resources it needs. This way the service account is the identity of the service, and the service account's permissions control which resources the service can access.

A service account is identified by its email address, which is exclusive to the account.

- **Google cluster:** A Google cluster could also be a named assortment of Google accounts and repair account. Every cluster contains a particular email address that is associated with the cluster. Users will be able to notice the e-mail address that is associated with a Google cluster by clicking on the homepage of any Google cluster. Google team's square measure a convenient because of apply access policy to a bunch of users. Enterprise will be able to grant and alter access controls for a full cluster directly instead of granting or kinetic access controls one-at-a-time for individual users or service accounts. Companies will be able to in addition merely add members to require away members from a Google cluster instead of amendment a Cloud IAM policy to feature or take away users.

- **G Suite domain:** A G Suite domain represents a virtual cluster. It is area unit for all the Google accounts created in organization's G Suite account. G Suite domains represent organization's Internet name (such as example.com). Once organization adds a user to their G Suite domain, a replacement Google account is made for the user inside this virtual cluster (such as username@ example.com). Similar to Google groups, G Suite domains cannot be used to establish identity, but they enable convenient permission management.

- **Cloud Identity domain:** A Cloud Identity domain is sort of a G Suite domain. It represents a virtual cluster of all Google accounts in a company. However,

Cloud Identity domain users do not have access to G Suite applications. Here are the different types of users.

o `allAuthenticatedUsers`: This is a special user that represents anyone who is attested with a Google account or a service account. Users, who aren't attested, like anonymous guests, aren't enclosed.

o `allUsers`: This is a special user that represents someone who is on the net, together with attested and unauthenticated users. Note that some GCP arthropod genus need authentication of any user accessing the service, and in those cases, `allUsers` can solely imply authorization for all attested users.

There are three types of roles in Cloud IAM:

- Primitive roles, that includes the Owner, Editor, and Viewer roles that existed before the introduction of Cloud IAM.

- Predefined roles, which offer granular access for a specific service and managed by GCP.

- Custom roles, which offer granular access as per a user-specified list of permissions.

Primitive roles

There are three types of roles that existed before the introduction of Cloud IAM: Owner, Editor, and Viewer. These roles area unit concentric; that's, the Owner role includes the permissions within the Editor role, and therefore, the Editor role includes the permissions within the Viewer role.

The following table summarizes the permissions that the primitive roles embody across all GCP services:

Name	Title	Permissions
`roles/viewer`	Viewer	Permissions for read-only actions that do not affect state, such as viewing (but not modifying) existing resources or data.
`roles/editor`	Editor	All viewer permissions, plus permissions for actions that modify state, such as changing existing resources. **Note: While the roles/editor role contains permissions to create and delete resources for most GCP services, some services (such as Cloud Source Repositories and Stackdriver) do not include these permissions.**

roles/owner	Owner	All editor permissions and permissions for the following actions:
		Manage roles and permissions for a project and all resources within the project.
		Set up billing for a project.

The user can apply primitive roles at the project or service resource levels by using GCP Console, the API, and the gcloud command-line tool.

Invitation flow, users cannot grant the owner role to a member for a project using the Cloud IAM API or the gcloud command-line tool. Users can only add owners to a project using the GCP Console. An invitation will be sent to the member via email and the member must accept the invitation to be made an owner of the project.

Note that invitation emails aren't sent in the following cases:

- When someone is granting a role other than the owner.
- When an organization member adds another member of their organization as an owner of a project within that organization.

Predefined roles

Over and above primitive roles, Cloud IAM provides additional predefined roles. These roles provide granular access to specific GCP resources and help to protect unwanted access to other resources.

A particular role can be granted to this resource type or in most cases any type above it in the GCP hierarchy. Organization can grant multiple roles to the same user. For example, the same user can have network admin and log viewer roles on a project and also have a publisher role for a Pub/Sub topic within that project.

Custom roles

Along with predefined roles, Cloud IAM also provides additional ability to create customized Cloud IAM roles. Admin/organization can create a custom Cloud IAM role with one or more permissions and then grant that custom role to users who are part of organization.

Application Engine

An App Engine app is made up of a single application resource that consists of one or more services. Each service further can be configured to use different runtimes and to operate with different performance settings. Within each service, the user deploys version of that service. Each version then runs within one or more instances, depending on how much traffic user has configured it to handle.

Build and deploy applications on a fully managed platform. It helps to scale applications seamlessly from zero to planet scale without having to worry about managing the underlying infrastructure. With zero server management and zero configuration deployments, developers can focus only on building great applications without the management overhead. With App Engine, the developers can stay more productive and agile by supporting popular development languages and a wide range of developer tools.

The following screenshot shows how the App Engine service can be enabled from GCP:

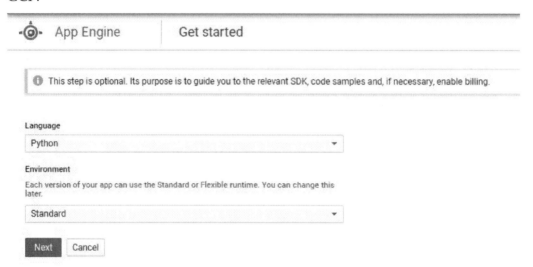

Figure 1.13: Creating an App Engine Instance

Below screenshot shows the different types of services available within App Engine:

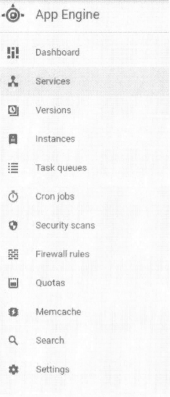

Figure 1.14: Google App Engine

Google App Engine (often said as **GAE** or just **App Engine**) could be a PaaS and cloud computing platform for developing and hosting net applications in Google-managed information centers. Applications are sandboxed and see multiple servers. App Engine offers automatic scaling for net applications—as the number of requests will increase for associate in nursing application, App Engine mechanically allocates a lot of resources for the online application to handle the extra demand.

Google App Engine is unencumbering to an explicit level of consumed resources and solely in customary setting however not in versatile setting. Fees are charged for extra storage, bandwidth, or instance hours needed by the applying. It had been 1st free as a preview version in Gregorian calendar month 2008 and came out of preview in Gregorian calendar month 2011.

Quickly build and deploy applications and it supports several of the favored languages like Java, PHP, Node.js, Python, C#, .Net, Ruby and Go or bring own language runtimes and frameworks. Start quickly with zero configuration deployments in App Engine. Manage resources from the statement, rectify ASCII text file in production and run API backends simply mistreatment business leading tools like Cloud SDK, Cloud supply Repositories, IntelliJ plan, Visual Studio, and PowerShell.

The App Engine app is created under GCP project when company plans to create an application resource. The App Engine application is a top-level container that comprises of the service, version, and instance resources that make up an app. When the user creates their App Engine app, all their resources are created in the region that they select, including their app code along with a collection of settings, credentials, and their app's metadata. Each App Engine application includes at least one service, the default service, which can hold as many versions of that service.

The following diagram demonstrates the hierarchy of an App Engine app running with multiple services. In the diagram, the app has two services that contain multiple versions, and two of those versions are actively running on multiple instances:

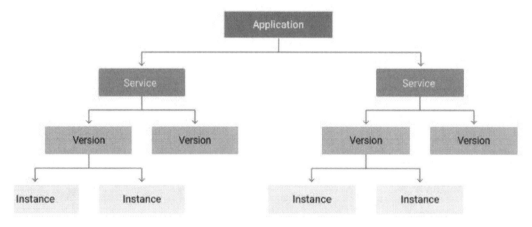

Figure 1.15: Hierarchy of an App Engine

Some of the other GCP services, for example cloud datastore, are shared across App Engine application.

Services

Services are used in App Engine to factor large apps into logical components that can securely share App Engine features and communicate with one another. App Engine services acts like microservices. Therefore, user can run their whole app in a single service, or they can design and deploy multiple services to run as a set of microservices.

For example, an app that handles customer requests might include separate services that each handles different tasks, such as:

- API requests from mobile devices.

- Internal, administration-type requests.
- Backend processing such as billing pipelines and data analysis.

Each service in App Engine consists of the ASCII text file from app and therefore the corresponding App Engine configuration files. The set of files that user just deploy to a service represent one version of that service and every time that they just deploy there to service, you're making further versions inside that very same service.

Versions

Having multiple versions of app inside every service permits them to quickly switch between completely different versions of that app for rollbacks, testing, or different temporary events. User will be able to route traffic to one or additional specific versions of app by migrating or cacophonic traffic.

Instances

The versions inside your services run on one or additional instances. By default, App Engine scales your app to match the load. Your apps can rescale the quantity of instances that square measure running to supply consistent performance or scale all the way down to minimize idle instances and reduces prices.

Application requests

Each of app's services and every version inside those services should have a singular name. The user will be able to then use those distinctive names to focus on and route traffic to specific resources victimization URLs, for example:

http://my-version.my-service.my-project-id.appspot.com

https://my-version-dot-my-service-dot-my-project-id.appspot.com

Incoming user requests square measure routed to the services or versions that square measure designed to handle traffic. You'll be able to conjointly target and route requests to specific services and versions.

Limits

The maximum number of services and versions that user can deploy depends on their app pricing:

Maximum instances per manual/basic scaling version		
Free app	Paid app US	Paid app EU
20	25 (200 for us-central)	25

Compute Engines

Google Compute Engine allows to create and run virtual machines on the Google infrastructure. Compute Engine offers scale, performance, and value that allow easily launch of large compute clusters on Google's infrastructure. There are no upfront investments and one can run thousands of virtual CPUs on a system that has been designed to be fast, and to offer strong consistency of performance.

The following screenshot shows how the compute engine services can be enabled with one of the VM is in running state:

Figure 1.16: GCP VM Instances

The following screenshot shows the different options available within the Compute Engine GCP service:

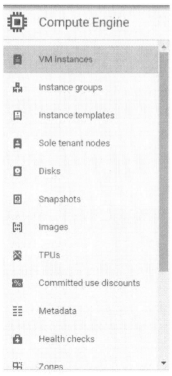

Figure 1.17: Compute Engine

Compute Engine instances will run the general public pictures for UNIX and Windows Server that Google provides likewise as non-public custom pictures that just will produce or import from existing systems. The user will conjointly deploy jack containers, which area unit mechanically launched on instances running the Container-Optimized OS public image.

Users can opt for the machine properties of their instances, like quantity of virtual CPUs and also the amount of memory, by employing a set of predefined machine sorts or by making own custom machine sorts.

Instances

Each instance belongs to a GCP Console project, and a project will have one or more than one instances. Once you produce an instance in a very project, specify the zone, operating system, and machine style of that instance. Once it is deleted an instance, it's far from the project. Here are some of the properties of an instance:

- **Instances and storage choices:** By default, every reckon Engine instance encompasses a tiny boot persistent disk that contains the OS. Once applications running on instance may need a lot of space for storing, add extra storage choices to their instance.

- **Instances and networks:** A project will have up to five VPC networks, and every reckon Engine instance belongs to at least one VPC network. Instances within the same network communicate with one another through neighborhood area network protocol. An instance uses the Web to speak with any machine, virtual or physical, outside of its own network.

- **Instances and containers:** Compute Engine instances support a declarative methodology for launching applications victimization containers. Once making a VM or an instance model, the user will give a jack image name and launch configuration. Reckon Engine should beware of the remainder together with supply an up-to-date Container-Optimized OS image with jack put in and launching your instrumentation once the VM starts up.

- **Tools to manage instances:** To create and manage instances, use a variety of tools, including the Google Cloud Platform Console, the gcloud command-line tool, and the REST API. To configure applications on instances, connect to the instance using Secure Shell (SSH) for Linux instances or Remote Desktop Protocol (RDP) for Windows Server instances.

Users can run their Windows applications on Google Compute Engine and take advantage of many benefits available to virtual machine instances such as reliable storage options, the speed of the Google network, and Autoscaling.

Compute Engine provides several tools to help bring Windows applications and services to the cloud:

- Use Windows Server images to create instances with a basic Windows environment upon which can build applications. For Windows Server 2016 and 2012 R2 images, select from either the Windows Server with Desktop Experience or Windows Server Core configurations.

- Use SQL Server images to start instances that have Windows Server with SQL Server preinstalled. Pay for both Windows Server and SQL Server licenses only when you use them. Windows Server images receive per-second billing and SQL Server images receive per-minute billing.

- Run .NET applications on your Compute Engine instances.

- Deploy Active Directory to your instances and bring your domain services to the cloud.

- Run IIS web servers to host your web content on Windows instances.

- If user has existing licenses for SQL Server or other applications that run in a Windows environment, use existing Microsoft application licenses through the Microsoft License Mobility program.

Google Compute Engine provides **graphics processing units (GPUs)** that can add to virtual machine instances. Users can use these GPUs to accelerate specific workloads on their instances such as machine learning and data processing.

The following screenshot shows how a user can create a compute engine using GCP Console:

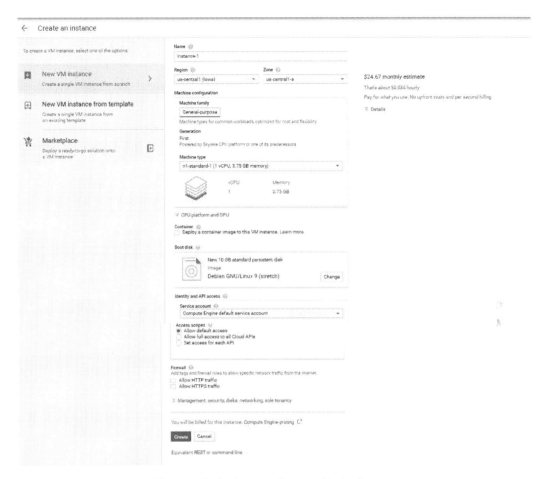

Figure 1.18: Setting up a Compute Engine Instance

Container Engines

Software containers are a convenient way to run applications in multiple isolated user-space instances. Users can run containers on Linux or Windows server public VM images, or on a Container-Optimized OS image. Containers allow applications to run with fewer dependencies on the host virtual machine and run independently from other containerized applications that deploy to the same virtual machine instance. These characteristics make containerized applications more portable, easier to deploy, and easier to maintain at scale.

Run containers on Compute Engine when needs complete control over user container environment and their container orchestration tools. Alternatively, users can use Google Kubernetes Engine to simplify cluster management and container orchestration tasks so that do not need to manage the underlying virtual machine instances.

Container technologies that run on Compute Engine

In general, Compute Engine instances can run almost any container technology or tool. Users can run several different types of containers on modern Linux operating systems and they can also run Docker on Windows Server2016 or later. The following list includes several common tools that use to run and manage containerized applications:

- Docker and rkt are two popular container technologies that allow you to easily run containerized applications.

- Kubernetes is a container orchestration platform that you can use to manage and scale your running containers across multiple instances or within a hybrid-cloud environment.

- Containers on Compute Engine are an easy way to deploy containers to Compute Engine VM instances or managed instance groups.

- User can convert their existing systems into LXD images and run them within Compute Engine virtual machine instances for a simple lift-and-shift migration solution. LXD runs on Ubuntu images.

Additionally, you can use Container Registry to manage container image versions. Container Registry serves as a central location to store and manage your container images before you deploy those images to Kubernetes on Compute Engine or to Google Kubernetes Engine clusters.

Container-optimized VM images

Compute Engine provides several public VM images that you can use to create instances and run your container workloads. Some of these public VM images have a minimalistic Container-Optimized operating system that includes newer versions of Docker, rkt, or Kubernetes preinstalled. The following public image families are designed specifically to run containers:

- Container-Optimized OS from Google
- Includes: Docker, Kubernetes
- Image project: cos-cloud
- Image family: cos-stable
- CoreOS
- Includes: Docker, rkt, Kubernetes
- Image project: coreos-cloud
- Image family: coreos-stable
- Ubuntu
- Includes: LXD

- Image project: ubuntu-os-cloud
- Image family: ubuntu-1604-lts
- Windows
- Includes: Docker
- Image project: windows-cloud
- Image family: windows-1809-core-for-containers

If you need to run specific container tools and technologies on images that do not include them by default, install those technologies manually. The following screenshot shows how to set up Kubernetes engine clusters:

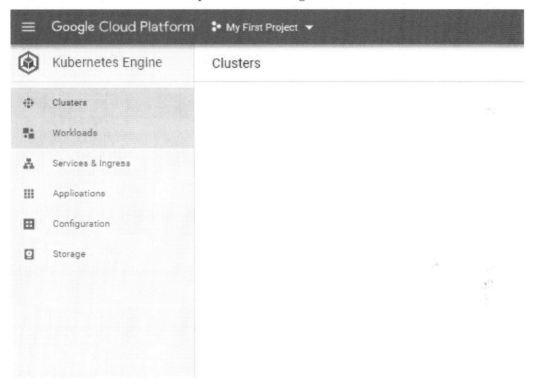

Figure 1.19: *Kubernetes Engine*

Cloud Functions

Google Cloud Functions enables a serverless execution atmosphere for building and connecting cloud services from the command line. With Cloud Functions, a user writes straightforward, single-purpose functions that are hooked up to events emitted from cloud infrastructure and services. Cloud code executes in an exceedingly totally managed atmosphere within the GCP. There is no need to provision any infrastructure or worry regarding managing any servers.

Cloud Functions are often written in JavaScript, Python 3, or Go runtimes on GCP. Programmers will take their code to operate and run it in any commonplace Node. js (Node.js 6, 8 or 10), Python three (Python 3.7) or Go (Go one.11) atmosphere, that makes each moveableness and native testing a breeze.

Connect and extend cloud services

Cloud Functions provides a connective layer of logic that allows user to write code to attach and extend cloud services. Listen and answer a file transfer to cloud storage, a log amendment, or an incoming message on a Cloud Pub/Sub topic. Cloud Functions augments existing cloud services and permits anyone to deal with an increasing variety of use cases with whimsical programming logic. Cloud Functions have access to the Google Service Account credentials are so seamlessly each with the bulk of GCP services, together with Cloud AutoML Vision, still as several others. Additionally, Cloud Functions are supported by numerous Google Cloud shopper libraries, that any alter these integrations.

Events and triggers

Cloud events are things that happen in cloud atmosphere. These may be things like changes to information in an exceedingly info, files additional to a storage system, or a replacement virtual machine instance being created.

Events occur whether or not user selects to retort to them. The user produces a response to an occurrence with a trigger. A trigger could be a declaration that user just have an interest in an exceedingly bound event or set of events. Binding an operator to a trigger permits to capture and act on events.

Serverless

Cloud Functions removes the work of managing servers, configuring software system, change frameworks, and fixing operative systems. The software system and infrastructure are totally managed by Google and users simply add code. What is more important is provisioning of resources happens mechanically in response to events. This suggests that an operation will scale from many invocations daily to several invocations with no effort from user.

The following screenshot shows how to create a Google Cloud Function:

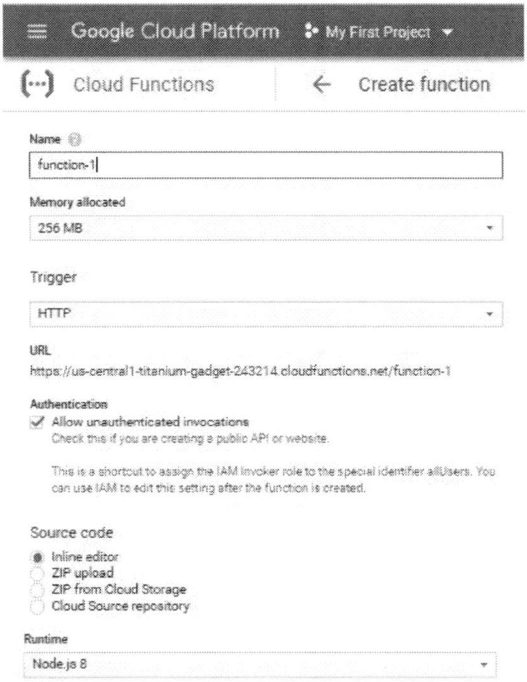

Figure 1.20: *Google Cloud Function*

Here's the sample code snippet for Cloud function:

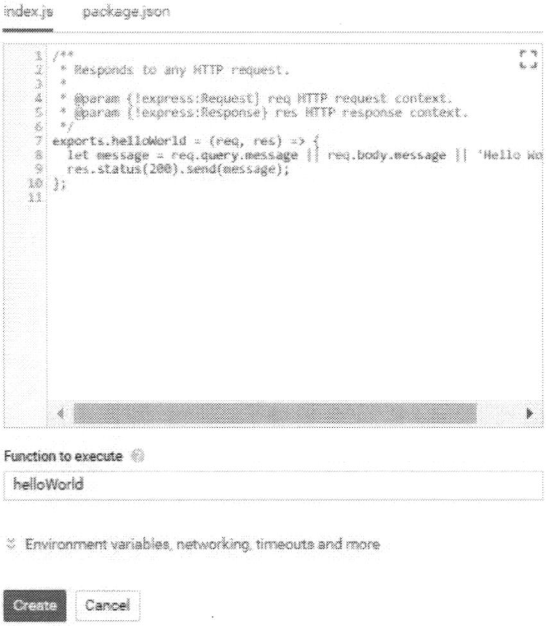

Figure 1.21: *Creating a Cloud Function*

Security via IAM

Cloud Identity & Access Management (Cloud IAM) helps administrators to drive and authorize users to act on specific resources. It also provides them full control and visibility to manage cloud resources centrally. For established enterprises with advanced structures, many workgroups, and many more, Cloud IAM provides a unified read into security policy across entire organization. Cloud IAM provides with constitutional auditing to ease compliance processes. Cloud IAM offers right tools to manage resource permissions with minimum hassle and high automation. It is easy to map job functions among any company to teams and roles. Users get access solely to what work they have to do, and admins will simply grant default permissions to entire teams of users.

Here's the screenshot of IAM service within GCP Console:

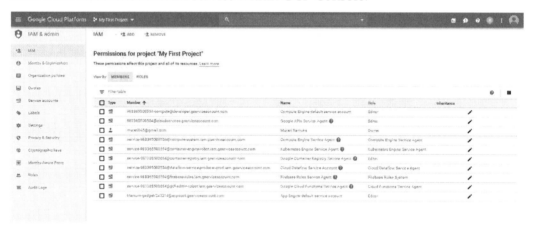

Figure 1.22: IAM Services

The admin can grant roles to users by making a Cloud IAM policy that could be assortment of statements that company has on access guide. A policy is connected to a resource and is employed to enforce access management whenever that resource is accessed as shown in the following diagram:

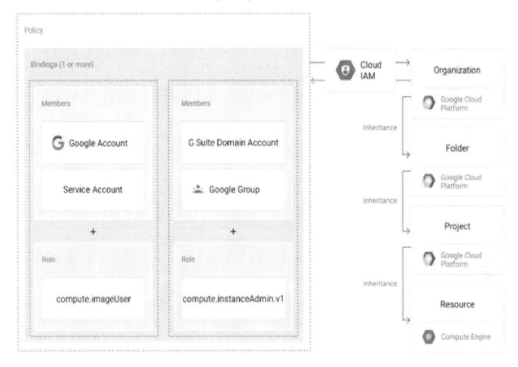

Figure 1.23: *Policy and Access Management*

A Cloud IAM policy is represented by the IAM Policy object. An IAM Policy object consists of a list of bindings. A binding binds a list of members to a role.

Individual role is the role admin (IAM Admin) want to assign to the member. The role is specified in the form of `roles/<name of the role>`.

For example, `roles/storage.objectAdmin`, `roles/storage.objectCreator`, and `roles/storage.objectViewer`.

Members contain a list of one or more identities as described in the concepts related to identity section above. Each member type is recognized with a prefix, such as a Google account (`user:`), service account (`serviceAccount:`), Google group (`group:`), or a G Suite or Cloud Identity domain (`domain:`).

In the following example , the `storage.objectAdmin` role is assigned to the following members using the appropriate prefix: `user:alice@example.com`, `serviceAccount:my-other-app@appspot.gserviceaccount.com`, `group:admins@example.com`, and `domain:google.com`. The `objectViewer` role is assigned to user: `bob@example.com`.

The following code snippet shows the structure of a Cloud IAM policy.

```
{
  "bindings": [
  {
    "role": "roles/storage.objectAdmin",
    "members": [
      "user:alice@example.com",
      "serviceAccount:my-other-app@appspot.gserviceaccount.com",
      "group:admins@example.com",
      "domain:google.com" ]
  },
  {
    "role": "roles/storage.objectViewer",
    "members": ["user:bob@example.com"]
  }
  ]
}
```

Cloud IAM and policy APIs

Cloud IAM provides a set of procedures that any organization can use to create and manage access control policies for GCP resources. These methods are exposed by the services that support Cloud IAM. For example, the Cloud IAM methods are exposed by the resource manager, Cloud Pub/Sub, and Cloud Genomics APIs; some more examples are as follows.

The Cloud IAM methods are:

- setIamPolicy(): Allows users to set policies on their own resources.
- getIamPolicy(): Allows users to get a policy that was previously set.
- testIamPermissions(): Allows users to test whether the caller has the specified permissions for a resource.

Policy hierarchy

GCP resources are organized hierarchically: the organization node is the root node in the hierarchy, the projects are children of the organization, and other resources are the descendants of projects. Each resource will have exactly one parent.

The following diagram is an example of a GCP resource hierarchy:

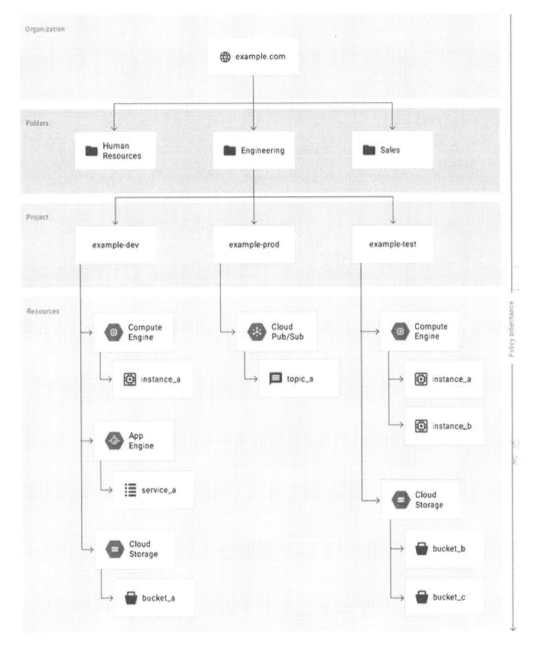

Figure 1.24: *Showing organization hierarchy*

Conclusion

In this chapter, we have understood about the cloud computing basic concepts along with types of models supported. There are different vendors who have different composition for their public cloud services. Google Cloud Platform basic services have been described along with billing, region, and zones concepts.

Questions

1. What is the different model provided within cloud computing?

2. Please highlight important features and services provided by GCP.

3. Explain about the compute and Kubernetes Engines in GCP.

4. What are region and zones in GCP and the difference between them?

5. How does the access control work in GCP?

CHAPTER 2
Google Cloud Platform Storage

In the previous chapter, we discussed about the **Google Cloud Platform (GCP)** in detail and saw how it is different from other Cloud service providers. We also learned about the cloud service models. In GCP, we have seen how does billing, IAM, and other important features (App Engine, Compute Engine, and more) work and can be enabled as and when required. In this chapter, we will understand the GCP's different types of Storages services. This chapter will enable us to learn in which scenarios which GCP storage should be utilized. There are multiple types of GCP storage service that are available to cater different storages (that is, Cloud Storage, Datastore, Cloud SQL, Cloud Spanner, Big Table, Big Query, and more). The main objective of this chapter is to make users aware of the GCP storage and help them to choose the correct storage service within GCP whenever required based on the features of each.

As discussed earlier, there are different types of storage available in GCP, which are as follows:

- Cloud Storage
- Cloud Datastore
- Cloud SQL
- Cloud Spanner
- Cloud Firestore
- Cloud Bigtable

- Cloud Big Query
- Cloud Memorystore

The following diagram shows the complete storage options provided by GCP. It is categorized into different buckets like objects, relational, non-relational, and more. Users can select a proper storage service as per their requirements keeping the following parameters in mind:

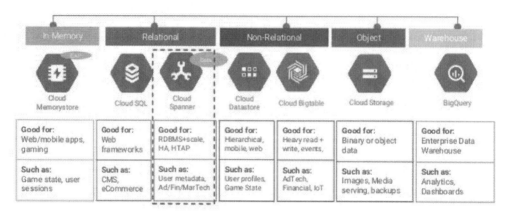

Figure 2.1: Different Cloud Storage services within GCP

The following flowchart will enable the user to decide which GCP storage needs to be selected as per the use cases and requirement. This flowchart is self-explanatory and contains the different types of structured and non-structured storage services provided within GCP:

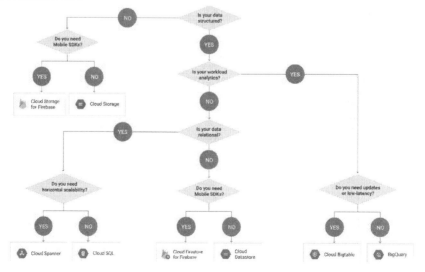

Figure 2.2: Flowchart to select GCP storage options

Cloud Storage

Cloud Storage is a type of storage supported by GCP which integrates storage into apps and a single unified API. Cloud Storage supports four storage classes with object lifecycle management which can optimize price/performance. As far as availability is concerned, cloud storage data can be accessed instantly from any storage class and designed for security and durability.

Overview of storage classes

In Cloud Storage, there is a concept called *bucket* which is the actual storage that is created by the user to store the data and files. While creating a bucket, three properties need to be specified. These properties are a globally unique name, a location where the bucket and their contents are stored, and a default storage class for objects which are added to the bucket.

Cloud Storage comes with four different storage classes:

- Multi-regional Storage
- Regional Storage
- Nearline Storage
- Coldline Storage

Low latency and high durability are the default properties for all storage classes. Along with the above properties, there are some additional properties like minimum storage duration, availability, and storage pricing and access which help them to distinguish between the storage classes.

Comparison of storage classes

The following table suggests a storage class based on data storage needs. The following table describes each storage class in more detail:

Type of storage class	Storage class properties	Use cases
Multi-regional storage	>99.99% typical monthly availability, Geo-redundant, SLA of 99.95% availability.	Multi-regional storage is used in case of storing data which is frequently accessed (hot objects) across the world, that is, website content, streaming videos, or gaming and mobile applications. Since Multi-Regional Storage data is stored in dual-regional locations, the user gets optimized performance when accessing GCP products which are in one of the associated regions.

Regional storage	99.99% typical monthly availability, storage per GB cost is low, data is stored in a narrow geographic region, 99.9% availability SLA, redundant across availability zones.	Storage of data which needs to be accessed frequently in the same region is used in data analytics via Cloud Data Proc.
Nearline storage	99.95% typical monthly availability in multi-regional locations; 99.9% typical monthly availability in regional locations, 99.9% availability SLA in multi-regional locations, 99.0% availability SLA in regional locations, data retrieval costs, per GB storage cost is very low, data retrieval costs, higher per-operation costs, minimum storage duration is 30 days.	Data access should not be quite often (that is, no more than once per month). Perfect for back-up and long-tail multimedia content service.
Coldline storage	99.95% typical monthly availability in multi-regional locations, 99.9% typical monthly availability in regional locations, 99.9% availability SLA in multi-regional locations, 99.0% availability SLA in regional locations, lowest cost per GB stored, data retrieval costs, higher per-operation costs, minimum storage duration is 90 days.	Expectation of Data access is not so often (that is, no more than once per year). Typically, this type of storage is used in disaster recovery scenario, or in data which is archived and may or may not be needed at some future time.

Prices listed are general storage prices, which apply to storing data in utmost locations. Some locations have a separate pricing structure. In addition to storage pricing, there are costs for process like operations, data egress, and early deletion.

All the above-mentioned storage classes are designed for the following:

- Creating buckets in locations worldwide.
- Using the same tools and APIs in order to access data, including the XML API and JSON API, the command-line gsutil tool, the GCP Console, and the client libraries.
- Using the same OAuth and granular access controls to secure data.

- 99.999999999% (11 9's) annual durability, achieved by redundantly storing objects across multiple devices which are located in multiple availability zones. Checksums are stored and frequently revalidated to proactively confirm the data integrity of all data at rest and to detect corruption of data in transit. Multi-regional and dual-regional locations offer supplemental protection against region-wide failures by storing data in at least two geographically different locations.

- No minimum object sizes.

- The same data security through encryption at rest.

- Low latency (time to receive first byte is typically tens of milliseconds).

- Using other Cloud Storage features like object versioning, object notification, access logging, lifecycle management, per-object storage classes, and composite objects and parallel uploads.

- Paying only for what you use.

- Providing unlimited storage that can be accessed worldwide.

Bucket

A storage class in a bucket and object setting can be managed easily. While creating a bucket, a default storage class needs to be specified. Objects will get added to the bucket as default storage classes unless they are overwritten.

The default storage class of the bucket can be changed as and when required. However, this will only affect the default storage class for objects that will be added newly going forward. It will not impact the storage class of objects that are already in the bucket. The following screenshot shows how a bucket can be created within the GCP Console:

Figure 2.3: Enabling a bucket from GCP Console.

Please note that while creating a bucket via the API and if we have not specified a default storage class, the bucket is assigned the Standard Storage class, which is similar to either multi-regional storage or regional storage and depends on the bucket's location settings.

Moving data flawlessly across storage classes: Generally, when users kick off their project, it is hard to be aware about the classes which suit their project. It is a good option to get started with anyone for the time being and then, it is very easy to switch tiers. As per the changes needed, object lifecycle management can automatically optimize price/performance across classes. Data redundancy will be maintained while moving from one class to another class within a multi-region or regional location.

The following snippet gives the example to move the storage classes:

```
{
  "lifecycle": {
    "rule": [
    {
      "action": {
        "type": "SetStorageClass",
        "storageClass": "NEARLINE"
      },
      "condition": {
        "age": 365,
        "matchesStorageClass": ["MULTI_REGIONAL", "STANDARD", "DURABLE_
REDUCED_AVAILABILITY"]
      }
    },
    {
      "action": {
        "type": "SetStorageClass",
        "storageClass": "COLDLINE"
      },
      "condition": {
        "age": 1095,
        "matchesStorageClass": ["NEARLINE"]
      }
```

```
        }
    ]
  }
}
```

Some of the important key features of Cloud Storage are as follows:

- Single API across storage classes
- Easily scalable to additional data bytes
- Designed for 99.999999999% durability
- Very high availability across all storage classes
- Time to first byte in milliseconds
- Strongly consistent listing

Cloud Datastore

Cloud Datastore is a highly scalable NoSQL database which can support any applications. Cloud Datastore has some inbuilt features like sharding and replication, providing you with a highly available and durable database that scales automatically to handle your application's load. Cloud Datastore offers a lot of capabilities such as ACID transactions, which are similar to SQL queries, indexes, and much more. The following screenshot shows how to create Datastore within the GCP console. Cloud Datastore supports maximum up to 10 TB of data size:

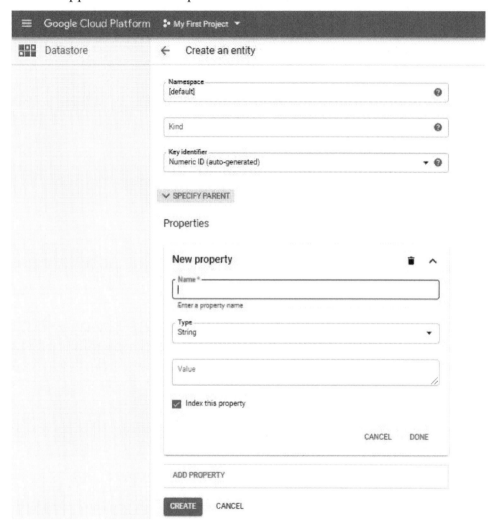

Figure 2.4: Enabling Datastore service from the GCP Console.

Some of the important characteristics of Cloud Datastore are as follows:

- **Simple and integrated:** Easy access of data by any deployment target with Cloud Datastore's RESTful interface. It helps to build solutions that span across App Engine and Compute Engine and rely on Cloud Datastore as the integration point.
- **Highly scalable and fast:** With this feature, it provides with building your applications without thinking much about provisioning and load anticipation. Applications need to maintain high performance since they can

receive more traffic and hence, one of the most important features is that Cloud Datastore scales seamlessly and automatically.

- **Support to use query language:** Datastore is a schema-less database, which allows your application to evolve and make changes without worrying about the underlying data structure. Datastore comes with a powerful query engine that allows you to query for data across multiple properties and sort as and when required. Some of the examples are as follows:

```
// List Google companies with fewer than 400 employees.
var companies = query.filter('name =', 'Google').filter('size <', 400);
```

Cloud Datastore is a NoSQL document database designed for automatic scaling, high performance, and ease of application development. Cloud Datastore includes the following:

- **Atomic transactions:** Cloud Datastore will execute a collection of operations wherever; either all succeed, or none occur.

- **High convenience of reads and writes:** Cloud Datastore executes in Google information centers and hence uses redundancy to reduce the impact from points of failure.

- **Massive quantifiability with high performance:** Cloud Datastore aligns with a distributed design to manage scaling mechanically. Cloud Datastore uses a collection of indexes and question constraints. Thus, queries will scale with the scale of the result set and not the scale of actual information set.

- **Flexible storage and querying of information:** Cloud Datastore integrates with object-oriented and scripting languages and is exposed to applications via multiple ways. It conjointly offers a SQL-like search language.

- **Balance of robust and ultimate consistency:** Cloud Datastore makes sure that entity lookups by key and relation queries always receive powerfully consistent information. All other queries are eventually consistent. The consistency models permit your application to deliver a good user experience while handling large amount of information and users. Cloud Firestore, the most recent version of Cloud Datastore, helps to make all queries powerfully consistent.

- **Encryption at rest:** Cloud Datastore mechanically encrypts all information before it's written to disk and mechanically decrypts the data when read by a licensed user.

- **Fully managed with no planned period:** Google takes care of the administration of the Cloud Datastore service. Thus, the organization will be able to concentrate on their application. Applications will still use Cloud Datastore once the service receives a planned upgrade.

Cloud Firestore in Datastore mode

Cloud Firestore is the latest version of Cloud Datastore and comes with many more advance enhancements on Cloud Datastore. The existing Cloud Datastore community will access these enhancements by making a replacement Cloud Firestore in the Datastore mode info instance. In future, all existing Cloud Datastore databases are generally moved and upgraded to Cloud Firestore in Datastore mode.

Comparison of Cloud Datastore and Cloud Firestore with ancient databases

While the Cloud Datastore interface has several identical options as ancient databases, as a NoSQL database it differs from them in the way it describes relationships between information objects.

Here is a high-level comparison of Cloud Datastore, Cloud Firestore, and relational database:

Properties	Cloud Datastore	Cloud Firestore	Relational database
Type of object	Kind	Collection group	Table
One object is called as	Entity	Document	Row
Individual data for an object	Property	Field	Column
Unique ID for an object	Key	Document ID	Primary key

Unlike rows in a database table, Cloud Datastore entities of the same kind will have completely different properties and totally different entities will have properties with the same name but with different price options. These distinctive characteristics imply a unique way of planning and managing knowledge to take advantage of the flexibility to scale mechanically.

Cloud Datastore is good for applications that require confidence in extremely structured data at scale. It will be able to use Cloud Datastore to store and question all the subsequent kinds of data:

- Product catalogues that give real-time inventory and product details for a distributor.
- User profiles that deliver a customized experience based on the users' past activities and preferences.
- Transactions based on ACID properties, for instance, transferring funds from one checking account to a different. For other storage and info choices, Cloud Datastore isn't ideal for each use case. For instance, Cloud Datastore isn't a computer database, and it's not a good resolution for analytic knowledge.

Here are some common eventualities wherever the user ought to most likely contemplate another to Cloud Datastore:

- If the user would like a computer database with full SQL support for a web dealing and transactional process system, then consider Cloud SQL.
- If the user doesn't need support for ACID transactions or if your knowledge isn't extremely structured, then consider Cloud Bigtable.
- If the user would like interactive querying in a web analytical process (OLAP) system, then contemplate BigQuery.
- If the user would like to store massive immutable blobs like massive pictures or movies, then contemplate Cloud Storage.

Cloud Firestore

Cloud Firestore is advance and the latest version of Cloud Datastore and removes many Cloud Datastore limitations. The following screenshot explains how to enable the Cloud Firestore service from the GCP Console:

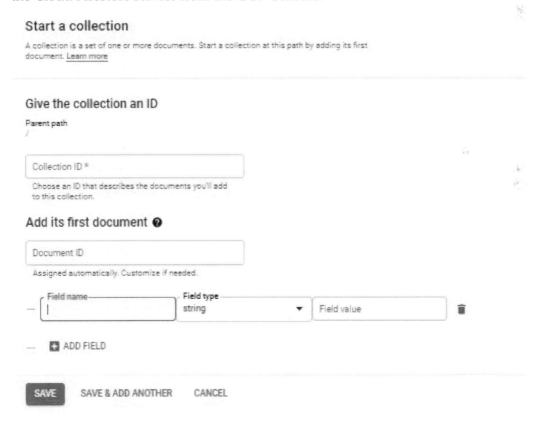

Figure 2.5: Enabling a Cloud Firestore service from the GCP Console

Features of Cloud Firestore are as follows:

- **NoSQL database engineered for international apps:** Cloud Firestore is a quick, absolutely serverless, managed, cloud-native NoSQL document info that simplifies storing, syncing, and querying data for mobile, web, and IoT apps at the international level. Its consumer libraries give live synchronization and offline support, whereas its security measures and integrations with base of operations and GCP accelerate building serverless apps.

- **Accelerate development rate with serverless infrastructure:** Cloud Firestore is a cloud native database that provides automatically scaling resolution from the bottom up to require advantage of GCP's powerful infrastructure. It's designed to produce an excellent developer experience and modify app development with live sync, offline support, and ACID transactions across many documents and collections. Cloud Firestore is integrated with each GCP and base of operations and Google's mobile development platform. The user can connect to Cloud Firestore from mobile or net purchasers for a really serverless resolution. No need to created negotiator server to manage access to data. This is often nice for prototyping, iterating, and obtaining a production system up in running quickly.

- **Sync information across devices, online or offline:** With Cloud Firestore, your applications may be updated in close to real time once the information on the backend changes. This cannot be solely nice for building cooperative multi-user mobile applications; however, it suggests that you'll be able to keep your data in synchronization with individual users who may need to use your app from multiple devices. Cloud Firestore has a full offline support; therefore, you'll be able to access and build changes to your data, and changes are synced to the cloud once the shopper comes back online. Intrinsic offline support leverages native cache to serve and store data, and so your app remains responsive no matter the network latency or web property.

- **Simple and easy:** Cloud Firestore's robust shopper libraries make it simple for you to update and receive new data while worrying less about establishing network connections or unforeseen race conditions. It will scale effortlessly as app grows. Cloud Firestore permits to run subtle queries against your data. This provides a lot of flexibility in the manner in which you structure your data and might usually mean that you have to do less filtering on the shopper that keeps your network calls and data usage a lot of economical.

Enterprise-grade, ascendable NoSQL Cloud Firestore is a fast and fully managed NoSQL cloud database. It's engineered to scale and takes advantage of GCP's powerful infrastructure, with automatic horizontal scaling in and out, in response to application's load. Security access controls for data are inbuilt and enable you to handle data validation via a configuration language. Cloud Firestore is a versatile, scalable, real-time database. It's straightforward enough for fast prototyping nevertheless ascendable and versatile enough to grow with you to any size. Cloud

Firestore is a real-time database, which means that users will be able to track data in Cloud Firestore and be notified in real-time when it changes. This feature helps to build responsive apps that work no matter the network latency or web property. Cloud Firestore is a cloud-hosted NoSQL database.

Cloud Firestore is a NoSQL, document-oriented database. Unlike an SQL database, there aren't any tables or rows. Instead of storing data in documents it follows to store in organized into collections. Each document contains a group of key-value pairs. Cloud Firestore is optimized for storing giant collections of little documents. All documents should be kept in collections. Documents will contain sub collections and nested objects; each of which might embrace primitive fields like strings or advanced objects like lists.

Collections and documents are created implicitly in Cloud Firestore.

Documents

In Cloud Firestore, the storage unit is the document. A document may be a light-weight record that contains fields that map to values. Every document is known by an identifier.

A document representing a user `JohnTape` might look like this:

```
class JohnTape
first : "John"
last : "Tape"
born : 1815
```

Please note that Cloud Firestore works well with different variety of data types for values: binary blob, Boolean, number, string, geo point, and timestamp. There is choice to also use arrays or nested objects which are called *maps* and these maps help to structure data within a document.

Complex, nested objects in a document are called *maps*. For example, a user could structure the user's name with a map like this:

```
class JohnTape
  name :
    first : "John"
    last : "Tape"
born : 1815
```

Documents are like JSON. There are some variances (for example, documents support extra data types and are limited in size to 1 MB), but in general, you can treat documents as lightweight JSON records.

Collections

The following diagrams show how collection, document and data are managed:

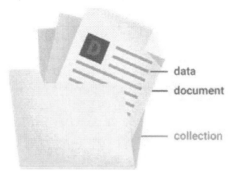

Figure 2.6: Management of data, document, and collection

Documents reside in collections, which are simply containers for documents. For example, an organization could have a user's collection to contain their various users, each represented by a document:

```
collections_bookmark users
   class JohnTape
      first : "John"
      last : "Tape"
      born : 1815
   class TomPaine
      first : "Tom"
      last : "Paine"
      born : 1912
```

Cloud Firestore is schema less, so it gives you complete freedom over what fields you need to be put in each document and what data types need to be stored in respective fields. Documents within the same collection can contain dissimilar fields or store different types of data in respective fields. However, it is always good to have the same fields and data types across multiple documents, which helps query the documents more easily.

A collection comprises documents. It can't directly contain raw fields with values, and it can't comprise other collections.

The names of documents inside a collection are unique. Users have the flexibility to provide their own keys such as user IDs, or even allow Cloud Firestore to generate random IDs automatically.

Cloud SQL

Cloud SQL is a fully-managed database service that makes it easy to set up, maintain, manage, and administer you relational PostgreSQL, MySQL, and SQL server databases within the cloud. Some of unique features which are offered by Cloud SQL are high performance, scalability, and convenience to use. As it is hosted on GCP, Cloud SQL comes with a database infrastructure for applications running from any place.

Some important characteristics are highlighted as follows:

- **Focus on your application:** Let Google manage the database, so users can target their applications. Cloud SQL is ideal for Word Press sites, ecommerce applications, CRM tools, geospatial applications, and other applications that are compatible with the MySQL, PostgreSQL, or SQL Server.

- **Simple and fully managed:** Cloud SQL is simple to use. It doesn't need any software installation. It automates all your backups, replication, patches, and updates while guaranteeing larger than 99.95% handiness, anywhere in the world.

- **Performance and scalability:** Cloud SQL delivers high performance and scalability with up to 10 TB of storage capability, 40,000 IOPS, and 416 GB of RAM per instance.

- **Reliability and security:** Easily configure replication and backups to guard data. Go beyond by enabling automatic failover by creating database highly available (HA). Your data is automatically encrypted, and Cloud SQL is SSAE 16, ISO 27001, and PCI DSS v3.0 compliant and supports HIPAA compliance.

- **Discounts without lock-in:** Cloud SQL comes with per-second billing, automatic sustained-use discounts, and instance sizes to suit any budget. Database instances are straightforward to prevent and begin. There's no up-front commitment and with sustained-use discounts, consumers will automatically get discounted prices for databases which are running continuously. As discussed earlier, Cloud SQL is a fully-managed database service that makes it easy to set up, maintain, manage, and administer relational databases on GCP.

Cloud SQL database comes with two different databases:

- Cloud SQL for MySQL
- Cloud SQL for PostgreSQL

The following are features of Cloud SQL for MySQL:

- This is a fully managed MySQL Community Edition database which is hosted within the cloud environment.

- Second Generation instances support MySQL 5.6 or 5.7. It also supplies up to 416 GB of RAM and data storage of 30 TB, with the choice to increase the storage size as per requirement.

- First generation instances support MySQL 5.5 or 5.6 and supply up to 16 GB of RAM and data storage of 500 GB.

- Create and manage instances within the GCP Console.

- Instances obtainable in US, EU, or Asia.

- Google's internal networks take care of Customer data encryption and are kept in information tables, temporary files, and backups.

- Secure external connections are supported with the Cloud SQL Proxy or with the SSL/TLS protocol.

- Data replication between multiple different zones with automatic failover.

- Importing and exporting of databases can be achieved using `mysqldump`, or import and export CSV files.

- There are supports available for MySQL wire protocol and normal MySQL connectors.

- Different types of backups like automated as well as on-demand, and point-in-time recovery.

- Helps in Instance cloning.

- Integration with Stack driver for logs and monitoring.

- ISO/IEC 27001 compliant.

The following screenshot shows how an instance of cloud MySQL DB can be set up within GCP:

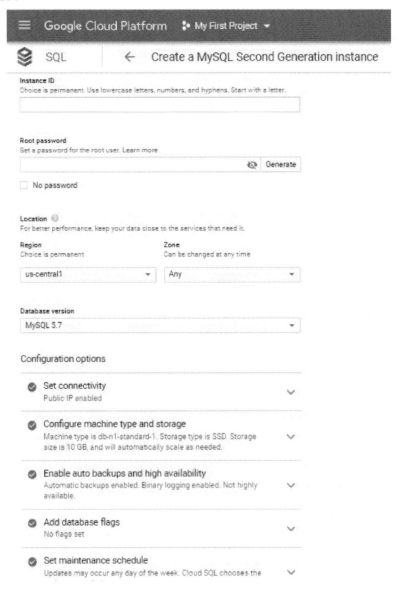

Figure 2.7: Enabling Cloud SQL (My SQL) from GCP Console

Supported languages: Java, Python, PHP, Node.js, Go, and Ruby are some of the preferred languages for Cloud SQL MySQL with App Engine applications. Cloud SQL for MySQL can be accessed with external applications via the standard MySQL protocol.

Cloud SQL instance for MySQL can be connected from:

- Via a MySQL client
- Can be accessed via SQL Workbench or Toad for MySQL which are third-party tools
- External applications
- App Engine applications
- Applications running on Compute Engine
- Applications being executed on Google Kubernetes Engine
- Cloud Functions
- Google Apps Script scripts

Comparison between Cloud SQL and standard MySQL based on their functionality

In general, the MySQL functionality given by a Cloud SQL instance is the equal to the functionality offered by a locally hosted MySQL instance. Still, there are some differences between a standard MySQL and Cloud SQL for MySQL instance.

Some of the features that are not supported are follows:

- User defined functions
- InnoDB memcached plugin
- Federated Engine
- The SUPER privilege

Some of SQL statements which are not supported are listed below. The following SQL statements will trigger an error with the message `Error 1290: The MySQL server is running with the Google option so it cannot execute this statement`:

- `LOAD DATA INFILE`

Note that `LOAD DATA LOCALINFILE` is supported.

- `SELECT .... INTO OUTFILE`
- `SELECT .... INTO DUMPFILE`
- `INSTALL PLUGIN ....`
- `UNINSTALL PLUGIN`
- `CREATE FUNCTION .... SONAME ....`

Unsupported functions are as follows:

- `LOAD_FILE()`

Cloud SQL for PostgreSQL

This is another type of Cloud SQL database offered by GCP. Here are some of the important features of Cloud SQL for PostgreSQL:

- It is a fully managed PostgreSQL database in the cloud and it is based on the Cloud SQL Second Generation platform.

- It comes in custom machine types which come with up to 416 GB of RAM and 64 CPUs.

- Up to 30 TB of default storage available with the functionality to automatically increase storage size as required.

- The GCP Console can be used to create and manage instances easily.

- As discussed in *Chapter 1: GCP Overview and Architecture* about the regions and zones, the instances of PostgresSQL are available in US, EU, or Asia.

- Google's internal networks help in customer data encryption and in database tables, temporary files, and backups.

- Data replication between multiple zones with automatic failover options.

- Secure external connections with the Cloud SQL Proxy or with the SSL/TLS protocol are supported.

- Importing and exporting of databases is easy using SQL dump files.

- Support for PostgreSQL client-server protocol and standard PostgreSQL connectors.

- Automated and on-demand backups.

- Can come up with Instance cloning.

- Easy to integrate with Stackdriver logging and monitoring.

The following screenshot helps to spin up a Cloud SQL PostgreSQL instance within the GCP console:

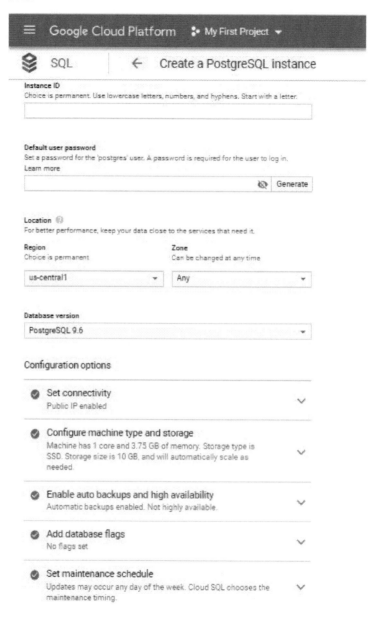

Figure 2.8: Enabling Cloud SQL (PostgreSQL) from GCP Console

Some PostgreSQL features are not yet available for Cloud SQL:

- Point-in-time recovery (PITR)

- Importing/exporting in CSV file format through the GCP Console or the gcloud command-line tool

Some of the PostgreSQL 11.1 features that are not yet available for Cloud SQL:

- Logical replication
- Allow setting WAL size during initdb
- JIT plan compilation

Supported procedural languages: Cloud SQL for PostgreSQL supports the PL/pgSQL SQL procedural language.

Supported languages: Cloud SQL for PostgreSQL with App Engine applications executing in the flexible environment that are written in Java, Python, PHP, Node.js, Go, and Ruby. Cloud SQL for PostgreSQL can be leveraged with external applications using the standard PostgreSQL client-server protocol.

You can connect to a Cloud SQL instance for PostgreSQL from the following:

- A psql client
- Third-party tools that use the standard PostgreSQL client-server protocol
- External applications
- App Engine applications
- Applications running on Compute Engine
- Applications running on Google Kubernetes Engine
- Cloud Functions

Differences between Cloud SQL and the standard PostgreSQL functionality

In general, the PostgreSQL functionality provided by a Cloud SQL instance is the same as the functionality provided by a locally hosted PostgreSQL instance. However, there are some differences between a standard PostgreSQL instance and a Cloud SQL for PostgreSQL instance.

Unsupported features: Any features which need SUPERUSER privileges are not supported.

Notable differences: There are multiple PostgreSQL options and parameters that are not enabled for editing as Cloud SQL flags.

Cloud Spanner

Cloud Spanner is a relational database which comes with full relational semantics. It can accommodate schema changes as an online operation with zero planned downtime. For querying the data, it reuses existing SQL skills in Cloud Spanner using the familiar industry standard ANSI 2011 SQL.

SQL, transactions, and strong consistency at scale: When it comes to scalability, enterprise-grade, globally distributed, and strongly consistent database service, Cloud Spanner is the first. Cloud Spanner is designed for the cloud to take the advantage of the relational database structure with non-relational scaling horizontally. This combination brings high-performance transactions along with strong consistency across rows, regions, and continents with the best in class 99.999% availability SLA, zero planned downtime, and enterprise-level security. Cloud Spanner transforms database administration and management and helps to make application development more efficient.

The following table describes the database properties with respect to different types of relational and non-relational databases:

Properties	Cloud Spanner	Traditional relational	Traditional non-relational
Schema	Yes	Yes	No
SQL	Yes	Yes	No
Consistency	Strong	Strong	Eventual
Availability	High	Failover	High
Scalability	Horizontal	Vertical	Horizontal
Replication	Automatic	Configurable	Configurable

Some of the use cases are explained in the following table which indicates the implementation of Cloud Spanner:

Use case	Before cloud spanner	With cloud spanner
Financial trading	Inconsistencies lead to possible monetary loss during reconciliation. Global synchronous replication of trades is not feasible.	Cost reduction and a consistent, unified, global view.
Insurance	Inconsistencies lead to partial views of customers.	Current customer views offer more precise, real-time data.
Global call centers	Eventual and out-of-touch.	Real-time and up-to-date.
Supply-chain management and manufacturing	Global supply chain presents an inconsistent global view and/or data must be shipped in batches.	Global, real-time, consistent view helps in real-time decision making.
Logistics and Transportation	Reaching to regional region by joining many systems together.	Universal reach with lesser latency and a consistent view.

Gaming	Each server or cluster is its private universe.	Consistent and universal view delivers a combined experience.
E-commerce (high availability)	Limited availability SLA or no SLA guarantees.	Guaranteed downtime of max 5 min (including planned downtime) on paper as well as in practice.

Multiple industries can leverage Cloud Spanner to deliver value to their customers. Most databases today need to make compromises between scale and consistency. With Cloud Spanner, you get the finest relational database structure and non-relational database scale and performance with external strong consistency across rows, regions, and continents. One of property of Cloud Spanner is that it scales horizontally and it serves data with low latency while maintaining transactional consistency and best in class 99.999% (five 9s) availability - 10x less downtime than four nines (< 5 minutes per year). Cloud Spanner helps future-proof your database backend. It can scale to indiscriminately giant database sizes to assist avoid rewrites and migrations. The use of multiple databases or sharded databases as an alternative solution introduces spare quality and price. IT admins and DBAs are inundated with thankless tasks. With Cloud Spanner, you can specialize in value-add and innovation rather than maintenance. Making or scaling a globally replicated info for mission-critical apps takes just one or two clicks. Industry-leading high-availability and Google-grade security as defaults, not pricey add-ons, facilitate apps to stay online and secure. When architecting apps, Cloud Spanner has an easy request model that doesn't charge additional over your configuration selection for high-availability, replication, or guaranteeing safer, international powerfully consistent data. Cloud Spanner is a relational database with full relative linguistics and handles schema changes as an internet operation with no planned period of time. You can utilize existing SQL skills to query data in Cloud Spanner victimization acquainted, industry-standard ANSI 2011 SQL. You can deliver better experiences for end users with external, robust consistency. Cloud Spanner is battle tested by Google's own mission-critical applications and services. It comprises Google-grade security, encryption by default in transit and at rest, granular identity and access management, comprehensive audit logging, custom-manufactured hardware, hardware tracking and disposal, and the Google-owned and controlled international network.

Some of the schema design considerations in Cloud Spanner are as follows:

- Defining a proper primary key which could be a combination of one or more columns. Also, hashing of the keys can be utilized.
- **Database splits:** Cloud Spanner divides your data into chunks called splits, where an individual splits can move independently from each other and get assigned to different servers, which can be in different physical locations.

- **Load based splitting of data:** Cloud Spanner performs load-based splitting to mitigate read hotspots.

Cloud Bigtable

Cloud Bigtable is a sparsely populated table which can scale to billions of rows and thousands of columns, enabling you to store terabytes or maybe petabytes of data. One price in every row is indexed; this price is thought because of the row key. Cloud Bigtable is good for storing massive amount of single-keyed data with very low latency. It supports high read and write throughput at low latency, and it's a perfect data source for MapReduce operations.

Cloud Bigtable is exposed to applications through multiple consumer libraries, together with a supported extension to the Apache HBase library for Java. As a result, it integrates with the prevailing Apache scheme of open-source massive data software.

Cloud Bigtable's powerful back-end servers provide many key benefits over a self-managed HBase installation:

- **Incredible scalability:** Cloud Bigtable scales in direct proportion to the number of machines in your cluster. A self-managed HBase installation features a style bottleneck that limits the performance once a threshold is reached. Cloud Bigtable doesn't have this bottleneck, thus users can scale their cluster up to handle additional reads and writes.

- **Simple administration:** Cloud Bigtable handles upgrades and restarts transparently, and it automatically maintains high data durability. To copy data, merely add a second cluster to the existing instance, and replication starts mechanically. No additional managing masters or regions; simply style table schemas, and Cloud Bigtable can handle the remaining for your organization.

- **Cluster resizing without downtime:** Users can increase the scale of a Cloud Bigtable cluster for several hours to handle an outsized load, and then cut back the cluster's size again—all with no downtime. Once a user modifies a cluster's size, it usually takes simply a few minutes under load for Cloud Bigtable to balance performance across all the nodes in the cluster.

Cloud Bigtable benefits are that it is good for applications that require very high throughput and scalability for non-structured key/value data, where each value is usually smaller than 10 MB. Cloud Bigtable conjointly excels as a storage engine for batch MapReduce operations, stream processing/analytics, and machine-learning applications.

Companies can use Cloud Bigtable to store and query all the subsequent forms of data:

- Time-series data like central processing unit and memory usage over time for multiple servers.
- Marketing data like purchase histories and client preferences.
- Financial data like transaction histories, stock costs, and currency exchange rates.
- Internet of Things data like usage reports from energy meters and residential appliances.
- Graph data like info regarding how users are connected to one another.

Cloud Bigtable storage model

Cloud Bigtable stores data in massively scalable tables, each of which is a sorted key / value map. The table consists of rows, each of which usually describes one entity, and columns that contain individual values for every row. Every row is indexed by one row key, and columns that are associated with each other are usually classified together into a column family. Every column is known by a mixture of the column family and a column qualifier that could be a distinctive name within the column family.

Each row/column intersection will contain multiple cells, or versions, at totally different timestamps, providing a record of how the stored data has been altered over time. Cloud Bigtable tables are sparse; if a cell doesn't contain any data, it doesn't take up any space.

Cloud Bigtable architecture

The following diagram shows a simplified version of Cloud Bigtable's overall architecture:

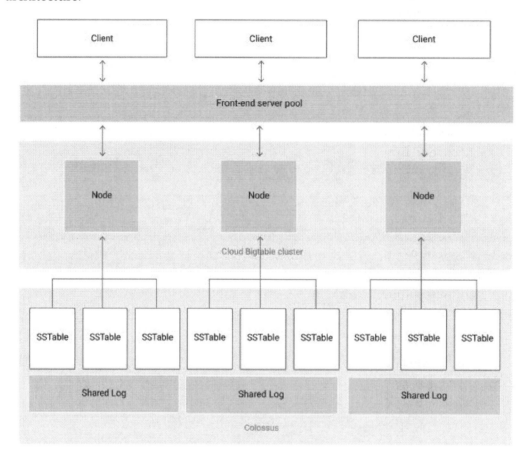

Figure 2.9: Cloud Bigtable architecture

As the diagram shows, all consumer requests undergo a front-end server before they're sent to a Cloud Bigtable node. The nodes are organized into a Cloud Bigtable cluster that belongs to a Cloud Bigtable instance, which is a container for the cluster.

Each node within the cluster handles a subset of the requests to the cluster. By adding nodes to a cluster, you will be able to increase the quantity of simultaneous requests that the cluster can handle as well as the maximum throughput for the whole cluster. If users enable replication by adding a second cluster, they will be able to additionally send differing types of traffic to different clusters, and they will be able to fail over to at least one cluster if the opposite cluster becomes unavailable.

A Cloud Bigtable table is sharded into blocks of contiguous rows, called tablets, to assist balance the workload of queries. Tablets are stored on Colossus, Google's file system, in the SSTable format. An SSTable provides a persistent, ordered immutable map from keys to values, where both keys and values are whimsical byte strings. Every tablet is related to a selected Cloud Bigtable node. In addition to the SSTable files, all writes are stored in Colossus's shared log as they are acknowledged by Cloud Bigtable, providing increased durability.

Importantly, data isn't stored in Cloud Bigtable nodes themselves; every node has pointers to a set of tablets that are stored on Colossus. As a result:

- Rebalancing tablets from one node to a different is very quick because the data isn't copied. Cloud Bigtable merely updates the pointers for every node.

- Recovery from the failure of a Cloud Bigtable node is extremely quick because only data must be migrated to the replacement node.

- When a Cloud Bigtable node fails, data lost is zero.

Cloud Bigtable treats all data as raw byte strings for many functions. The sole time Cloud Bigtable tries to determine the sort is for increment operations, where the target should be a 64-bit integer encoded as an 8-byte big-endian price.

Cloud Bigtable isn't a relative database; it doesn't support SQL queries or joins, nor does it support multi-row transactions. Also, it's not an honest solution for storing but 1 TB of data.

For Cloud Bigtable schema, keep the following points in mind:

- Each table has only one index, the row key. There are no secondary indices.

- Rows are sorted lexicographically by the row key, from the lowest to the highest byte string. Row keys are sorted in big-endian, or network, byte order, the binary equivalent of alphabetical order.

- Columns are grouped by the column family and sorted in the lexicographic order within the column family.

- All operations are atomic at the row level. For example, if you update two rows in a table, it's possible that one row will be updated successfully, and the other update will fail. For this reason, follow these guidelines:

  o Avoid schema designs that require atomicity across rows.

  o Mostly keep all information for an entity in a single row. However, if your use case doesn't require you to make atomic updates or reads to an entity, you can split the entity across multiple rows. Splitting across multiple rows is recommended if the entity data is large (hundreds of MB).

- Ideally, both reads and writes should be distributed evenly across the row space of the table.

- Related entities should be stored in adjacent rows, which make reads more efficient.

- Cloud Bigtable tables are sparse. Empty columns don't take up any space. As a result, it often makes sense to create a very large number of columns, even if most columns are empty in most rows.

Cloud BigQuery

BigQuery is an offering within GCP which a serverless, highly scalable enterprise data warehouse. BigQuery is designed to help data analysts who make them more productive with unmatched price-performance. Since there is no infrastructure to manage, an organization can focus on discovering meaningful insights using familiar SQL and do not need to engage a database administrator.

BigQuery helps in analyzing all batches and streaming data by making a logical data warehouse over managed columnar storage; furthermore, as data from object storage and spreadsheets. It can produce blazing-fast dashboards and reports with the in-memory metal Engine. It can build and operate in machine learning solutions or do geospatial analysis using easy SQL. Firmly share insights inside an organization and on the far side as datasets, queries, spreadsheets, and reports. BigQuery's powerful streaming captures and analyses data in real time, enabling certain insights. Along with that, analysis up to 1 TB of data and storing 10 GB of data for free per month.

Some of the important characteristics are as follows:

- **Focus on the analytics, not your infrastructure:** Get up and run quick. Set up your data warehouse in seconds and begin to query data like a shot. BigQuery runs blazing-fast SQL queries on gigabytes to petabytes of data and makes it simple to affix public or industrial datasets together with your data. Train an machine learning model in minutes or drive geospatial analysis with plain SQL. Ingest streaming data and visualize insights. Eliminate the long work of provisioning resources and scale back your period of time with a serverless infrastructure that handles all current maintenance, together with patches and upgrades. BigQuery supports acquainted ANSI-compliant SQL and provides ODBC and JDBC drivers to form integration with data quick and simple.

- **Scale seamlessly:** BigQuery separates storage and computes to alter elastic scaling that streamlines capabilities coming up for data warehouses. BigQuery meets the challenges of time period analytics by investment Google's serverless infrastructure that uses automatic scaling and superior streaming uptake to load data. BigQuery's managed columnar storage, massively parallel execution, and automatic performance optimizations empower users to quickly and at the same time, analyze data from your cloud data despite the number of users or datasize.

- **Accelerate your insights with powerful analysis:** Gain a full read of all of your data with seamless queries of information kept in BigQuery's managed columnar storage, Cloud Storage, Cloud Bigtable, Sheets, and Drive. BigQuery integrates with existing ETL tools like Informatica and Talend to counterpoint your data with dts. BigQuery supports well-liked BI tools like Tableau, MicroStrategy, Looker, and data Studio out of the box; thus, anyone will simply produce beautiful reports and dashboards. Automatically ingest and visualize Google Ads and promote data victimization BigQuery data Transfer Service to line up a high-powered promoting data warehouse in only many clicks. Through BigQuery data Transfer Service, users additionally gain access to data connectors that assist you simply transfer data from Teradata and Amazon S3 to BigQuery.

- **Protect your business data and investments:** BigQuery makes it simple to maintain a powerful security and governance foundation. Eliminate data operation burdens with automatic data replication for disaster recovery and high availability of process for no further charge. BigQuery provides a 99.9% SLA subject to terms and follows the Privacy defend Principles.

- **Control prices and cut back TCO:** It solely charges for the storage and cipher resources that are being employed because of BigQuery's serverless design. BigQuery's separation of storage and cipher makes it simple to scale severally and endlessly on demand, leading to low-priced, economical storage. BigQuery will lower the whole price of possession by 56%–88%.

We will be discussing the architecture and more details of BigQuery in the upcoming chapters.

Conclusion

In this chapter, we learned about the different types of storage services provided by GCP. It is a very important aspect of designing for any solution to choose the best option which is suitable for particular use cases. Each service has a set of properties, characteristics, and use cases which has been explained in detail to help end users in order to take appropriate decisions.

Questions

1. What are different types of storage which can be used to unstructured data in the GCP?

2. Highlight some difference between Cloud Big Table and Cloud SQL.

3. Which all database options are available within the Cloud SQL service in the GCP?

4. Which scenario user should opt for Cloud Spanner service of the GCP?

CHAPTER 3

Data Processing and Message with Dataflow and Pub/Sub

Introduction

In this chapter, we discuss about data processing and messaging techniques using **Google Cloud Platform (GCP)**. GCP supports multiple different services to achieve data processing and real-time messaging. It depends on one's use case to select which services to use in order to get accurate output along with cost and performance. Once data is stored and persisted in any GCP environment, it needs to be processed as per business requirement to make it worthy. In this chapter, we will discuss about Dataflow and Pub/Sub services which enable users to apply data transformation and push real-time messages within GCP.

Structure

This chapter covers the details of Cloud Dataflow and Cloud Pub/Sub in below structure:

- Cloud Dataflow
- Cloud Pub/Sub

Objectives

The objective of this chapter is to explain the different concepts of Cloud Dataflow and Cloud Pub/Sub with the help of use cases. Readers will get well versed with the architecture, features of each service and can select appropriate services based on requirement.

Cloud Dataflow

There are multiple fully managed serviced offered by GCP. Cloud Dataflow is one of them which provide help in data transformation, data enrichment, and multiple data processing features. It supports both stream (real-time) and batch (historical) modes with equal reliability and fluency. There were always challenges around implementing complex transformations and there were complex workarounds and compromises for the same. Cloud Dataflow overcomes those challenges while transforming and processing the data. As this is a fully managed service, serverless mechanism for resource provisioning and management is being used within Dataflow. It can scale as per need and have access to virtually limitless capacity to resolve biggest data processing challenges. Dataflow charges as per the usage (only for what is being used) and hence, limits the cost and expenses.

Multiple industries use Cloud Dataflow to resolve data transformational problems. Some of the use cases include the following:

- Clickstream and event stream, point-of-sale and different types of segmentation analysis in banking and retail sector industries.
- Fraud, risk, and financial crime detection in banking and financial services.
- Help in enabling unique user experience in gaming.
- IoT data analytics in multiple industries across healthcare, manufacturing, and logistics.

The following diagram shows that cloud dataflow is a fully managed service within the GCP:

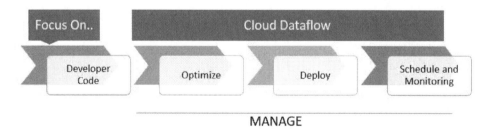

Figure 3.1: Explaining Dataflow

As discussed earlier, Dataflow is a GCP-based service and hence, works on a serverless method. With this approach, performance, scaling, availability, security, and compliance are handled automatically by eliminating operational overhead cost. This helps users to focus on programming rather than managing server clusters and other operational aspects. Since Cloud Dataflow is a managed service, it takes care of optimizing, deploying, and monitoring the code.

Cloud Dataflow integrates easily and smoothly with Stackdriver. Stackdriver is GCP's integrated monitoring solution which helps to track, monitor, logs and fine-tune pipelines when they are executing. It has very attractive dashboards, logging and advanced alerting to facilitate the unseen problems and reply to the same. One of the main advantages of Stackdriver is that it seamlessly integrates with Cloud Dataflow and other GCP services for ingesting streaming events (Cloud Pub/Sub) and GCP services like BigQuery for data warehousing and cloud machine learning for machine leaning solutions and many other services.

Custom extensions can be built on a beam-based SDK and provides additional choice of another execution engines like Apache Spark via Cloud Dataproc or on-premises.

Cloud Dataflow ensures quick, simple pipeline development through expressive SQL, Java, and Python APIs within the Apache Beam SDK. Beam's exclusive, integrated development model supports to reuse a lot of code over streaming and batch pipelines. Apache Beam SDK also supports a wide range of windowing and session analysis primitives as well as a system of source and sink connectors.

Cloud Dataflow SQL allows to use SQL queries to develop and run Dataflow jobs from the BigQuery web UI. Dataflow SQL integrates with Apache Beam SQL and supports a variant of the ZetaSQL query syntax. ZetaSQL's streaming extensions can be used to define streaming data parallel-processing pipelines and provides additional features as below:

- With SQL skills, it is easy to develop and run streaming pipelines from the BigQuery web UI. A user does not need to set up an SDK development environment or know how to program in Java or Python.

- Join streams (such as Pub/Sub) with snapshotted datasets (such as BigQuery tables and Cloud Storage filesets).

- Query streams or static datasets with SQL by associating schemas with objects such as tables, Cloud Storage filesets, and Pub/Sub topics.

- Write results into a BigQuery table for analysis and dashboarding.

Google Cloud Dataflow is one among Apache Beam runners and is designed on top of Google Compute Engine which means during the Dataflow job execution, it is getting executed on Google Compute Engine instances. During initiation of job, Apache Beam SDK is installed on every worker along with other libraries which are specified, and then it is executed. For the Dataflow job, it is important to specify the type of GCE virtual machine as well as size of the hard disk. Of course, depending on the number of workers which process data, VM can be enhanced during run time.

There is a feature called **Dataflow Shuffle**, which can be used for shuffle phase, in transforms such as `GroupByKey`. These combinations are executed on managed service (of course there is some VM at the bottom, however that's hidden) and not on Dataflow worker VM and hence shuffle can be considerably quicker.

The following diagram of Cloud Dataflow integrates seamlessly with other GCP services:

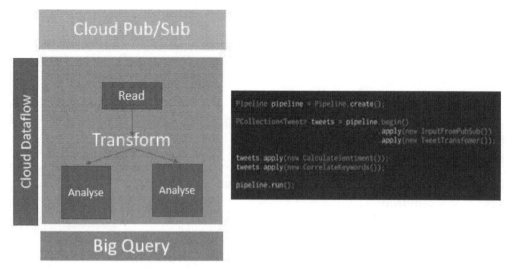

Figure 3.2: Dataflow integration with source and target

Dataflow is designed to support the rest of Google's existing cloud portfolio. If Google BigQuery is already being used, then Dataflow will help to transform, prep, and filter data before it gets written to BigQuery. Along with writing the data into BigQuery, Dataflow can also be used to read from BigQuery to join BigQuery data with other sources. Once data is integrated with other source systems and processed, it can also be written back to BigQuery.

Cloud Dataflow templates

Cloud Dataflow templates execute from a variety of environments (that is, source and targets) and allow you to stage your pipelines on Cloud Storage. Users can use one of the Google provided templates or create their own in case of specific requirements.

Templates provide with additional benefits compared to traditional Cloud Dataflow deployment such as:

- Since Pipeline is considered as a template which is inbuilt and hence execution of the same need not require recompilation of the code every time.
- Users can execute pipelines in the absence of the development environment and associated dependencies that are common with traditional deployment. This is useful in case of scheduling recurring batch jobs.
- With runtime parameters, you can customize the execution of the pipeline.
- Non-technical users also can execute the templates easily from the GCP Console, gcloud command-line tool, or the REST API.

There is some limitation of updating an existing pipeline that uses a Cloud Dataflow template which is not currently supported.

Traditional versus templated job execution

Cloud Dataflow templates come with a new development and execution workflow that varies from the traditional job execution workflow. The template workflow splits the development step from the staging and execution steps. Let's see them one by one:

- **Traditional Cloud Dataflow jobs:** Apache Beam pipeline development and job execution all happen within a development environment. A typical workflow for traditional Cloud Dataflow jobs:

    1. In order to develop the pipeline, developers build a development environment and then develop the pipeline. As discussed earlier, this development environment should have the Apache Beam SDK and other dependencies.

    2. The pipeline can be executed from the development environment. It is the responsibility of Apache Beam SDK to stage files in Cloud Storage, create a job request file and then submit the file to the Cloud Dataflow service.

- **Templated Cloud Dataflow jobs:** In the preceding section, we saw how a traditional dataflow jobs works. Now, let's quickly talk about the template-based cloud dataflow. When Cloud Dataflow templates are being used, staging and execution are separate steps. With addition of this split, flexibility comes into the picture which helps to decide who can run jobs and where the jobs are run from. Typical workflow for templated Cloud Dataflow jobs are as follows:

    1. In order to develop the pipeline, developers build a development environment and then develop the pipeline. As discussed earlier, this development environment should have the Apache Beam SDK and other dependencies.

    2. Developers execute the pipeline and create a template. The Apache Beam SDK stages files in Cloud Storage, creates a template file (like job request), and saves the template file in Cloud Storage.

    3. This enables non-developer users to easily execute jobs with the GCP Console, gcloud command-line tool, or the REST API to submit template file execution requests to the Cloud Dataflow service.

Cloud Dataflow templates which are a set of open source templates provided by Google. Some of the Google provided templates are as follows:

- **Streaming templates:** Templates for processing data in stream flow:
    o   Cloud Pub/Sub Subscription to BigQuery

- o Cloud Pub/Sub Topic to BigQuery
- o Cloud Pub/Sub to Cloud Pub/Sub
- o Cloud Pub/Sub to Cloud Storage Avro
- o Cloud Pub/Sub to Cloud Storage Text
- o Cloud Storage Text to BigQuery (Stream)
- o Cloud Storage Text to Cloud Pub/Sub (Stream)
- o Data Masking/Tokenization using Cloud DLP from Cloud Storage to BigQuery (Stream)

- **Batch Dataflow templates:** Templates for processing data in bulk:
  - o Cloud Bigtable to Cloud Storage Avro
  - o Cloud Bigtable to Cloud Storage SequenceFiles
  - o Cloud Datastore to Cloud Storage Text
  - o Cloud Spanner to Cloud Storage Avro
  - o Cloud Spanner to Cloud Storage Text
  - o Cloud Storage Avro to Cloud Bigtable
  - o Cloud Storage Avro to Cloud Spanner
  - o Cloud Storage SequenceFiles to Cloud Bigtable
  - o Cloud Storage Text to BigQuery
  - o Cloud Storage Text to Cloud Datastore
  - o Cloud Storage Text to Cloud Pub/Sub (Batch)
  - o Cloud Storage Text to Cloud Spanner
  - o Java Database Connectivity (JDBC) to BigQuery

- **Utility templates:**
  - o Bulk Compress Cloud Storage Files
  - o Bulk Decompress Cloud Storage Files
  - o Cloud Datastore Bulk Delete

Data transformation with Cloud Dataflow

Cloud Dataflow integrates seamlessly with Google cloud services and supports any type of data transformation/processing which is shown in the following diagram:

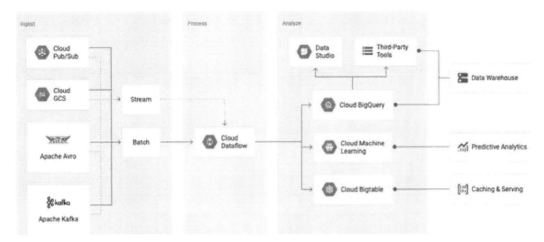

Figure 3.3: Data movement from source to target using Dataflow

The preceding diagram shows how the dataflow jobs can be used a data transformation pipeline. It can receive the data in the Batch and Streaming mode and then process it as per business requirement (applying transformation) and then load into the target data storage which could be Cloud BigQuery, Cloud Bigtable, and more. Further, these transformed and cleansed data can be used for multiple different use cases (that is, predictive analytics, advanced reporting, and more).

The following are the steps for executing large data text processing pipeline in Cloud Dataflow:

1. **Overview:**

    In order to develop and execute a wide range of data process, data transformation patterns and continuous computation, GCP provided a unified programming model and managed service supported called Dataflow. Dataflow is a managed service which will assign resources on-demand as and when required to maintain high utilization efficiency and low latency. In this section, we will discuss about the setup and requirements needed for processing big data text in Cloud Dataflow.

    The Dataflow pipeline supports both type of data processing, which is a batch and stream process; therefore, developers don't need to create trade-offs between accuracy, charge, and processing time.

    In the following examples, we will understand about a Dataflow pipeline which counts the occurrences of unique words in a text file.

2. **Setup and requirements:**

    1. Start with login into GCP via the GCP Console, that is, **console.cloud. google.com** in order to create a new project as shown in the following

screenshot if not existing one (Project ID is an exclusive name across all Google Cloud projects):

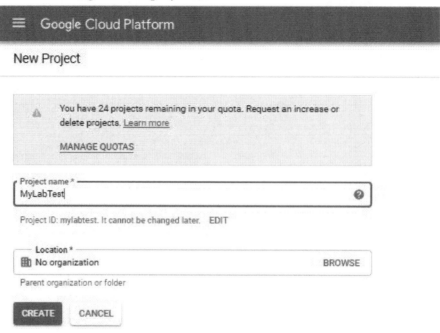

Figure 3.4: Creating a new project from the GCP Console

2. Once the project is created, go to the **Menu** icon and click on the **API Manager** page to **Enable** the following APIs, as shown in the following screenshot:

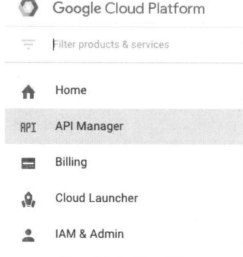

Figure 3.5: Enabling API's

3. Please search for **Google Compute Engine API**, as shown in the following screenshot:

Figure 3.6: Search for GCE API

4. Once GCE APIs are found, enable/invoke that API, as shown in the following screenshot, via the GCP Console:

Figure 3.7: Showing APIs and Services List

5. Enable the following APIs from the APIs and services page of the GCP Console:

- Google Dataflow API
- API for Stackdriver Logging
- Google Cloud Storage
- Google Cloud Storage JSON API
- API for BigQuery

- Google Cloud Pub/Sub API
- API for Google Cloud Datastore

3. **In order to create a new Cloud Storage bucket below are the steps:**

   1. Please click on the Storage option once log in into the GCP Console via the **Menu** icon.

   2. In order to initiate a new storage bucket, go to the `Create bucket` button and fill all the information as per required in the displayed form (make sure to enter the globally unique bucket name).

   3. After successfully creating the bucket, a prompt message is shown as `There are no objects in this bucket:`

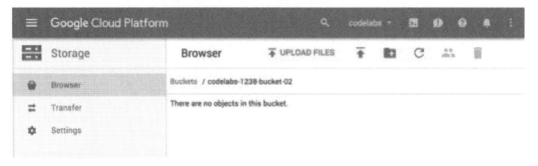

Figure 3.8: Google storage with no objects

4. **Start Cloud Shell:**

   1. In order to start cloud shell, execute the following command which will set up the default Project ID:

   ```
   gcloud config set project <PROJECT_ID>
   ```

5. **Create a Maven project:**

   1. Once the preceding command gets executed successfully, the project ID is set and then kick-off a Maven project which contains Cloud Dataflow SDK for Java.

   2. Execute the following command in Cloud Shell in order to set up the Maven project:

   ```
   mvn sampletype:generate

   mvn sampletype:generate \

   -DsampletypeArtifactId=google-cloud-dataflow-java-
   sampletypes-examples \

   -DsampletypeGroupId=com.google.cloud.dataflow \

   -DsampletypeVersion=1.9.0 \

   -DgroupId=com.example \
   ```

```
-DartifactId=sample-dataflow \
-Dversion="0.1" \
-DinteractiveMode=false \
-Dpackage=com.example
```

3. A new directory is created called sample-dataflow under the current directory once the preceding commands get executed successfully. As discussed earlier, it will contain a Maven project which consists of the Cloud Dataflow SDK for Java and pipelines.

6. **Execute Cloud Dataflow pipeline for text processing pipeline:**

1. Define two environment variables for project ID and Cloud Storage bucket names as per the following commands:

```
export PROJECT_ID=<sample_project_id>
export BUCKET_NAME=<sample_bucket_name>
```

2. With the help of Cloud Shell, change the directory and go to the `sample-dataflow` directory:

3. Let's create a new pipeline and name it `WordCount` which reads text, tokens, and takes a frequency count on each of these words.

4. In order to begin the pipeline, execute the following command in Cloud Shell or the Terminal window:

```
mvn compile exec:java
```

5. Set up the environment variable like –project, –stagingLocation, and –output arguments with the following command references which have been set up earlier in this step:

```
mvn compile exec:java \
-Dexec.mainClass=com.example.WordCount \
-Dexec.args="-project=${PROJECT_ID} \
-stagingLocation=gs://${BUCKET_NAME}/staging/ \
-output=gs://${BUCKET_NAME}/output \
-runner=BlockingDataflowPipelineRunner"
```

7. **Let's verify if the jobs are successful:**

   1. Go to the Cloud Dataflow Monitoring UI where all the jobs created earlier are shown and then check whether the status of this WordCount job is successful or not:

Figure 3.9: Successful execution of Dataflow job

In the following screenshot, the dataflow job is captured:

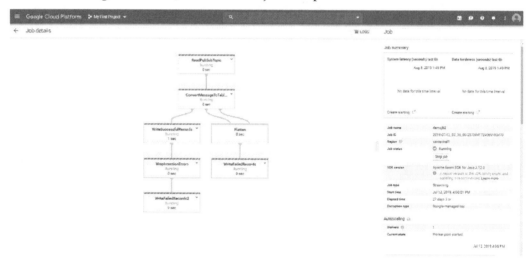

Figure 3.10: Dataflow job

   2. When the job starts, it is in the running state, and it may take 4-5 minutes to complete this job.

   3. Since the output is specified as a bucket, remember that when the pipeline is executed, it will create a different output and staging file, as shown in the following screenshot:

Storage	**Browser** ⬆ UPLOAD FILES ⬆ UPLOAD FOLDER 🗂 CREATE FOLE	
🪣 Browser	Buckets / my-wordcount-storage-bucket	
⇄ Transfer	☐ Name	Size	Type
⚙ Settings	☐ 🗋 OUTPUT.txt-00000-of-00009	5.41 KB	text/plain
	☐ 🗋 OUTPUT.txt-00001-of-00009	5.12 KB	text/plain
	☐ 🗋 OUTPUT.txt-00002-of-00009	5.29 KB	text/plain
	☐ 🗋 OUTPUT.txt-00003-of-00009	5.4 KB	text/plain
	☐ 🗋 OUTPUT.txt-00004-of-00009	5.2 KB	text/plain
	☐ 🗋 OUTPUT.txt-00005-of-00009	5.01 KB	text/plain
	☐ 🗋 OUTPUT.txt-00006-of-00009	5.15 KB	text/plain
	☐ 🗋 OUTPUT.txt-00007-of-00009	5.76 KB	text/plain
	☐ 🗋 OUTPUT.txt-00008-of-00009	5.45 KB	text/plain
	☐ 📁 staging/	—	Folder

Figure 3.11: Output file in a Bucket

8. **Shut down resources:**

Once the pipeline execution is completed, jump to the storage buckets from the console and shut down resources so that the bucket can be deleted which is created earlier, as shown in the following screenshot. Using the Drain option to stop the job makes sure that the Dataflow service finishes the job in its current state. The Dataflow job stops ingesting new data from input sources soon after receiving the drain request (typically, within a few minutes). However, the Dataflow service preserves any existing resources such as worker instances to finish processing and writing any buffered data in the pipeline. When all pending processing and write operations are complete, the Dataflow service cleans up the Google Cloud resources associated with the job which includes storage as well which is shown in the following screenshot:

Figure 3.12: Storage Bucket

Pick a bucket inside the storage bucket:

Figure 3.13: Buckets in Storage

The following screenshot shows how to select a bucket which needs to be deleted post processing:

Delete bucket?

All of its contents will also be deleted. You cannot undo this action.

CANCEL   DELETE

Figure 3.14: Delete bucket confirmation box

In the preceding example, you saw how to enable a data flow pipe. Once it is successfully executed, delete all the dependent resources, including the bucket.

As discussed in the earlier section about the Dataflow template to perform WordCount exercise, let's see how it works.

Example of the WordCount Template

The WordCount template is a batch pipeline. The WordCount template reads text from Cloud Storage which is treated as the source and then tokenizes the text lines into individual words. Finally, it comes up with a frequency count on each of the words.

Here are template parameters which need to be defined:

Parameter	Description
inputFile	The Cloud Storage input file path.
output	The Cloud Storage output file path and prefix.

There are multiple ways to execute Cloud Dataflow jobs. These are via the GCP Console, gcloud commands, and APIs.

Here are the steps to run the WordCount template Dataflow job from the GCP Console:

1. Open the GCP Console and go to the Cloud Dataflow page.

2. On the **Cloud Dataflow** page, click on **CREATE JOB FROM TEMPLATE** as shown in the following screenshot:

Figure 3.15

3. There are multiple dataflow templates present as stated earlier. Hence, from the drop-down menu, select the WordCount template from the Cloud Dataflow template.

4. Name that dataflow template job in the **Job Name** field. The Dataflow job name should be valid and must match the regular expression [a-z]([-a-z0-9]{0,38}[a-z0-9]).

5. Enter parameter values in the provided parameter fields.

6. Click on **Run** Job.

Once the WordCount template dataflow jobs get successfully executed, there will be an output file that will get generated at the mentioned output parameter on Cloud storage.

Apache Beam

Apache Beam SDK is used to build a Dataflow program. Apache beam is an open source and unified model which is leveraged for both batch- and streaming-data parallel-processing pipelines. The Apache Beam programming model helps in simplifying the development of large-scale data processing. One of the Apache Beam SDKs can be leveraged to build a program which defines the pipeline. Another Apache Beam's SDK supported distributed processing backends such as Cloud Dataflow and helps to execute the pipeline. This model enables a programmer to concentrate on the logical composition of data processing job, rather than on the physical orchestration of parallel processing. With this approach, a programmer can focus on what their data processing jobs need. A programmer does not need to focus on how that job gets executed and other aspects.

The Apache Beam model provides useful abstractions that insulate from low-level details of distributed processing such as coordinating individual workers, sharding datasets, and other such tasks. Cloud Dataflow fully takes care of these low-level details.

The following are the basic concepts and components of Apache Beam:

- **Pipelines:** A pipeline encapsulates the whole series of computations involved in reading input data, transforming that data, and writing output data. The input source and output sink can be the same or of various varieties, permitting you to convert data from one format to a different format as required. Apache Beam programs start by constructing a `Pipeline` object, and then use that object as the basis for creating the pipeline's datasets. Every pipeline represents a single, repeatable job.

- **PCollection:** A `PCollection` signifies a potentially distributed, multi-element dataset that acts as the pipeline's data. Apache Beam transforms use `PCollection` objects as inputs and outputs for each and every step in your pipeline. A `PCollection` has the capability to hold a dataset of a fixed set size or an unbounded dataset from a continuously updating data source.

- **Transforms:** A transform is the main component of the Apache beam and represents a processing operation during transformation of data. A transform takes one or more `PCollection` objects as input, performs an operation that is defined on every element in this collection, and generates one or more `PCollection` objects as the output. A transform can perform any kind of processing operation, including performing mathematical computations on data, changing data from one format to another, grouping data together, reading and writing data, filtering data to output, or combining data elements into single values.

- **ParDo:** `ParDo` is a core parallel processing operation within the Apache Beam SDKs, which invoke a user-specified function on each and every element of the input `PCollection`. `ParDo` assembles zero or more output elements into an output `PCollection`. The `ParDo` transform processes each element independently and possibly in parallel.

- **Pipeline I/O:** Apache Beam I/O connectors allow you to read and write data into your pipeline. An I/O connector contains a source and a sink. All Apache Beam sources and sinks are transforms that allow the pipeline to work with data from a variety of various data storage formats which will additionally write a custom I/O connector.

- **Aggregation:** Aggregation is the method of computing some value from multiple input elements. The first computational pattern for aggregation in Apache Beam is to group all elements with a common key and window. Then, it combines every group of elements using an associative and commutative operation.

- **User defined Functions (UDFs):** Some operations within Apache Beam enable executing user-defined code as a way of configuring the transform. For ParDo, user-defined code specifies the operation to apply to each element, and for combine, it specifies how values should be combined. A pipeline can contain UDFs written in a completely different language than the language of your runner. A pipeline may also contain UDFs written in a lot of different languages.

- **Runner:** Runners are the software that accepts a pipeline and executes it. Most runners (Direct Runner, Dataflow Runner, Flink Runner, Spark Runner, and more) are translators or adapters to massively parallel big-data processing systems. Other runners play an important role for native testing and debugging.

The following are the advanced concepts in Apache Beam:

- **Event time:** The time a data event happens is determined by the timestamp on the data element itself. This can be contrasted with the time when the data element gets processed at any stage inside the pipeline.

- **Windowing:** Windowing allows grouping operations over unbounded collections by dividing the collection into windows of finite collections according to the timestamps of the individual elements. A windowing function tells the runner a way to assign elements to an initial window, and the way to merge windows of grouped elements. Apache Beam permits you to outline different sorts of windows or use the predefined windowing functions.

- **Watermarks:** Apache Beam tracks a watermark. This system is a notion of when all data in a certain window will be expected to arrive within the pipeline. Apache Beam tracks a watermark which results into data isn't guaranteed to arrive in a pipeline in time order or at predictable intervals. Along with that, there are no guarantees that data events can appear in the pipeline in the same order that they were generated.

- **Trigger:** Triggers determine when to emit aggregated results as data arrives. For bounded data, results are emitted after the input has been processed. For unbounded data, results are emitted when the watermark passes the end of the window, indicating that the system believes that all input data for that window has been processed. Apache Beam provides many predefined triggers and lets you combine them.

Different parameters which need to be configured while executing a Dataflow pipeline are shown in the following table:

Field	Type	Description	Default value
runner	Class (NameOf Runner)	The `PipelineRunner` to use. This field allows you to determine the `PipelineRunner` at runtime.	`DirectRunner` (local mode)
streaming	boolean	Specifies whether the streaming mode is enabled or disabled; true if enabled.	If your pipeline reads from an unbounded source, the default value is true. Otherwise, false.

project	String	The project ID for your Google Cloud project. This is required if you want to run your pipeline using the Dataflow managed service.	If not set, defaults to the currently configured project in the Cloud SDK.
gcpTemp Location	String	Cloud Storage path for temporary files. Must be a valid Cloud Storage URL, beginning with gs://.	
staging Location	String	Cloud Storage path for staging local files. Must be a valid Cloud Storage URL, beginning with gs://.	If not set, defaults to what you specified for tempLocation.
autoscaling Algorithm	String	The autoscaling mode for your Dataflow job. Possible values are THROUGHPUT_BASED to enable autoscaling, or NONE to disable. See Auto tuning features to learn more about how autoscaling works in the Dataflow managed service.	Defaults to THROUGHPUT_BASED for all batch Dataflow jobs that use Dataflow SDK for Java version 1.6.0 or later; defaults to NONE for streaming jobs or batch jobs using earlier versions of the Dataflow SDK for Java.
numWorkers	int	The initial number of Google Compute Engine instances to use when executing your pipeline. This option determines how many workers the Dataflow service will kick off when job begins.	If unspecified, the Dataflow service determines an appropriate number of workers.
maxNum Workers	int	The maximum number of Compute Engine instances to be made available to your pipeline during execution. Note that this can be higher than the initial number of workers (specified by numWorkers to allow your job to scale up, automatically or otherwise.	If unspecified, the Dataflow service will determine an appropriate number of workers.
region	String	Specifying a regional endpoint allows you to define a region for deploying your Dataflow jobs.	If not set, defaults to us-central1.

zone	String	The Compute Engine zone for launching worker instances to run your pipeline.	If you specified the region parameter, the zone parameter will default to a zone from the corresponding region. You can override this behavior by specifying a different zone.
dataflow KmsKey	String	Specifies the **customer-managed encryption key (CMEK)** used to encrypt data at rest. You can control the encryption key through KMS. You must also specify gcpTempLocation to use this feature.	If unspecified, Dataflow uses the default Google Cloud encryption instead of a CMEK.
network	String	The Compute Engine network for launching Compute Engine instances to run your pipeline. See how to specify your network.	If not set, Google Cloud assumes that you intend to use a network named default.
subnetwork	String	The Compute Engine subnetwork for launching Compute Engine instances to run your pipeline. See how to specify your subnetwork.	The Dataflow service determines the default value.
disk SizeGb	int	The disk size, in gigabytes, to use on each remote Compute Engine worker instance. The minimum disk size is 30 GB, to account for the worker boot image and local logs. If your pipeline shuffles data, you should allocate more than the minimum.	Set to 0 to use the default size defined in your Cloud Platform project. Warning: Lowering the disk size reduces available shuffle I/O. Shuffle-bound jobs may result in increased runtime and job cost.

Working of Apache Beam code

The MinimalWordCount is a pipeline that includes multiple transforms for reading data into the pipeline, cleansing or transforming the data, and finally writing out the results. A transformation can consist of an individual operation, or can contain multiple nested transforms (which is a composite transform) within a transformation.

As discussed earlier, each transform can accept the input data and then generate some output data. The input and output data are denoted by the SDK class PCollection. PCollection is a special class, which is provided by the Beam SDK and can be used to indicate a dataset of virtually any size, including unbounded datasets. The following diagram shows the different transformations in a Dataflow pipeline:

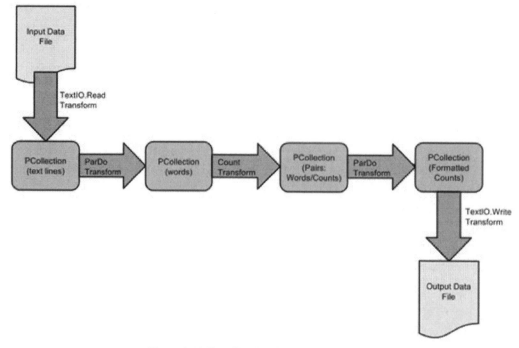

Figure 3.16: Dataflow Pipeline Transformation

The MinimalWordCount pipeline comprises five transforms as shown in the preceding diagram:

1. The input data read() transform is applied to the Pipeline object and then it generates a PCollection as output. Each element in PCollection which is an output signifies a single line of text from the incoming file. This example uses the input data stored in a publicly available Google Cloud Storage bucket (gs://):

   ```
   p.apply(TextIO.read().from("gs://apache-beam-test/JohnTom/*"))
   ```

2. Splitting the lines in PCollection<String> is performed by the next transform, where every element is a separate word in John Tom's collected texts. As an alternate option, you can use a ParDo transform that calls a **DoFn (defined in-line as an anonymous class)** on each element that tokenizes the text lines into individual words. The PCollection of text lines is generated by the previous TextIO. The read() transform is used as an input for this transform. The ParDo transform produces a new PCollection, where each element describes an individual word in the text:

   ```
   .apply("ExtractWords", FlatMapElements
   ```

```
.into(TypeDescriptors.strings())
.via((String word) -> Arrays.asList(word.split("[^\\p{L}]+"))))
```

3. The SDK provides a universal transform which is the Count transform. It takes any type of `PCollection` and generates a `PCollection` of key-value pairs. Each key signifies a unique element from the input collection and each value indicates the number of times that key appeared in the input collection.

   In this sample pipeline, which is shown in preceding diagram, the input to generate Count is the `PCollection` of separate words generated by the previous `ParDo`, and the output is a `PCollection` of key/value pairs where each key signifies an exclusive word in the text and the associated number is the occurrence count for each:

```
.apply(Count.<String>perElement())
```

4. The next transform formats each of the key-value pairs of unique words and occurrence counts into a printable string suitable to write to an output file.

   The map transform is a higher-level composite transform that performs a simple `ParDo`. For each element in the input `PCollection`, the map transform applies a function that produces precisely one output element:

```
.apply("FormatResults", MapElements
  .into(TypeDescriptors.strings())
  .via((KV<String, Long> wordCount) -> wordCount.getKey() + ": " +
wordCount.getValue()))
```

5. This transform takes input as the final `PCollection` of formatted strings and writes each element to an output text file. Each element in the input `PCollection` represents a single line of text in the resultant output file:

```
.apply(TextIO.write().to("wordcounts"));
```

The preceding steps explain how the different types of transformations work in the Apache Beam SDK.

Now, let's see a sample Apache Beam code for WordCount:

```
package com.google.cloud.teleport.templates;

import org.apache.beam.sdk.Pipeline;
import org.apache.beam.sdk.io.TextIO;
import org.apache.beam.sdk.metrics.Counter;
import org.apache.beam.sdk.metrics.Metrics;
import org.apache.beam.sdk.options.Description;
import org.apache.beam.sdk.options.PipelineOptions;
```

```java
import org.apache.beam.sdk.options.PipelineOptionsFactory;
import org.apache.beam.sdk.options.ValueProvider;
import org.apache.beam.sdk.transforms.Count;
import org.apache.beam.sdk.transforms.DoFn;
import org.apache.beam.sdk.transforms.MapElements;
import org.apache.beam.sdk.transforms.PTransform;
import org.apache.beam.sdk.transforms.ParDo;
import org.apache.beam.sdk.transforms.SimpleFunction;
import org.apache.beam.sdk.values.KV;
import org.apache.beam.sdk.values.PCollection;

/**
 * An template that counts words in Shakespeare.
 */
public class WordCount {
  static class ExtractWordsFn extends DoFn<String, String> {
      private final Counter emptyLines = Metrics.counter(ExtractWordsFn.
class, "emptyLines");

    @ProcessElement
    public void processElement(ProcessContext c) {
      if (c.element().trim().isEmpty()) {
        emptyLines.inc();
      }
      // Split the line into words.
      String[] words = c.element().split("[^a-zA-Z']+");
      // Output each word encountered into the output PCollection.
      for (String word : words) {
        if (!word.isEmpty()) {
          c.output(word);
        }
      }
    }
  }

  /** A SimpleFunction that converts a Word and Count into a printable
string. */
```

```java
public static class FormatAsTextFn extends SimpleFunction<KV<String,
Long>, String> {
  @Override
  public String apply(KV<String, Long> input) {
    return input.getKey() + ": " + input.getValue();
  }
}
/**
  * A PTransform that converts a PCollection containing lines of text
into a PCollection of
  * formatted word counts.
  */
public static class CountWords extends PTransform<PCollection<String>,
     PCollection<KV<String, Long>>> {
  @Override
  public PCollection<KV<String, Long>> expand(PCollection<String> lines)
{
    // Convert lines of text into individual words.
    PCollection<String> words = lines.apply(
        ParDo.of(new ExtractWordsFn()));

    // Count the number of times each word occurs.
    PCollection<KV<String, Long>> wordCounts =
        words.apply(Count.<String>perElement());
    return wordCounts;
  }
}
/**
  * Options supported by {@link com.google.cloud.teleport.templates.
WordCount}.
  * <p>Inherits standard configuration options.
  */
public interface WordCountOptions extends PipelineOptions {
  @Description("Path of the file to read from")
  ValueProvider<String> getInputFile();
  void setInputFile(ValueProvider<String> value);
```

```
@Description("Path of the file to write to")
ValueProvider<String> getOutput();
void setOutput(ValueProvider<String> value);
}


public static void main(String[] args) {
    WordCountOptions options = PipelineOptionsFactory.fromArgs(args).
withValidation()
      .as(WordCountOptions.class);
    Pipeline p = Pipeline.create(options);
    p.apply("ReadLines", TextIO.read().from(options.getInputFile()))
     .apply(new CountWords())
     .apply(MapElements.via(new FormatAsTextFn()))
     .apply("WriteCounts", TextIO.write().to(options.getOutput()));

    p.run();
  }
}
```

Using the following command, run the self-executing JAR on Cloud Dataflow:

```
java -jar target/beam-examples-bundled-1.0.0.jar \
  --runner=DataflowRunner \
  --project=<TEST_GCP_PROJECT_ID> \
  --tempLocation=gs://<TEST_GCS_BUCKET>/temp/
```

With the preceding commands, the Apache Beam jar file can be executed.

Cloud Pub/Sub

In order to perform real-time analytics, it is important to have a robust system which captures real-time events. Cloud Pub/Sub one of the important services in GCP which is scalable, durable and takes care of real-time event ingestion and delivery system. In modern stream analytics pipeline, Cloud Pub/Sub serves as a foundation for messaging service. Along with this, Cloud Pub/Sub brings the flexibleness and reliability of enterprise message-oriented middleware to the cloud. Cloud Pub/Sub provides the environment for secure, safe and highly available communication between standalone configured applications by enabling many-to-many, asynchronous messaging which decouples senders and receivers. Cloud Pub/Sub properties like low latency, durable messaging that enable quicker integration with systems which are hosted on the GCP. Pub/Sub is similar to cloud implementation of Kafka on-premises messaging service.

Here are the core components of Pub/Sub:

- **Topic:** A named resource which is used to send the messages by publishers.
- **Subscription:** A named resource for the stream of messages from a single, specific topic, which needs to be delivered to the subscribing application.
- **Message:** Data and (optional) attributes are combined to make a message, which then a publisher sends to a topic and is ultimately delivered to subscribers.
- **Message attribute:** A key-value pair that a publisher will define for a message. For example, `xyz.org/language_tag` and when en is added to messages, it helps to identify that it is readable by an English-speaking subscriber.

Publisher-subscriber relationships

The main usage of a publisher application is to create and sends messages to a topic. Subscriber applications are used to create a subscription to a topic so that messages can be received from it.

As shown in the following figure, there could be different ways of communication which are one-to-many called as fan-out, many-to-one called as fan-in, and many-to-many:

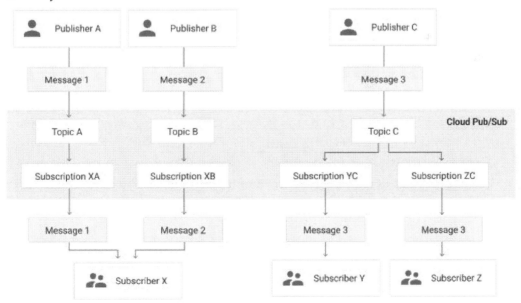

Figure 3.17: Publisher/Subscriber relationship

Cloud Pub/Sub message flow

The following diagram shows an overview of the components in the Cloud Pub/Sub system and how messages flow between them:

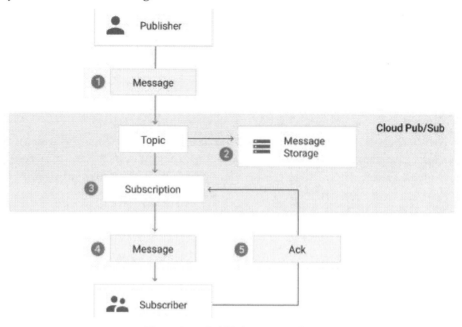

Figure 3.18: Pub/Sub Message Flow

The following steps explain the Pub/Sub message flow:

1. Generating a topic in the Cloud Pub/Sub service and sending messages to the topic is done via a publisher application. A payload and optional attributes make a message which describes the payload content.

2. The service makes sure that published messages are saved on behalf of subscriptions. Until a published message is acknowledged by any subscriber, which confirms consumption of messages from that subscription, it is retained for a subscription.

3. Cloud Pub/Sub sends messages from a topic to all subscriptions individually. There are two mechanisms of subscription receiving the messages. One is via Cloud Pub/Sub pushing them to the subscriber's chosen endpoint and other by the subscriber pulling them from the service.

4. All the pending messages are received by the subscriber from its subscription and acknowledge each one to the Cloud Pub/Sub service.

5. Once post message is acknowledged by the subscriber; it is then removed from the subscription's message queue.

Cloud Pub/Sub integrations

Cloud Pub/Sub messaging services integrate smoothly with other Google cloud services, which is shown in the following diagram:

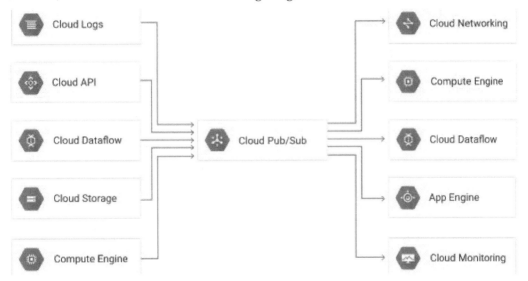

Figure 3.19: Integration of Pub/Sub with other GCP services.

As described in the preceding diagram, in order to make global messaging event ingestion simple and easy, enable Google Pub/Sub. There are multiple benefits of Google Pub/Sub.

Google Pub/Sub provides tremendous support in the following features:

- **Ingesting events at any scale:** Data ingestion is the backbone for analytics and machine learning. There could be different types of data ingestion such as building stream data, batch mode, or unified pipelines. Cloud Pub/Sub not only provides an easy but also a reliable staging location for event data towards process, storage, and analysis.

With Cloud Pub/Sub, data engineers can do the following:

1. Easily scale without provisioning, partitioning, or load isolation concerns.
2. Increase applications and pipelines to new regions merely with global topics.
3. Use Cloud Dataflow to enrich, remove duplicate, order, summarize, and land events.
4. Combine real-time and batch processing via Cloud Pub/Sub's into durable storage.

- **Streamline development of event-driven microservices:** Creating events available via messaging middleware is a vital early step; whether it is simply starting a lifecycle to event-driven asynchronous microservices or moving to an existing system. GCP application developers' trust on Cloud Pub/Sub to reliably transport every event to all the services that must respond to it.

Upon event published to Cloud Pub/Sub:

1. Delivering the event to serverless apps which run in Cloud Functions, App Engine, or Cloud Run is via Push subscriptions.

2. Make it available to a lot of complex stateful services running in Google Kubernetes Engine or Cloud Dataflow Pull subscriptions.

3. Multi-region environments operate seamlessly as a result of Cloud Pub/Sub's global nature.

- **Enables organization to be production prepared from day one:** Cloud Pub/Sub is a premium service which helps Google Cloud users specialize in application logic. The service is minimal and easy to begin with and reduces the operational, scaling, compliance, and security glitches that unavoidably expose themselves in IT projects.

Hence, Cloud Pub/Sub comes with the following always on features:

1. End-to-end encryption, IAM, and audit logging.

2. NoOps, automated scale up and down and provisioning with virtually unlimited throughput.

3. Synchronous cross-zone replication with extreme data durability and availability.

4. Native client libraries in almost all major languages and an open-service API.

The above supported features in Pub/Sub make Pub/Sub a complete differentiator within multiple messaging service which are available in market.

Fundamentals of a Publish/Subscribe service

Cloud Pub/Sub stands for publish/subscribe (Pub/Sub) service. It is a messaging service. In this message service, senders are completely decoupled from the receivers of messages. There are key concepts in a Pub/Sub service which are described in the above sections:

- **Message, Topic, Subscription, Publisher:** This is referred as a producer which creates messages and sends (publishes) them to the messaging service on such a topic.

- **Subscriber:** This is referred as a consumer and receives messages on a specified subscription.

The basic flow of messages through Cloud Pub/Sub is summarized in the following diagram:

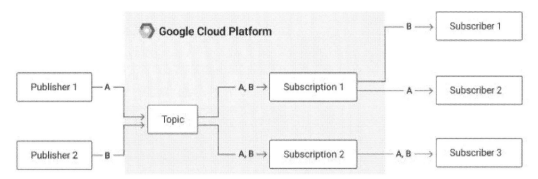

Figure 3.20: *Flow of messages via Cloud Pub/Sub*

In the preceding diagram, there are two publishers which are publishing messages on one topic. As shown in the diagram, there are two subscriptions to this topic. The primary subscription has two subscribers; this indicates that messages will be load-balanced across them, with every subscriber receiving a subset of the messages. The second subscription has one subscriber that will receive all the messages. The bold letters in the preceding diagram (which is **A, B**) represent messages. Message **A** comes from **Publisher 1** and is sent to **Subscriber 2** via **Subscription 1** and to **Subscriber 3** via **Subscription 2**. Message **B** comes from **Publisher 2** and is sent to **Subscriber 1** via **Subscription 1** and to **Subscriber 3** via **Subscription 2**.

Judging performance of a messaging service

Messaging services are evaluated based on mainly three characteristics. These characteristics are scalability, availability, and latency. Since these three factors are interdependent and typically at odds with one another, and hence, require compromises on one to improve the other two.

The terms scalability, availability, and latency refers to different properties of a system and hence the following sections describe how they're outlined in Cloud Pub/Sub:

- **Scalability:** A scalable service should be ready to handle increases in load without noticeable degradation of latency or availability. Various dimensions of usage in Cloud Pub/Sub can refer to load. Some of them could be:
  o Total number of topics
  o Count of publishers
  o Quantity of subscriptions
  o Amount of subscribers
  o Number of messages

o Size of messages

o Rate of messages (throughput) published or consumed

o Size of backlog on any given subscription

- **Availability:** In a distributed system, the types and severity of issues can vary depending on multiple factors. When it comes to systems availability, it is measured on how well it deals with different kinds of problems, graciously failing over in a way that is unnoticeable to end users. Failures can occur anywhere in hardware (for example, disk drives not working or network connectivity problems), or in software because of load. Failure due to load could happen generally when explosion in traffic in the service (or in other software components running on identical hardware or in software dependencies) results in resource scarcity. Availability can also degrade due to human error, where one makes mistakes in building or deploying software or configurations.

- **Latency:** Latency is a time-based measure of the performance of a system. A service usually needs to minimize latency wherever possible. For Cloud Pub/Sub, the two most important latency metrics are as follows:

o The amount of time it takes to acknowledge a published message.

o The amount of time it takes to deliver a published message to a subscriber.

It can be now concluded that scalability, availability, and latency are the most important characteristics and basic necessities for any services.

Cloud Pub/Sub basic architecture

This section explains the design of Cloud Pub/Sub to indicate how it is tackling with the service which attains its scalability and low latency while retaining availability. This system is supposed to be horizontally scalable, where an increase within the number of topics, subscriptions, or messages can be handled by increasing the number of instances of running servers.

As this is a Google cloud platform enabled service, cloud Pub/Sub servers run in most GCP regions around the world. This allows the service to offer fast, global data access, while giving users control over where messages are stored. Cloud Pub/Sub also encapsulates global data access in that publisher and subscriber clients. They are not aware of the location of the servers to which they connect or the services that route the data.

Cloud Pub/Sub's load balancing mechanisms direct publisher traffic to the closest GCP data center where data storage is allowed, which is defined within the Resource Location Restriction section of the IAM & admin console. This implies that publishers in multiple regions might publish messages to one topic with low latency. Any individual message is stored in a single region. However, a topic might need messages to be stored in many regions. When a subscriber client requests messages published to this topic, it connects to the nearest server that aggregates data from all messages published to the topic for delivery to the client.

Cloud Pub/Sub is divided into a pair of primary parts: the data plane, which takes care of moving messages between publishers and subscribers, and the control plane, which is responsible for the assignment of publishers and subscribers to servers on the data plane. The servers within the data plane are mentioned as forwarders, and the servers within the control plane are known as routers. When publishers and subscribers are connected to their assigned forwarders, they do not need any information from the routers. Therefore, it's possible to upgrade the control plane of Cloud Pub/Sub while not affecting any clients that are already connected and sending or receiving messages.

Control plane

The Cloud Pub/Sub control plane distributes clients to forwarders in a way that it maintains scalability, availability, and low latency for all clients. Any forwarder can serve clients for any topic or subscription. When a client connects to Cloud Pub/Sub, the router decides the data centers the client needs to connect based on the shortest network distance, a measure of the latency on the connection between two points. At interval, any given data center the router tries to divide the overall load across the set of available forwarders.

The router needs to balance a pair of different goals when performing this assignment: (a) uniformity of load (that is, ideally, every forwarder is equally loaded); (b) stability of assignments (that is, ideally, a change in load or a change at intervals, the set of available forwarders changes the tiniest number of existing assignments). The router uses a variant of consistent hashing developed by Google research to maintain a tunable balance between consistency and uniformity. The router provides the client with an ordered list of forwarders which is considered for connecting. This ordered list might change based on forwarder availability and the form of the load from the client.

A client takes this list of forwarders and connects to one or more of them. The client prefers connecting to the forwarders most recommended by the router but also takes into consideration any failures that have occurred; for example, it may decide to try forwarders in a completely different data center if several attempts to the closest ones are unsuccessful. In order to abstract Cloud Pub/Sub clients away from these implementation details, there is a service proxy between the clients and forwarders that performs optimized connection on behalf of clients.

Data plane - The lifecycle of a message

The data plane collects messages from publishers and sends them to clients. Perhaps the most effective means of understanding Cloud Pub/Sub's data plane is by looking at the life of a message from the moment it's received by the service to the moment it's no longer present within the service. In this section, we assume that the topic on which the message is published has a minimum of one subscription connected to it. In general, a message goes through the following mentioned steps:

1. A publisher sends a message.
2. The message is written to storage.
3. Cloud Pub/Sub sends an acknowledgement to the publisher that it has received the message and makes sure its delivery to all involved subscriptions.
4. At the same time as writing the message to storage, Cloud Pub/Sub delivers it to subscribers.
5. Once messages are received by Subscribers, it sends an acknowledgement back to Cloud Pub/Sub that they have processed the message.
6. Once a minimum of one subscriber for each subscription has acknowledged the message, Cloud Pub/Sub deletes the message from storage.

In order to summarize, the Cloud Pub/Sub architecture consists of Control plane and Data Plane which has been described in the preceding section.

Features such as compliance, security, and integration make APIs very important for any messaging system and have been listed as follows:

- **At-least-once delivery:** This feature includes synchronous, cross-zone message replication. Also, per-message receipt tracking ensures at-least-once delivery at any scale.
- **Open:** Pub/Sub supports open APIs and client libraries in seven different languages which support cross-cloud and hybrid deployments.
- **Exactly once processing:** Cloud Dataflow establishes reliable, expressive, exactly once processing of Cloud Pub/Sub streams.
- **Global by default:** Publish from anyplace in the world and consume from anyplace, with consistent latency. No replication necessary.
- **No provisioning, auto-everything:** Cloud Pub/Sub doesn't have shards or partitions. Simply set the required quota, publish, and consume.
- **Compliance and security:** Cloud Pub/Sub is a HIPAA-compliant service, providing fine-grained access controls and takes care of end-to-end encryption.
- **Integrated:** Pub/Sub takes advantage of integrations with multiple services, like Cloud Storage and Gmail update events and Cloud Functions for serverless event-driven computing.
- **Seek and replay:** Rewind your backlog to any purpose in time or a snapshot, giving the ability to recycle the messages. Quick forward to discard outdated data.

Pub/Sub comes with rich features which have been described. It takes care of most of the important aspects and hence, makes it unique.

Cloud Pub/Sub implementation

In this section, let's concentrate on how the Cloud Pub/Sub service can be enabled and consumed from the Google cloud platform console. Here are the mentioned steps:

1. **Going to the Pub/Sub service from the GCP Console.**

   1. First, log in into Google Cloud Account using the existing username and password. In case you don't already have one, it is easy to sign up for a new account.

   2. Once logged in Create/Open a GCP Console project. Click on:
      o Project and select one or create one.
      o Open the Cloud Pub/Sub API for that particular project.

   3. Management and view of these resources can be done via the GCP Console at any time.

   4. Install and initialize the Cloud SDK. Please note that cloud shell can also be used to run gcloud commands without needing to install the Cloud SDK.

2. **Steps for creating a Topic:**

   1. Select the Cloud Pub/Sub topics page in the GCP Console.

   2. In order to create a topic, click on **CREATE TOPIC** which is shown in the following screenshot:

Figure 3.21: Creating a Pub/Sub Topic

   3. Enter a unique name for your topic, for example, `MyTopic`.

   4. It means that a new Cloud Pub/Sub topic has been created.

3. Add a subscription

1. Display the menu for the topic you just created and click on **New subscription**:

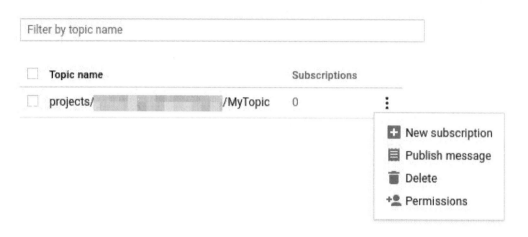

Figure 3.22: Creating a new subscription

2. Give a name for the subscription, for example: MySub:

Create a new subscription

A subscription directs messages on a topic to subscribers. Messages can be pushed to subscribers immediately, or subscribers can pull messages as needed.

Topic

projects/example-project/topics/MyTopic

Subscription name ❓

projects/example-project/subscriptions/MySub

Delivery Type ❓

◉ Pull

○ Push into an endpoint url ❓

https://

⩒ **More options**

Create   Cancel

Figure 3.23: Properties of a Subscription

3. Leave the delivery type as **Pull**. As per requirement, delivery can be Push as explained earlier.

4. Click on **Create**.

4. **Publish a message to the topic**

1. In the overflow menu for the topic, which is just created, click on **Publish Message**.

2. Enter Hello World in the **Message** field.

3. Click on **Publish**.

5. **Pull the message from the subscription**

In order to receive the message, which is just published, the subscription needs to perform a pull operation on the topic. One way of doing this is via the gcloud command-line tool. Cloud SDK which is installed before beginning of this task can be used. Alternately, Cloud Shell can be used to run the following gcloud commands:

```
gcloud init

gcloud pubsub topics create my-topic

gcloud pubsub subscriptions create --topic my-topic my-sub

gcloud pubsub topics publish my-topic --message "hello"

gcloud pubsub subscriptions pull --auto-ack my-sub
```

The message which is sent appears in the DATA field of the command output.

The preceding steps explain the setup of a Pub/Sub service through the GCP Console.

Conclusion

In this chapter, we discussed Cloud Dataflow and Google Pub/Sub in detail. Cloud Dataflow is a managed service offered by the GCP to apply all types of data processing in real time as well as in batch mode. GCP also supports some inbuilt templates which can be leveraged based on requirement and in order to serve customize data processing requirement, new data flow jobs can been developed using Apache Beam framework. We also learned about Google Pub/Sub. Google Pub/Sub is a real-time messaging service offered by GCP. A Pub/Sub message consists of message, topic, subscription, and message attribute.

Questions

1. What is Cloud Dataflow?

2. What are the different templates available within Cloud Dataflow?

3. What are different transformations/functions available in the Apache Beam SDK

4. What is Cloud Pub/Sub and why is it used?

5. How does a Pub/Sub service work?

6. How to publish and subscribe a message in the Pub/Sub topic?

CHAPTER 4

Data Processing with Dataproc and Dataprep

Introduction

In this chapter, we will discuss Cloud Dataproc and Dataprep **Google Cloud Platform (GCP)** services which are commonly used for Big Data use cases and data wrangling activity.

Structure

- Cloud Dataproc
- Cloud Data Prep

Objectives

The objective of this chapter is to explain the different concepts of Cloud Dataproc and Cloud Dataprep with the help of examples and enabling these services within the GCP Console. Readers will get well versed with the architecture, features of each service and can select appropriate services based on their requirements.

Cloud Dataproc

Cloud Dataproc is a managed Spark and Hadoop service. Cloud Dataproc is used for batch processing, querying, streaming, and machine learning and takes advantage of open source data tools. Cloud Dataproc automation helps to create clusters quickly and manage them easily, and when it is not required save money by turning off the clusters. Since this service takes less time and less money is spent on administration, a developer can focus on jobs and data.

Cloud Dataproc usage

Here are some of the usage patterns for Cloud Dataproc:

- When Cloud Dataproc is compared with traditional, on-premises products, and competitive cloud services, there are many exclusive benefits for clusters of three to many nodes:

- **Low price:** Cloud Dataproc is priced at only one cent per virtual CPU in your cluster per hour, on top of the other cloud platform resources which are being utilized. In addition to this low price, Cloud Dataproc clusters can include pre-emptible instances that have lower compute costs, reducing prices even further. Cloud Dataproc charges for what is being really used with second-by-second billing and a low, one-minute-minimum billing period, not just making the usage to rounding up to the nearest hour.

- **Super fast:** When Cloud Dataproc is not present, it generally takes from 5 to 30 minutes to make Spark and Hadoop clusters on-premises or through IaaS suppliers. When it is compared with other services, Cloud Dataproc clusters are fast to begin, scale, and shutdown, with each of these tasks taking 90 seconds or less, on average. With this approach, more time is available for hands-on working with data and less time waiting for clusters.

- **Integrated:** Cloud Dataproc has inbuilt features that integrate well with different GCP services like BigQuery, Cloud Storage, Cloud Bigtable, Stackdriver logging, and Stackdriver monitoring, and makes it more than simply a Spark or Hadoop cluster—which is an entire data platform. One of the use cases could be Cloud Dataproc that can be used to effortlessly to move and transform terabytes of raw log data directly into BigQuery for business intelligence.

- **Managed:** Since Cloud Dataproc is a managed service provided by GCP, it makes it easy to use Spark and Hadoop clusters without the involvement of an administrator or any new software. With the help of the GCP Console, it becomes easy to interact with clusters and Spark or Hadoop jobs, the Google Cloud SDK, or the Cloud Dataproc REST API. Making cluster switch off helps in saving money spent on an idle cluster. As discussed earlier, since integration of Cloud Dataproc is smooth with Cloud Storage, BigQuery, and Cloud Bigtable, data losses will not be there.

- **Simple and familiar:** Cloud Dataproc is simple and a developer does not need to learn new tools or APIs to use Cloud Dataproc. Spark, Hadoop, Pig, and Hive are frequently updated; hence, developers can be productive quicker.

Cloud Dataproc parts

When a cluster is created, normal Apache Hadoop system components are installed on the cluster. It also allows you to install additional components, known as *optional components*, on the cluster after creating the cluster. Adding non-mandatory components to a cluster is like adding components using initialization actions; however, these components have the following advantages:

- Quicker cluster start-up times.
- Cloud Dataproc versions compatibility testing.
- Leverage a cluster parameter at place of an initialization action script.
- Optional components are integrated with other Cloud Dataproc components. For example, when Anaconda and Zeppelin are installed on a cluster, Zeppelin which is an optional component will make use of Anaconda's Python interpreter and libraries.

Supporting and installation of optional components to clusters can be added with Cloud Dataproc version 1.3 and later.

Some of the available optional components are listed in the following table:

Optional component	Component name in gcloud commands and API requests	Image version	Release stage
Anaconda	ANACONDA	1.3 and later	GA
Druid	DRUID	1.3 and later	Alpha
Hive WebHCat	HIVE_WEBHCAT	1.3 and later	GA
Jupyter Notebook	JUPYTER	1.3 and later	GA
Presto	PRESTO	1.3 and later	Beta
Zeppelin Notebook	ZEPPELIN	1.3 and later	GA
Zookeeper	ZOOKEEPER	1.0 and later	Beta

In order to create a Cloud Dataproc cluster and install one or more optional components on the cluster, users can use the gcloud beta Dataproc clusters `create cluster-name` command with the `--optional-components` flag.

The following commands are used to spin up the Dataproc cluster:

```
gcloud dataproc clusters create cluster-name \
    --optional-components=COMPONENT-NAME(s) \
    --image-version=1.3 \
    ... other flags
```

Here are the steps to enable the Dataproc cluster from the GCP Console listed for the same:

1. Open the GCP Console and go to the Cloud Dataproc Clusters page.

2. The Create cluster option is used to create a new cluster. Go to the **Create Cluster** option.

3. The cluster needs to be named, so select some name such as example-cluster in the **Name** field.

4. It is mandatory to select the region and zones as specified in the earlier chapter. From the **Region and Zone** drop-down menus, select a region and zone for the cluster (global region and **us-central1-a** zone are shown selected in the following figure). Global region is the default value. This is a special multi-region endpoint that can deploy instances into any user-specified Compute Engine zone. Developers can also mention different regions, like **us-east1** or **europe-west1**, to segregate resources (including VM instances and Cloud Storage) and metadata storage locations utilized by Cloud Dataproc within the user-specified region. In the previous chapters, details about global and regional endpoints along with available regions and zones were described. Developers can also execute the `gcloud compute regions list` command to view the list of available regions.

5. Make sure that all the options should be left as default values while creating new a cluster as shown in the following screenshot:

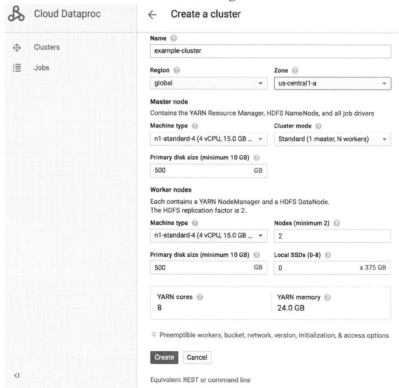

Figure 4.1: Setting up a Dataproc Cluster

6. After filling up all the details in all the options, click on **Create** to invoke the new cluster.

   Within a few seconds, a new cluster will appear in the **Clusters** list. The cluster status is listed as **Provisioning** until the cluster is ready to use, and then it changes to **Running**.

Once the cluster is up and running, it can be used to submit jobs to execute. Now, let's see the following steps for executing a sample Spark job:

1. Navigate to **Jobs** in the left navigation pane to switch to Dataproc's jobs view and then select the **Submit** job options.

2. A cluster needs be selected, so pick a new cluster `example-cluster` from the **Cluster** drop-down menu.

3. The cluster supports multiple types of jobs, so please select **Spark** from the **Job type** drop-down menu.

4. Specify the path of the JAR files. For example: `file:///usr/lib/spark/examples/jars/spark-examples.jar` in the JAR file field.

5. Type `org.apache.spark.examples.SparkPi` in the **Main class or jar** option as shown in the following screenshot.

6. In context of this example, enter `1000` in the **Arguments** field to set the number of tasks:

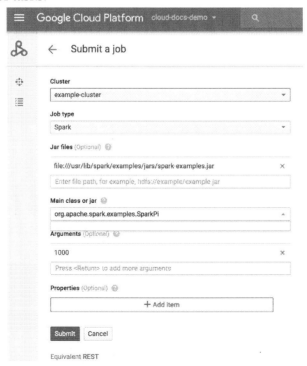

Figure 4.2: Submitting a Spark job in Dataproc Cluster

The cluster can also be updated and changed the number of worker instances by following the given steps:

1. Select **Clusters** in the left navigation pane to return to the Cloud Dataproc Clusters view.

2. Click on `example-cluster` in the Clusters list. By default, the page displays an overview of your cluster's CPU usage.

3. Go to **Configuration** to display the cluster's current settings.

4. Click on **Edit**. The number of worker nodes is now editable.

5. Put 5 worker nodes in the **Worker nodes** field as shown in the following screenshot.

6. Finally, click on **Save** to save the configuration. You can refer to the following screenshot:

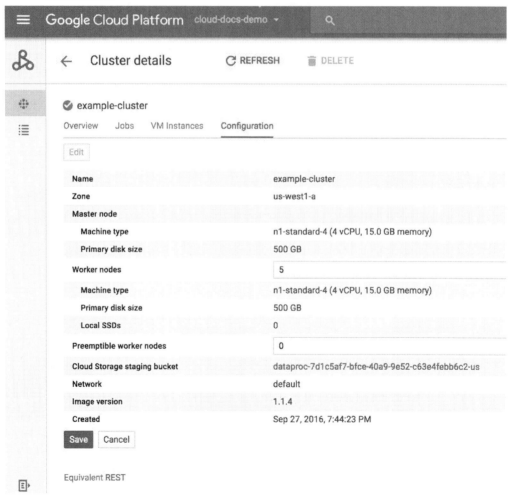

Figure 4.3: Updating existing cluster

In order to reduce the number of worker nodes to the original value, you can follow the same preceding steps.

Removing/Terminating the Dataproc Cluster

Since these services as charged as per usage, in order to avoid incurring charges to the GCP account for the resources, the Cloud Dataproc cluster can be deleted by following the given steps:

1. The cluster needs to be identified from the complete list of clusters which needs to be deleted. For example, select example-cluster in the **Cluster** page, and then select **Delete** to delete the cluster. There will be a prompt for confirmation. Confirm by clicking on **OK**.

2. Cloud Storage buckets which were created during the cluster spin up operation can also be removed by executing the following command:

    ```
    gsutil rm gs://bucket/subdir/**
    ```

The following flowchart enables you to select proper GCP services between Cloud Dataproc and Cloud Dataflow based on the use cases and problem statement:

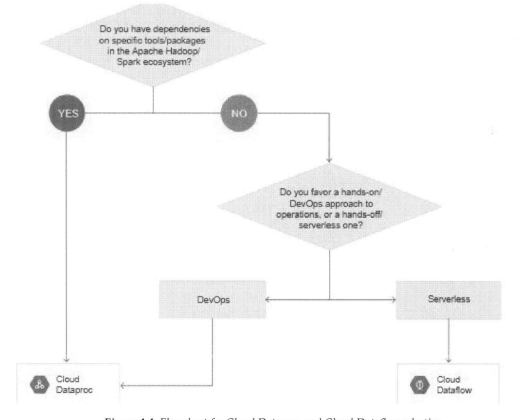

Figure 4.4: *Flowchart for Cloud Dataproc and Cloud Dataflow selection*

Moving on-premises Hadoop infrastructure to GCP

This section gives an overview of how to migrate on-premises Apache Hadoop system to GCP. This migration process not only moves your Hadoop work to GCP, but also helps to adapt your work to take advantages of a Hadoop system which is optimized for cloud computing. It also explains important concepts which need to be well understood to translate Hadoop configuration to GCP.

Let's start with listing down the benefits of moving to the GCP environment. As discussed in the earlier section, there are multiple ways in which enabling GCP can save time, cost, and effort in comparison to an on-premises hosted Hadoop solution. With adoption of a cloud-based approach in most cases, it makes solutions simpler and easy to manage.

The following are the benefits of moving on-premises Hadoop infrastructure to GCP:

- Inbuilt support for Hadoop: Hadoop and Spark environment is a managed service provided by GCP Cloud Dataproc. It helps to run most of their existing Cloud Dataproc with bottom alteration; therefore, users do not get to move far away from all the Hadoop tools they already know.

- Managed hardware and configuration: Hadoop on GCP takes care of hardware and hence, no one is worried regarding the physical hardware. It just needs to specify the configuration of the cluster and Cloud Dataproc make sure that the required resources are allocated to them. They can scale the cluster at any time when ever required.

- Simplified version management: It is always a challenge to keep open source tools up to date and manage a Hadoop cluster. With Cloud Dataproc, it is easy since a lot of that work is managed by Cloud Dataproc versioning.

- Flexible job configuration: A typical on-premises Hadoop setup uses a single cluster that serves several functions. Once it is moved to GCP, developers can concentrate on their individual tasks by making as many clusters as they need. With this, it eliminated a lot of the complexness of maintaining one cluster with growing dependencies and software configuration interactions.

- Planning on-premises migration: Migration from an on-premises environment to GCP needs a shift in approach. A typical on-premises Hadoop system consists of a monolithic cluster that supports several workloads, usually across multiple business areas. As a result, the system becomes a lot of complicated over time and might need administrators to create compromises to get everything working within the monolithic cluster. When the Hadoop system is moved to GCP, it will cut back the administrative complexity and make it easy and simple. However, in order to make this simplification and foremost economical process in GCP with the minimal price, it needs to be re-considered about the way to structure data and jobs. As Cloud Dataproc runs Hadoop on GCP, using a persistent Cloud Dataproc cluster to replicate on-premises setup may appear like the best answer.

However, there are some limitations to that approach:

- Keeping data in an exceedingly persistent HDFS cluster using Cloud Dataproc is costlier than storing data in Cloud Storage. But it also helps since keeping data in an HDFS cluster limits your ability to use data with different GCP products.

- Augmenting or replacing a number of open-source-based tools with different related GCP services are often a lot of economical or economical for specific use cases.

- Using one persistent Cloud Dataproc cluster for your jobs is tougher to manage than shifting to targeted clusters that serve individual jobs or job areas.

The most efficient and versatile way to migrate your Hadoop system to GCP is to shift away from thinking in terms of huge, multi-purpose, persistent clusters, and instead consider small, temporary clusters that are designed to run specific jobs. You can store data in Cloud Storage to support multiple, temporary process clusters. This model is commonly referred to as the ephemeral model because the clusters you utilize for process jobs are allotted as required and are released as jobs end.

The following diagram shows a theoretic migration from an on-premises system to a short-lived model on GCP:

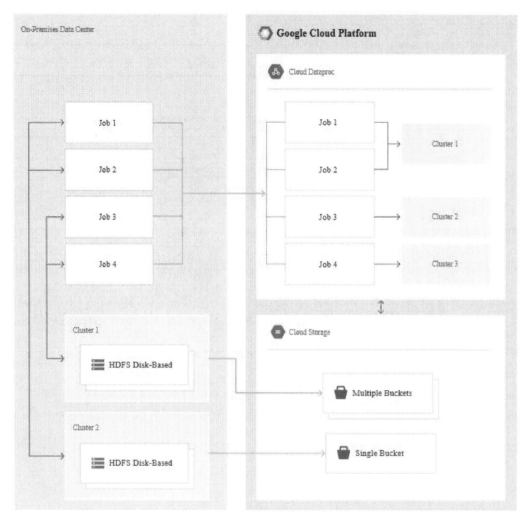

Figure 4.5: Migration from on-premises

The preceding example moves four jobs that run on two on-premises clusters to Cloud Dataproc. The ephemeral clusters that are accustomed to run the jobs in GCP are outlined to maximize efficiency for individual jobs. The primary two jobs use the same cluster, whereas the third and fourth jobs each run on their own cluster. Once these jobs are migrated, it will help them to be able to customize and optimize clusters for individual jobs or for groups of jobs as makes sense for your specific work. Cloud Dataproc helps quickly outline multiple clusters, bring them online, and scale them to fit as per needs.

The data in the preceding example is moved from two on-premises HDFS clusters to Cloud Storage buckets. The data within the first cluster is split among multiple buckets and the second cluster is moved to a single bucket. It can be customized to structure data in Cloud Storage to suit the needs as per applications and business.

The preceding example demonstrates all the states from start to end of an entire migration to GCP. This means a single step; however, results will be most effective if a one-time movement, complete migration to GCP is not considered. Instead, consider it as refactoring solutions to use a new set of tools in ways that weren't doable on-premises. To create such a refactoring work, it is suggested to migrate incrementally.

Best practices of Cloud Dataproc

Here are some of the best practices for Cloud Dataproc:

- **Specifying versions of cluster image:** Cloud Dataproc image versions are important and used to package operating systems and massive data elements (including core and elective components) and GCP connectors into one package that's deployed on a cluster. Cloud Dataproc defaults to the latest stable image version if the image version is not specified during its creation. For production environments, it is suggested that just continuously associate cluster creation step with a specific minor Cloud Dataproc version, as shown in the following example gcloud command:

```
gcloud Dataproc clusters create my-pinned-cluster --image-version
1.4-debian9
```

  This will ensure you know the precise OSS software versions that your production jobs require while Cloud Dataproc allows you to define a subminor version (that is, 1.4.xx instead of 1.4). In most environments, it's preferred to reference Cloud Dataproc minor versions solely (as shown within the gcloud command). Subminor versions are updated periodically for patches or fixes, hence new clusters automatically get security updates without breaking compatibility.

  New minor versions of Cloud Dataproc are made available during a preview, non-default mode before they become the default. With this approach, production jobs get tested and validated against new versions of Cloud Dataproc before creating the version substitution.

- **Understand when to use custom images:** Custom images from the most recent images in your target minor track need to be created if there are some dependencies that have to be shipped with the cluster like native Python libraries that have to be put on all nodes, or specific security hardening software or virus protection software needs for the image. This makes sure to enable those dependencies to be met every time. Users must update the subminor within their track every time they reconstruct the image.

- **Use the jobs API for submissions:** With the Cloud Dataproc Jobs API, it makes it easy and doable to submit a job to an already present Cloud Dataproc cluster with a job. Using the `gcloud` command-line tool or the GCP Console itself, the HTTPS call is submitted. It additionally makes it simple to divide and segregate the permissions of who has access to submit jobs on a cluster and permissions to achieve the cluster itself, without putting in place entry nodes or having to use something like Apache Livy.

The Jobs API makes it simple to develop custom tooling to run production jobs.

- **Control the location of initialization actions:** Initialization actions allow you to give your own customizations to Cloud Dataproc. A number of the most ordinarily installed OSS components and created example installation scripts the available are within Dataproc-initializaton-actions GitHub repository. While these scripts offer a simple way to start, once it is running in a production environment it must continually run these initialization actions from a location that you control. Typically, a primary step is to copy the Google-provided script into your own Cloud Storage location.

  As of now, the actions are not snapshotted and updates are typically created to the public repositories. If your production code merely references the Google version of the initialization actions, sudden changes might leak into your production clusters.

- **Keep a watch on Dataproc release notes:** Cloud Dataproc releases new subminor image versions each week. In order to remain on top of all the most recent changes, review the release notes that accompany every amendment to Cloud Dataproc. It is suggested to add this URL to your favorite feed reader.

- **Skills to research failures:** Even with these best practices in place, an error may still occur. When an error occurs due to something that happens among the cluster itself and not merely in a Cloud Dataproc API call, the first place to look will be your cluster's staging bucket. Typically, you may find the Cloud Storage location of cluster's staging bucket within the error message itself.

- **Analysis support choices:** Google Cloud is here to support production OSS workloads and help meet your business SLAs, with numerous tiers of support available. Additionally, Google Cloud Consulting Services also makes sure to facilitate and educate your team on best practices and provide guiding principles for specific production deployments.

Cloud Dataprep

Cloud Dataprep service within GCP is offered by Trifacta is a smart data service. This intelligent service helps in visually exploring, cleaning, and preparing structured and unstructured data for analysis, reporting, and machine learning. Since Cloud Dataprep is serverless, there is no infrastructure to deploy or manage and it can scale at any level when required. This is a UI-based tool and hence data transformation can be applied, suggested, and predicted with the UI-based input and there is no need to write the code. It also supports automatic schema, datatype, possible joins, and anomaly detection. It helps in skipping data profiling time and concentrate on data analysis.

Cloud Dataprep provides a lot of transformation which helps for data wrangling activities. In this section, the overviews of significant features of Cloud Dataprep are listed:

- **Cleanse tasks consist of these transformations:** Applying conditional transformations, changing column data type, comparing values, copying and pasting columns, replacing cell values, creating column by example, data reduplication, extracting values, dates formatting, managing string lengths, string values modification, normalizing numeric values, preparing data for machine processing, removing data, columns renaming, replacing groups of values, cleansing column names, and standardizing using patterns.

- **Discovery tasks provides these transformations:** Adding or editing recipe steps, analysis across multiple columns, metrics calculation across columns, comparing strings, compute counts, suggestions exploration, data filtering, locate outliers, parsing of fixed-width file and infer columns.

- **Data enrichment tasks:** Adding lookup data, adding two columns, appending datasets, generating primary keys, inserting metadata, and joining multiple datasets.

- **Import tasks is basically used to import the data into Cloud Dataprep:** Change file encoding, connecting to data, create dataset with parameters, disable type inference, excel data import, importing a file, importing a table, import from another flow, and removing initial structure.

- **Data structuring tasks:** Create aggregations, initial parsing steps, pivot data, reshaping steps, splitting column, working with arrays, and working with JSON.

The preceding listed data wrangling task can be invoked from the Cloud Dataprep web application. Let's get started using the Cloud Dataprep web application.

There are some initial setup needs to be performed before enabling Dataprep. As discussed in the earlier chapter, it is mandatory to have a Google account and GCP project to enable and use any service. As part of the initial setup, log in to the Google account and if not create one, and then set up a GCP project. The billing account needs to be set up for the same project. APIs for Cloud Dataflow, BigQuery, and Cloud Storage need to enabled from the console as part of the initial setup.

The New Cloud Storage bucket is also required, and it needs to be created by the steps which are explained in the earlier chapter. From the GCP console, go to the cloud storage browser and create a new bucket. In order to create a new bucket, put a unique name and select a storage class and a location where the bucket data needs to be stored and then click on create to enable a new Cloud storage bucket.

Setting up Cloud Dataprep service

This Google Cloud service is offered by Trifacta and users must accept the terms of service by logging into their Google account. The Cloud Dataprep console can be accessed from the GCP Console. While accessing Cloud Dataprep for the very first time, the project owner is requested to allow data access by Google and Trifacta. It is mandatory to select a Cloud Storage bucket to use with Cloud Dataprep. Once the preceding steps are completed, the Cloud Dataprep home page appears on the screen as shown in the following screenshot:

Figure 4.6: Home screen of Cloud Dataprep

Cloud Storage bucket folders are used by Cloud Dataprep for uploads, job runs, and temp storage, and they can be changed and updated by going to the Settings icon, which displays the first initial of the account owner's username, then selecting the full name from the drop-down menu as shown in the following screenshot:

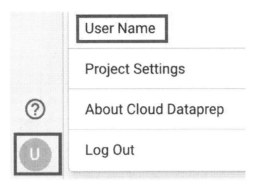

Figure 4.7: Selecting Full Name

On the user account setting page, all the Cloud Storage bucket paths for upload, **Job Run directory** and **Temp directory** are listed and can be changed as shown in the following screenshot:

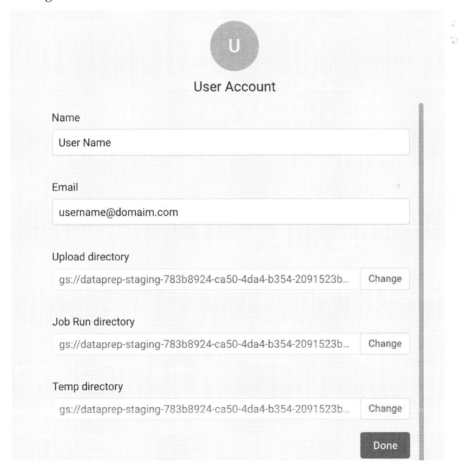

Figure: 4.8: *Showing different storage buckets*

Create a flow in Cloud Dataprep

Cloud Dataprep comes with flow workspace which is used to access and manipulate datasets. The data flow name and description need to be specified on the Cloud Dataprep home page in order to invoke the Dataprep flow, followed by clicking on **Create Flow**. In this example, sample data from *Federal Elections Commission 2016* is being used and hence naming it as FEC-2016, with a description that refers to this data:

Figure 4.9: Creating a Cloud Dataprep flow.

Go to the next page flow screen. The next step is to import the datasets:

Figure 4.10: Flow Screen

Import datasets: From the flow page, navigate to **Import & Add Datasets** to open the **Import Data and Add to Flow** page. Select **GCS** in the left panel. Under

Choose a file or folder, click on the **GCS** edit path pencil widget, then insert `gs://dataprep-sample/us-fec` in the **GCS** text box, and then click on Go as shown in the following screenshot.

Figure 4.11: Importing datasets

Add the cn-2016.txt dataset, name it `Candidate Master 2016`, and add the `itcont-2016.txt` dataset, name it `Campaign Contributions 2016`. After both the datasets are shown in the right pane, click on **Import & Add to Flow** to add the datasets:

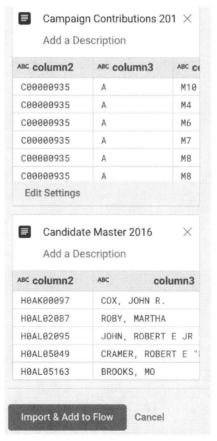

Figure 4.12: Listing, importing and adding datasets

Preparing one of the imported datasets, that is, Candidate file: On the `FEC 2016` flow page, where both the datasets are reflected, select the `Candidate Master 2016` dataset, then go to the `Add new Recipe` option:

Figure 4.13: Preparing imported dataset

As shown in the following screenshot, a new recipe icon appears on the screen. Then, click on `Edit Recipe`:

Figure 4.14: Adding and editing a Recipe

When you click on the `Edit` recipe, it opens a grid view, where data can be explored and transformation can be applied to the recipe using the `Recipe` pane displayed on the right-hand side of the page as highlighted in red.

To show the Recipe pane: In case the `Recipe` pane is not displayed in the Grid view, click on the Recipe icon at the top-right corner of the `Grid` view page:

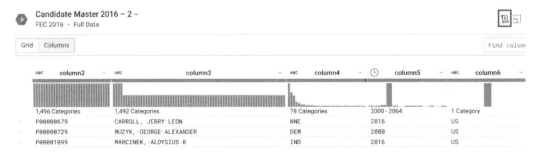

Figure 4.15: Sample data for column 5

As shown in the preceding screenshot, **column5 (Date/Time)** consists of year value. Drag and select the years 2016 and 2017 in the histogram:

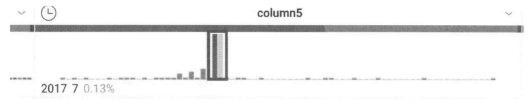

Figure 4.16: *Selecting Specific Year*

In the right pane which is titled as **Keep rows where value is in selected range**, select the **Add** option:

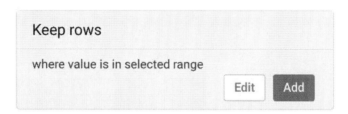

Figure 4.17: *Selecting option for Keep Rows for selected Range*

The following step is included in the recipe:

```
Keep rows where (date(2016, 1, 1) <= column5) && (column5 < date(2018, 1, 1))
```

Hover over and go to the mismatched (red) portion of the **column6** (state) header to select the mismatched rows:

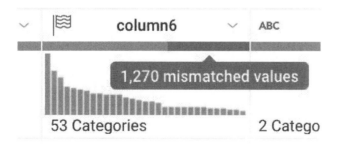

Figure 4.18: *Mismatched Rows*

Go to the end of the column. While scrolling, you will notice that the red highlighted (mismatched) items have the value US in **column 6** and "P" in **column 7** which indicate that these are presidential candidates. The mismatch happens since **column**

6 is defined as a **State** column (indicated by the flag icon), but it consists of non-state (such as **US**) values:

⚐ column6 ⌄	ABC
53 Categories	2 Catego
WI	H
WI	H
WI	H
WY	H
US	P
US	P
US	P
US	P
US	P
US	P
US	P
US	P
US	P
US	P
US	P
US	P
US	P
US	P

Figure 4.19: Mismatch value

To resolve this mismatch, mark it as a **String** column. Select **Cancel** in the right pane to cancel the transformation, then click on the flag icon above **column6** and select **String**:

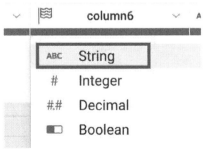

Figure 4.20: Resolving Mismatch Issue

The mismatch is removed, and the column marker is turned green. Now, in order to filter on just the presidential candidates in the histogram for **column7**, click on the **P** bin as shown in the following screenshot:

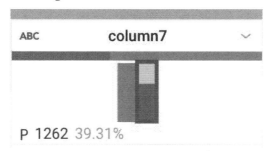

Figure 4.21: Selecting Column to apply Filter

Click on **Add** in the right pane recommendation to keep rows **where column7 is 'P'** as shown in the following screenshot:

Figure 4.22: Adding Filter for 'P'

Preparing and joining with the contributions file: Select **FEC 2016** in the upper left of the **Candidate Master 2016** grid view to return to the main dataset page. Select **Campaign Contributions 2016**, then go to **Add new Recipe**, and then click on

Edit Recipe to open the grid view for other contributions dataset as shown in the following screenshot:

Figure 4.23: Joining dataset

In the grid view, in order to removes extra delimiters from the contributions dataset, add a new step to the recipe. This can be done with following Wrangle language command in the **Search** box:

```
replacepatterns col: * with: '' on: `{start}"|"{end}` global: true
```

The transformation builder makes sure to parse the Wrangle command which has been passed and populates the find and replace transformation fields. Finally, click on **Add** to include the transform to the recipe as shown in the following screenshot:

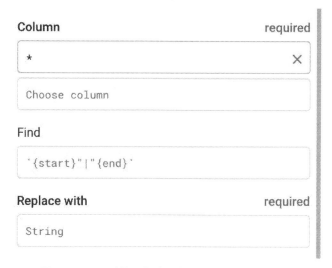

Figure 4.24: *Adding find and replace transformation*

Search for join transformation in order to add an additional new step to the recipe as shown in the following screenshot:

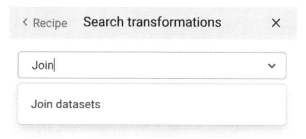

Figure 4.25: *Transformation Search*

In order to open the Join page, select the **Join datasets** link. Select Candidate Master 2016-2 (the Candidate Master file with the Recipe steps added above), then click on **Preview**:

Figure 4.26: *Join Dataset*

Select the **Join Keys** tab. Cloud Dataprep works on common keys. There are many common values that are recommended by Cloud Dataprep as join keys. Edit the **Join Keys** field as per the data. In this example, select column2 = column11 as the join keys as shown in the following screenshot:

Figure 4.27: Join Type and Join Column

Select the checkbox which is under the **Columns** label to add all or required columns of both the datasets to the joined dataset, and then finally, click on **Add to Recipe** to return to the grid view as shown in the following screenshot:

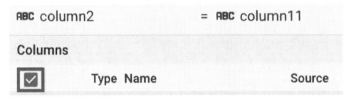

Figure 4.28: Adding Joining Columns to Recipe

Include the following steps in the recipe to generate a meaningful summary by aggregating, averaging, and counting the contributions in column 16 and grouping the candidates by IDs, names, and party affiliation in columns 2, 24, 8, respectively as follows:

```
pivot value:sum(column16),average(column16),countif(column16 > 0) group:
column2,column24,column8
```

Figure 4.29: Aggregating, averaging, and counting the column

The following screenshot is a draft sample of the joined and aggregated data which is displayed, representing a summary table of US presidential candidates and their 2016 campaign contribution metrics:

Figure 4.30: Joined and Aggregated Data

Further, you can make the data easier to understand by including the following renaming and rounding steps to the recipe.

```
rename type: manual mapping: [column24,'Candidate_Name'],
[column2,'Candidate_ID'],[column8,'Party_Affiliation'], [sum_
column16,'Total_Contribution_Sum'], [average_column16,'Average_
Contribution_Sum'], [countif,'Number_of_Contributions']

set col: Average_Contribution_Sum value: round(Average_Contribution_Sum)
```

Figure 4.31: Output Dataset after applying Transformation

In order to see more data, select the **Initial Sample** link which is at the top-left corner of the page to open the **Samples** panel. Select a random, quick sample, and then click on **Collect**:

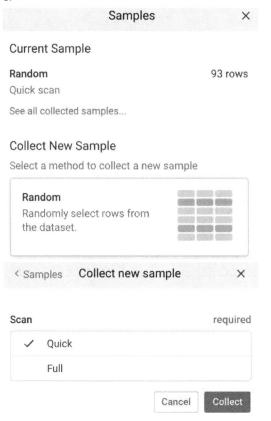

Figure 4.32: Applying Sample View Criteria

Once the job execution is completed, click on **Load Sample** in the **Samples** panel to view the data as shown in the following screenshot:

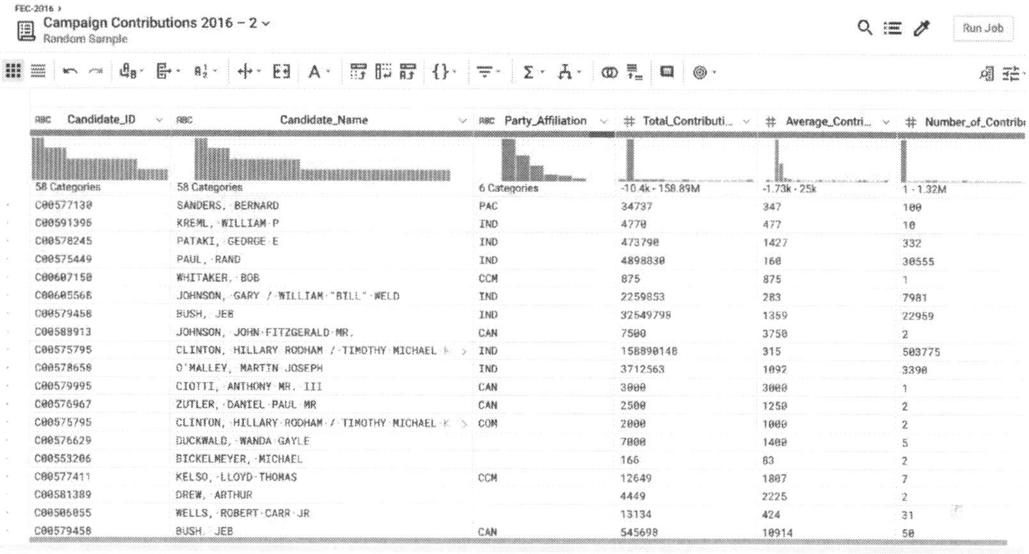

Figure 4.33: Sample View of Dataset

The preceding example explains the steps involved in Cloud Dataprep which is used for data transformation and wrangling.

We have discussed Cloud Dataflow, Cloud Dataproc, and Cloud Dataprep in detail. Now, let's see their comparison in following table:

Cloud Dataproc	Cloud Dataflow	Cloud Dataprep
Existing Hadoop/Spark application	New data processing pipeline	UI-driven data preparation
Machine learning/data science ecosystem	Unified streaming and batch	Scales on demand
Tuneable cluster parameters	Full-managed, no-ops	Fully managed, no-ops

Conclusion

In this chapter, we discussed about the Cloud Dataproc and Cloud Data Prep services of the Google cloud platform. Cloud Dataproc is a fully managed Hadoop cluster which enables you to implement big data oriented architecture. Cloud Data Prep is a product owned by Trifacta and is widely used to perform data wrangling and data transformation types of activities. It has a rich web user interface which gives users the flexibility to visualize and design the data pipe as per their requirements.

Questions

1. Highlight some of the benefits of moving on-premises Hadoop infrastructure to the Google cloud environment.

2. Set up Cloud Dataproc clusters from Google Cloud Console.

3. Highlight some of the important features of Cloud DataPrep.

4. What are the different types of transformations supported in Cloud DataPrep?

5. Highlight some of the differences between Cloud Dataflow, Cloud DataProc, and Cloud DataPrep.

CHAPTER 5

BigQuery and Data Studio

Introduction

In this chapter, we will discuss BigQuery and Cloud Data Studio **Google Cloud Platform (GCP)** Services which are used for large scale data warehouse (Online Analytical Processing) and data visualization activity.

Structure

- BigQuery
- Cloud Data Studio

Objectives

Understand the different concepts of BigQuery and Cloud Data Studio with the help of examples and enable these services within the GCP Console. Readers will be well versed with the architecture, features of each service and can select appropriate services based on requirement.

BigQuery

Google BigQuery is a fully-managed and cloud-based interactive query service for huge datasets. BigQuery is the external implementation of one of the company's core technologies which is called **Dremel**. This chapter discusses the uniqueness of the technology as a cloud-enabled massively parallel query engine, the differences between BigQuery and Dremel, and the way BigQuery compares with other technologies like MapReduce/Hadoop and existing data warehouse solutions.

BigQuery is serverless, extremely available, and petabytes scalable service that permits to run complex SQL queries fast and cloud-based interactive query service for large volume of datasets. It allows users to focus on analysis instead of thinking about infrastructure. The concept of hardware is totally abstracted and not visible to us, not when virtual machines.

BigQuery is a service offered by GCP; a set of product and services that has application hosting, cloud computing, database services, and many more on Google's scalable infrastructure.

Unique features of BigQuery are as follows:

- Service for interactive analysis of huge datasets (from TBs to PBs).
- Query billions of rows within seconds to write, seconds to return.
- Uses a traditional and familiar SQL-style query syntax.
- It's a service which can be accessed by an API.
- It is highly reliable, secure, and scalable easily to petabytes of data.
- Data is replicated across multiple sites for backup and disaster recovery purpose.
- Access is controlled through secured access control lists.
- Stores hundreds of terabytes.
- Cloud service which is based on pay only for what you use.
- It is very fast (really) for data retrieval.
- Designed to execute ad hoc queries on multi-terabyte data sets in seconds.

BigQuery is structured as a hierarchy with four different levels:

- **Projects:** This is the top-level container in the GCP that stores the data. Projects can be created within GCP under an organization through the GCP Console.
- **Datasets:** It is the next level of hierarchy which is defined within projects. Datasets consists of one or more tables of data.
- **Tables:** Under datasets, tables can be defined. Tables are row-column structures that hold the actual data.
- **Jobs:** This is the lowest level in the hierarchy and it is the tasks that are performed on the data like queries execution, loading data, and exporting data.

Google BigQuery architecture

Understanding BigQuery design helps us in controlling prices, optimizing query performance, and optimizing storage. BigQuery is made using the Google Dremel architecture. Dremel is a query service that enables to run SQL-like queries against massive datasets and obtain correct results in just a few seconds. It simply requires a basic knowledge of SQL to query extremely giant datasets in an ad hoc manner. Dremel will even execute a complex regular expression text matching on a large logging table that consists of about 35 billion rows and 20 TB, in just a few seconds. This can be the ability of Dremel; its super high scalability, and most of the time, it returns results within seconds or tens of seconds despite how massive the queried dataset is.

BigQuery is much more than just Dremel. Dremel is simply a query execution engine, whereas BigQuery relies on fascinating technologies like *Borg* (predecessor of Kubernetes) and *Colossus*. Colossus is that the successor to the **Google File System (GFS)** as shown in the following screenshot:

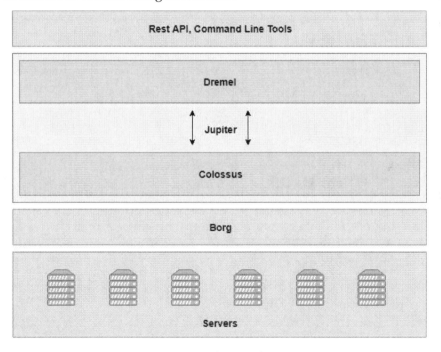

Figure 5.1: *BigQuery architecture*

Storing data in BigQuery

BigQuery stores data in a columnar format which is called **Capacitor** and it supports very high compression ratio and scan throughput. Unlike *ColumnarIO* (earlier version), BigQuery can directly function on compressed data without decompressing it.

Here are the advantages of columnar storage:

- **Traffic reduction:** When a query is submitted, the mentioned column values on each query are scanned and only those are shown on query execution. For example, a query `SELECT description FROM BOOK` would access the description column values only.

- **Better compression ratio:** Columnar storage can go up to a compression ratio of 1:10, whereas normal row-based storage can compress at roughly 1:3.

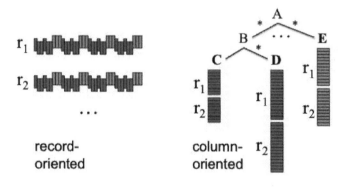

Figure 5.2: Row vs column storage

When it comes to updating existing records, columnar storage is not an efficient option for it. Due to this reason, Dremel doesn't support any update queries.

BigQuery execution

For data processing, BigQuery depends on Borg. Borg has the ability to concurrently instantiate hundreds of Dremel jobs across required clusters which are made up of thousands of machines. In addition to assigning compute capacity for Dremel jobs, Borg is capable of handling fault-tolerance as well.

Now, when a query is executed on thousands of nodes and fetches the result, it relies on the Tree architecture. This architecture makes a gigantically parallel distributed tree for breaking down a query to the tree and then aggregating the results from the leaves at a rapid fast speed. The following diagram shows the execution of query in Big Query.

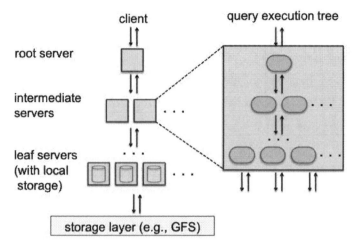

Figure 5.3: Execution of BigQuery

The Tree architecture is employed for dispatching queries and aggregating results across thousands of machines in a few seconds. Although, the technology has been standard as a data warehouse database design, Dremel is one of the primary implementations of a columnar storage-based analytics system that harnesses the computing power of many thousands of servers and is delivered as a cloud service.

Tree Architecture

One of the challenges Google had in designing Dremel was how to dispatch queries and collect results across tens of thousands of machines in a matter of seconds. The challenge was resolved using the Tree design. The design forms a massively parallel distributed tree for pushing down a query to the tree and then aggregating the results from the leaves at a blazingly quick speed. Google was able to implement the distributed style for Dremel and understand the vision of the massively parallel columnar-based database on the cloud platform.

These previous technologies are the explanation of the breakthrough of Dremel's incomparable performance and cost advantage. Google has been using Dremel in production since 2006 and has been endlessly evolving it for the last six years.

Samples of applications which are working on the Dremel architecture are listed as follows:

- Dremel is used for analysis of crawled net documents.
- Highly used to track and install data for applications within the Android market.

- Dremel is highly used for tracking Google product reporting such as crash reporting.
- Optical Character Recognition (OCR) results from Google Books.
- Search and investigation of spam emails.
- Debugging of map tiles on Google Maps.
- Tablet migrations in managed Bigtable instances
- Results of tests run on Google's distributed build system.
- Disk I/O statistics for many thousands of disks.
- Resource tracking for jobs run in Google's data centers.
- Finding symbols and dependencies in Google's codebase.

Dremel has been a very important core technology for Google, enabling nearly each a part of the company to work at *Google speed* with huge data.

Google BigQuery is an enterprise information warehouse designed using Bigtable and GCP. It is fully serverless and fully managed. BigQuery works excellently with all sizes of data, from a one hundred row stand out spreadsheet to as many petabytes of data. Most significantly, it will execute a complex query on that data within a few seconds. It needs to be noticed that BigQuery is not a transactional database. It takes around two seconds to run a straightforward question like `SELECT * FROM bigquery-public-data.table LIMIT 100` on a one hundred computer memory unit table with 5000 rows. Hence, it shouldn't be considered as an OLTP (Online Transaction Processing) database. BigQuery is generally for large volume of data.

BigQuery supports SQL-like query that makes it simple, easy and beginner friendly. BigQuery can also be accessed via the web UI, command-line tool, or client library (written in C#, Go, Java, Node.js, PHP, Python, and Ruby). It can conjointly benefit its REST APIs and obtain jobs done by sending a JSON request.

Now, let's dive deeper to know it better. Suppose for a data scientist (or analyst), it would like to research terabytes of data. If they select a tool like MySQL, the primary step before even thinking about any query is to own an infrastructure that may store this magnitude of information.

Designing this set up itself is going to be a troublesome task because users have to work out what's going to be the RAM size, DCOS or Kubernetes, and different factors. And if you've got streaming data returning, you ought to discover and maintain author cluster. In BigQuery, it has been a bulk transfer of the CSV/JSON file. BigQuery handles all the backend for you. Streaming data intake is needed and use of *Fluentd* is required. Another advantage is that BigQuery can connect Google Analytics with BigQuery seamlessly.

BigQuery can be accessed using the following method:

- BigQuery can access and run jobs from the web browser through the GCP Console. Developers can use the bq command line tool. It is a Python-based tool that can access BigQuery from the command line.
- Developers can also leverage the Service API:
    - o RESTful API to access BigQuery programmatically.
    - o Requires authorization by OAuth2.
    - o Google client libraries for Python, JavaScript, PHP, and more.
- It gets integrated with third-party tools for visualization and statistical tools like Tableau, QlikView, R, and more.
- BigQuery data can export data in a `.csv` file, `.json` or to Google Cloud Storage.

Querying data using BigQuery can be done in the following ways:

- BigQuery uses very familiar SQL-like language for querying and manipulating data.
- SQL statements are used to perform various database tasks such as querying data, creating tables, and updating databases.
- Queried result data is shown in a table called the result set.
- Basic queries contain the following components:
    - o `SELECT (required):` It identifies the columns to be included in the query.
    - o `FROM (required):` The table that contains the columns in the `SELECT` statement.
    - o `WHERE:` A condition to filter out records.
    - o `ORDER BY:` It is used to sort the result set.
    - o `GROUP BY:` It is used to aggregate data in the result set.

Let's see a query example:

```
SELECT month, country, is_male, gestation_weeks FROM [bigquery-public-data:samples.natality]
```

Sample query for time spent per session per user along with output screenshot:

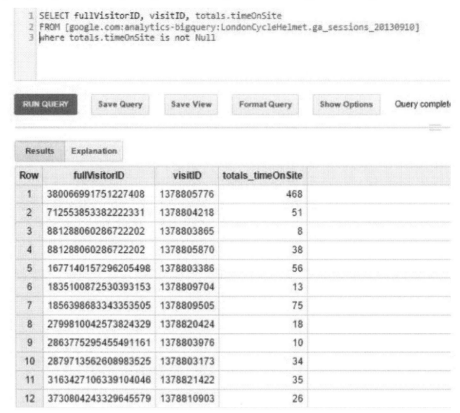

Figure 5.4: Sample screenshot of BigQuery web UI

BigQuery versus MapReduce

The key comparison between BigQuery and MapReduce are as follows:

- Dremel is designed as an interactive data analysis tool for large datasets.
- MapReduce is designed as a programming framework to perform batch process on large datasets.

Moreover, Dremel supports faster execution within seconds or tens of seconds and can even be used by non-programmers, whereas MapReduce takes much more time (sometimes, even hours or days) to process a query.

The following graph depicts the comparison on running MapReduce on a row and columnar DB in a chart format:

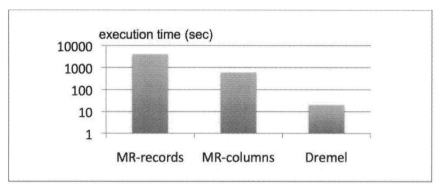

Figure 5.5: *Mapreduce vs Dremel execution time*

Another important thing to note is that BigQuery is used for analyzing structured data (SQL), but when processing of unstructured data is required, MapReduce plays an important role.

Comparing BigQuery and Redshift

In Redshift, you need to do allocation of different instance types by creating your own clusters. With this approach, it helps the user to tune the compute/storage to meet the required needs. However, you need to be aware of (virtualized) hardware limits and scale up/out based on that. Each instance spinning up is being charged by the hour.

In BigQuery, it is very easy since you just need to upload the data and then query it. It is a truly managed service. BigQuery is charged for storage when it comes to streaming inserts and queries.

Since both are cloud-based OLAP solutions, there are more commonalities in both the data warehouses than the differences.

Users will prefer to take benefits of the hybrid cloud (GCE + AWS) by utilizing different services offered by both the service providers.

Getting started with Google BigQuery

The following example helps to get started with BigQuery quickly:

1. BigQuery has many public datasets, which can be used to explore BigQuery. Let's make use of the `bigquery-public-data:teststackoverflow` dataset.

In order to add the dataset, click on the **Add Data** option on the left-hand side of the panel and select datasets as shown in the following screenshot:

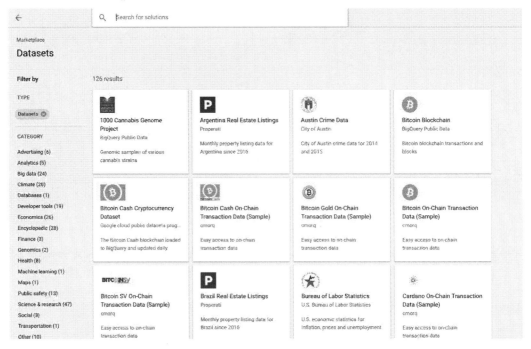

Figure 5.6: Selecting public dataset to BigQuery

2. Once the dataset is added, it is ready to query for analysis. Create the following query to do that.

3. Now, run the query and get results as shown in the following screenshot:

Figure 5.7: Query Execution in Console

4. Users will get the following results:

Row	questions	tag	mean_geo_minutes	median
1	114684	c	27.12	16
2	825005	javascript	37.49	18
3	223101	c++	40.84	21
4	580225	python	49.17	23
5	70699	ruby	54.56	30
6	602270	java	56.31	26
7	8221	rust	59.16	39
8	23422	go	67.98	41
9	45374	scala	107.28	62

Figure 5.8: Execution and result of BigQuery

Introduction to partitioned tables

A partitioned table is a special table that's divided into multiple sections known as partitions. With this partitioned table, it gets easier to manage and query data. By dividing an oversized table into smaller partitions, benefits like improved query performance and control prices by reducing the amount of bytes scan by a query can be achieved.

There are two forms of table partitioning in BigQuery:

- **Based on ingestion time:** BigQuery tables are partitioned to support the data's ingestion (load) date or arrival date.
- **Date/time partitioned tables:** BigQuery tables are partitioned based on a TIMESTAMP or DATE column.

Ingestion-time based partitioned tables

In ingestion-time-based partitioning, tables are partitioned by ingestion time or arrival time. BigQuery loads data into daily, date-based partitions which come from the data's ingestion date or arrival date. Pseudo column and suffix identifiers enable you to restate (replace) and redirect data to partitions for a particular day.

Partitioned tables, which are based on ingestion time, add a pseudo column named `_PARTITIONTIME` that contains a date-based timestamp that is loaded into the table. When querying against time-partitioned tables, it makes sure that the whole data is not scanned by passing the `_PARTITIONTIME` filters that represent a partition's location. The whole data within the given partition is scanned by the query; however, the `_PARTITIONTIME` predicate filter restricts the number of partitions scanned.

When the ingestion-time based partitioned tables option is used, the partitions will have identical schema definition of the table. In order to load data into a partition with a schema that's not consistent within the partition, you need to update the schema of the table before loading the data. Or else, use schema update options to update the schema of the table in a load job or query job.

Date or timestamp partitioned tables

BigQuery permits partitioned tables based on a particular `DATE` or `TIMESTAMP` column present in the data. Data written to a date/timestamp partitioned table is mechanically delivered to the appropriate partition based on the date value (expressed in UTC) within the partitioning column.

Date/timestamp partitioned tables don't need a `_PARTITIONTIME` pseudo column. Queries against date/timestamp partitioned tables will specify predicate filters based on the partitioning column to scale back the quantity of data scanned.

When date/timestamp partitioned tables are formed, the following two special partitions are created:

- The `__NULL__` partition represents rows with `NULL` values within the partitioning column.
- The `__UNPARTITIONED__` partition represents data that exists outside the allowed range of dates.

Except for the `__NULL__` and `__UNPARTITIONED__` partitions, all data within the partitioning column matches the date of the partition symbol. This permits a query to check which partitions contain no data that satisfies the filter conditions. Queries that filter data on the partitioning column will prohibit values and fully prune supererogatory partitions.

Partitioning versus sharding

Sharding is an alternate option to partitioned tables. Shard tables employ a time-based naming approach like `[PREFIX]_YYYYMMDD`. This is referred to as creating date-sharded tables. Using either normal SQL or legacy SQL, you can specify a query with a UNION operator to limit the tables scanned by the query.

Partitioned tables perform better than tables sharded by date. Once date-named tables are produced, BigQuery should maintain a replica of the schema and information for every date-named table. Also, when date-named tables are used, BigQuery can be required to verify permissions for each queried table. This practice additionally adds overhead and impacts query performance. The suggested best practice is to use partitioned tables rather than date-sharded tables.

Partitioned table quotas and limits

Limit is the maximum rate of incoming requests and enforces appropriate quotas on a per-project basis in BigQuery. With these quotas, limit restriction can be applied to a limit in order to perform certain set of activities (that is, querying, streaming, loading, and more). Specific policies vary as per resource availability, user profile, history of service usage, and other factors, and also are subjected to change without notice.

Query Jobs:

In order to perform interactive queries, the following limits apply to query jobs and also to jobs which get submitted programmatically using the `jobs.query` and query-type `jobs.insert` method calls.

> **There are total 100 concurrent queries limit for interactive concurrent (queries at the same time) queries.**

Queries with results that are returned from the query cache count against this limit for the duration it takes for BigQuery to determine that it is a cache hit. Dry run queries do not count against this limit. Without having actual query execution, users have the option to dry run query using the `--dry_run` flag or by setting the `dryRun` property in a query job.

BigQuery supports external data sources query and to support this concurrent rate limit for interactive queries against Cloud Bigtable, external data sources are limited to four concurrent queries.

> **There are 1,000 updates per table per day is supported as part of daily update limit for destination table.**

As BigQuery follows the Dremel columnar structure, updating of destination tables should be avoided and have a limit of 1,000 updates per table per day. Updated DML includes append operations and overwrite operations performed via a query through the console, the classic BigQuery web UI, the bq command-line tool, or by invoking the `jobs.query` and query-type `jobs.insert` API methods.

> **Query execution duration has six hours' maximum time limit: A query can run for a maximum time of six hours continuously.**

Load jobs:

This limit applies to jobs created automatically by loading data using the command-line tool, the GCP Console, or the classic BigQuery web UI. The limits also apply to load jobs submitted programmatically using the load-type `jobs.insert` API method.

The following limits apply when loading data into BigQuery.

- In total 1000 load jobs per table per day which includes failures.
- In total 100,000 load jobs per project per day including failures.
- There could be maximum 10,000 columns per table.

Dataset limits:

The following limits apply to datasets:

- There is no restriction in the number of datasets per project: The number of datasets per project is not limited and not subject to a quota; however, as with thousands of datasets in a project, classic web UI performance begins to worsen, and listing datasets becomes sluggish.

- There is no restriction in the number of tables per dataset: Once 50,000 or more tables in a dataset are created, enumerating them becomes slower. Enumeration performance suffers whether you use an API call or the classic BigQuery web UI. Currently, the BigQuery web UI in the GCP Console allows you to display only 50,000 tables per dataset. The minimal parameter can be used to limit the number of tables displayed to 30,000 tables per project to improve the classic BigQuery web UI.

- There are total 2,500 number of authorized views in a dataset's access control list. An authorized view is created to control the access of source data. An authorized view consists of those columns which users want to query on excluding some of the columns and created using a SQL query. Up to 2,500 authorized views can be added to a dataset's access control list.

Table limits:

The following limits apply to BigQuery tables.

- **All tables:**
  - **There could be a maximum 16,384 characters length of a column description:** Text for column description for explanation could be at most 16,384 characters.
- **Standard tables:**
  - **There are 1,000 number of table operations per day:** You are limited to 1,000 operations per table per day which includes operations such as appending data to a table, overwriting a table, or using a DML `INSERT` statement to write data to a table.

The combined total of all loading, copying, and querying jobs which append or overwrite a destination table or that use a DML `INSERT` statement to write data to a table is included as part of maximum number of table operations.

For example, if there are 500 copy jobs being executed that append data to `testtable` and 500 query jobs that append data to the same `testtable`, your quota is reached.

o **There can be in total five operations every 10 seconds per table rate of table metadata update operations:** The table metadata update limit includes all metadata update operations performed using the GCP Console, the classic BigQuery web UI, the bq command-line tool, the client libraries, or by calling the `tables.insert, tables.patch, or tables.update` API methods. This limit also applies to job output.

o There can be a maximum 10,000 columns in a table, query result, or view definition

- **Partitioned tables:**

  o There can be a maximum of 4,000 partitions per partitioned table.

  o There can be a maximum of 40,000 partitions modified by a single job: Every query/load job operation can impact an upper limit of 4,000 partitions. When it tries to impact more than 4,000 partitions, it is rejected and failed by BigQuery.

  o Maximum number of partition modifications per ingestion time partitioned table — 5,000.

  o Maximum number of partition modifications per column partitioned table—30,000: It permits to a limited total of 5,000 partition modifications per day for ingestion time partitioned table and 30,000 partition changes for a column partitioned table. An operation that appends or overwrites data in the partition can be used to modify a partition. Some of the operations which update partitions include a load job, a query that writes results to a partition, or a DML statement (`INSERT, DELETE, UPDATE,` or `MERGE`) which modifies data in a partition.

  There could be a scenario where more than one partition may be impacted by a single job. For example, the `UPDATE` DML statement can update data in multiple partitions (for both ingestion-time and partitioned tables). Query jobs and load jobs can also write to multiple partitions but only for partitioned tables. BigQuery utilizes the number of partitions affected by a job when defining how much of the quota the job consumes. Streaming inserts do not impact this quota.

  o **Maximum rate of partition operations — 50 partition operations every 10 seconds**

View limits:

- There can be a maximum of 16 nested view levels: Generally, 16 levels of nested views are supported in BigQuery. In case of more than that, an `INVALID_INPUT` error is produced.

- There can be a maximum of 256K character length of a standard SQL query used to define a view: When a view is created, the text of the standard SQL query can be at most 256 K characters.

- Maximum number of authorized views in a dataset's access control list — 2,500: An authorized view is created to restrict access within the source data. An authorized view is created using a SQL query that excludes columns which is not required by the users to see when they query the view. It can add up to 2,500 authorized views to a dataset's access control list.

Streaming inserts:

The following limits apply for streaming data into BigQuery. The `insertId` field is not populated while inserting rows. Currently, these quotas apply only to the US multi-region location, and you must complete the BigQuery Streaming V2 beta enrollment form in order to use them.

- Maximum of 1,000,000 rows can be ingested in a second: If the `insertId` field for each row inserted is not populated, then it is limited to 1,000,000 rows per second, per project. This quota is cumulative. It can use this quota on one table or can use this quota to stream data to several tables in a project. If the amount is exceeded, it will cause `quotaExceeded` errors.

- Maximum limit of 1 Gigabytes data can be streamed in seconds: If the `insertId` field for each row inserted is not populated, it is limited to 1 GB per second, per project. This limit applies at the project level. It does not apply to individual tables. Exceeding this amount will cause `quotaExceeded` errors.

Assign a project-level Cloud IAM role to data analysts

In order to query the view, data analysts need permission to run query jobs. The `bigquery.user` role includes permissions to run jobs, including query jobs within the project. If a user or group is granted the `bigquery.user` role at the project level, the user can create datasets and run query jobs against tables in those datasets. The `bigquery.user` role does not give users permission to query data, view table data, or view table schema details for datasets the user did not create.

Assigning data analysts the project-level `bigquery.user` role does not give them the ability to view or query table data in the dataset containing the tables queried by the view. Most individuals (data scientists, business intelligence analysts, data analysts) in an enterprise should be assigned the project-level `bigquery.user` role.

For the following example, data analysts are in a group named `test@example.com`. This group name is for example purposes only. When this group is added to an IAM role, the email address and domain must be associated with an active Google Account or Google Apps account.

To assign the data analysts group to the `bigquery.user` role at the project level, follow the given steps via the GCP Console:

1. Go to the IAM page in the Google Cloud Platform Console.
2. Then, click on **Select a project**.
3. Select your project and click on **Open**.
4. On the **IAM** page, click on **Add**.
5. In the **Add members** dialog:
   - For **Members**, type the group name: `test@example.com`.
   - For **Roles**, click on select a role and choose `BigQuery > BigQuery User`.
6. Click on **Add**.

Assign access controls to the dataset containing the view

In order for data analysts to query the view, they need to be provided with the `bigquery.dataViewer` role on the dataset containing the view. The `bigquery.user` role gives data analysts the permissions required to create query jobs, but they cannot successfully query the view unless they also have at least `bigquery.dataViewer` access to the dataset that contains the view.

To give your data analysts' `bigquery.dataViewer` access to the dataset via the GCP Console, perform the given steps:

1. In the **Resources** section, select the `shared_views` dataset, and then click on **Share dataset**.
2. In the `Dataset permissions` panel, click on `Add members`.
3. Type `data_analysts@example.com` in the `New members` text box.
4. Click on select role and select `BigQuery > BigQuery Data Viewer`.
5. Click on Done.

Authorize the view to access the source dataset

Once access controls for the dataset containing the view are created, add the view as an authorized view in the source dataset. This gives the view access to the source data, not data analysts group.

To authorize the view to access the source data via the GCP Console, perform the following steps:

1. Open the `github_source_data` dataset from **Resources** and click on **Share dataset**.
2. In the **Dataset permissions** panel, click on the **Authorized views** tab.
3. Under the Share authorized view:
   - For select project, verify your project is selected.
   - For select dataset, choose `shared_views`.
   - For select view, type the view name: `github_analyst_view`.
4. Click on **OK**.
5. Click on **Add** and then click on **Done**.

Introduction to external data sources

An external data source (also referred to as a federated data source) is a data source which will query directly even if the data doesn't hold on in BigQuery. Rather than loading or streaming the data, a table can be created which references the external data source.

BigQuery offers support for querying data directly from:
- Cloud Bigtable
- Cloud Storage
- Google Drive

The following are the use cases for external data sources:
- Loading and cleansing data in one travel by querying the data from an external data source (a location external to BigQuery) and writing the clean result into BigQuery storage.
- Having a small quantity of often changing data that join with alternative tables. As an external data supply, the often-dynamic data need not be reloaded every time it's updated.

The external data source limitations embrace the following:
- BigQuery doesn't guarantee data consistency for external data sources. Changes to the underlying data while a query is running may end up in surprising behavior.
- Query performance for external data sources is not high as compared to querying data in a native BigQuery table. If speed may be a priority, load data into BigQuery rather than fitting an external data supply. The performance of a query that has an external data source depends on the external storage sort. For example, querying data hold on in Cloud Storage is quicker than querying data hold on in Google Drive. In general, query performance for external data sources should be like reading the info directly from the external storage.

- Use of the `TableDataList` JSON API method is not allowed to retrieve data from tables that reside in an external data supply. In order to work around this limitation, save query ends up in a destination table and then use the `TableDataList` method on the results table.

- Running a BigQuery job that exports data from an external data source is not allowed. To work around this limitation, save query results in a destination table and then run an export job against the results table.

- Referencing an external data supply in a wildcard table query is not permissible.

- External data sources don't support table partitioning or a cluster.

- When querying an external data source, the results aren't cached. This makes sure that, charges for every query against an external table even though an equivalent query is executed multiple times. In case of repeatedly issues of a query against an external table that doesn't modify, take into account writing the query results to a permanent table and run the queries against the permanent table instead.

BigQuery best practices for controlling prices

In this section, we will look at the best practices for controlling prices.

Avoid selecting *

Best practice: Use only that column which is necessary and required.

Using * (all columns) is the costliest way to query data. Once * is included in the query, BigQuery does a full scan of each column within the complete table. Also, it is a good practice to use info preview choices rather than selecting * during experimenting with data or exploring data. Also, if the `LIMIT` clause is applied to choose the * query, it doesn't impact the quantity of data scan. It consumes the entire free tier quota by reading all bytes within the entire table. If it needs queries against each column in a table, solely against a set of data, consider the following:

- Create a materialized result target table and then query that table instead.

- Make sure that tables are properly partitioned by date and then query the relevant partition; for example, wherever `_PARTITIONDATE="2019-02-01"` solely scans the Feb 1, 2019 partition.

Use the preview option while sample data exploitation

Best practice: Not to run queries to preview table data.

During experimentation with or exploring data, use table preview choices to look at data for free and without considering quotas.

BigQuery provisions the subsequent data preview options:

- Sampling/previewing of data can be done via a **Preview** tab in the GCP Console or the classic web UI on the table details page.
- Via the command line interface, a set of specific number of rows to preview can be previewed through the bq head command.
- In the API, use `tabledata.list` to retrieve the table data from a fixed set of rows.

Price queries before executing them

Best practice: Estimating the cost of queries using the preview option before actual execution of queries.

Queries are charged as per the number of bytes scan. In order to estimate prices before a query gets executed, perform the following:

- View the question validator within the GCP Console or the classic web UI
- Leverage evaluation calculator within the GCP
- Do a test exercise by using the:
  - o   `--dry_run` flag in the CLI
  - o   `dryRun` parameter when submitting a query job using the API

Using the query validator

When a query is written within the GCP Console or the classic web UI, the query validator verifies the query syntax and provides an estimate of the amount of bytes scan. This estimate can be used to calculate the query price within the pricing calculator.

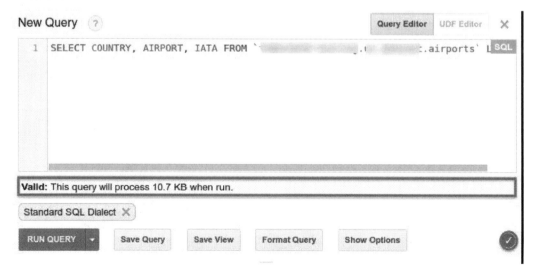

Figure 5.9: Volume of data process in BigQuery

Performing a dry run:

Restrict query costs by limiting the number of bytes billed.

Best practice: Under the Setting option, use the maximum bytes billed to limit query costs.

In order to limit the number of bytes to be billed for a query, maximum bytes billed setting can be used. When maximum bytes billed is enabled and queries try to read bytes beyond the limit, the query breaks without incurring a charge. If a query fails because of the maximum bytes billed setting, an error like the following is displayed:

```
Error: Query exceeded limit for bytes billed: 2000000. 10484860 or higher
required.
```

The following steps are used to configure the maximum bytes billed:

1. In the classic BigQuery web UI, enter a number in the **Maximum Bytes Billed** field in the query options. This option is currently not supported in the GCP Console. Refer to the following screenshot:

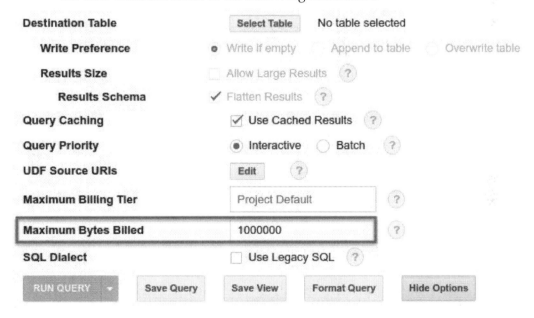

Figure 5.10: Setting up maximum byte limits

2. This option can be set via the CLI using the bq query command with the --maximum_bytes_billed flag.

```
bq query --maximum_bytes_billed=1000000 \
--use_legacy_sql=false \
'SELECT text  FROM `bigquery-public-data`.samples.books'
```

3. Also via an API, the `maximumBytesBilled` property can be set in the query job configuration.

LIMIT doesn't impact any cost

Best practice: The `LIMIT` clause should not be used as a method of cost control.

Including a `LIMIT` clause within a query does not affect the amount of data which is being read. It only limits the results set output. However, billing is applied for reading all bytes in the table as specified by the query. Despite the presence of a `LIMIT` clause, the amount of data read by the query counts against free tier quota.

View costs using a dashboard and query your audit logs

Best practice: In order to control BigQuery usage, users can develop a dashboard to view billing data. While developing a billing dashboard, streaming audit logs to BigQuery also needs to be considered to make it helpful to analyze usage patterns.

It is easy to export the billing data to BigQuery and then visualize it in a tool such as Google Data Studio. Audit logs can be streamed to BigQuery and analyzed for usage patterns such as query costs by users.

Partition data by date

Best practice: Partition BigQuery tables by date.

Make sure that BigQuery tables are partitioned by date. Partitioning tables make sure that relevant subsets of data are queried which improves performance and reduces expenses.

For example, when a query is executed on partitioned tables, apply filter on the `_PARTITIONTIME` pseudo column to filter for a specific date or a range of dates. The query processes data only in the partitions that are specified by the date or range.

Materialize query results in stages

Best practice: If possible, materialize query results in stages.

If a large multi-stage query is being executed each time on a huge dataset, all the records are read which is required in BigQuery. Since all the data is read each time, bill charges will be high and hence, breaking query into stages where each stage materializes the query results by writing them to a destination table will help to reduce the cost. Also, a query process on smaller destination tables reduce the amount of data that is read and lower costs. As we already know that cost of storing the materialized results is lesser than the cost of processing large amount of data.

Think of large result sets price

Best practice: It is suggested to apply the default table expiration time to delete the data when it's no longer needed when writing large query results to a destination table.

Keeping large result sets in BigQuery storage has a cost. If permanent access to the results is not needed, use the default table expiration to automatically delete the data when it expires.

Use streaming inserts with caution

Best practice: Use streaming inserts only when data must be immediately available and data is required in real time.

As discussed earlier, there is no charge for loading data into BigQuery. However, there is a charge for streaming data into BigQuery. Unless your data needs to be immediately available, load data rather than streaming it.

Optimizing query computation

- **Avoid repeated joins and sub queries**
    - o Consider revisiting the table if the same tables are repeatedly joined together.
    - o Use nested and repeated fields in such situations which may result into better performance (saving I/O costs that are incurred reading and writing the same data).
- **Materializing large result sets**
    - o Writing large result sets has the performance and cost impacts.
    - o BigQuery limits the cached results to approximately 128 MB compressed.
    - o Queries that return results overtake this limit and frequently result in the following error: Response too large.
- **Normalization**
    - o Remove data redundancy from data as much as possible.
    - o Work towards improving data integrity.
- **Denormalization in BigQuery**
    - o Denormalization in BigQuery make queries much faster.
    - o Data integrity is not an issue because data is not being modified.
    - o Extra cost is often outweighed by faster query times.
- **Denormalize data whenever possible**
    - o Performance of BigQuery is at its peak when it processes denormalized data.
    - o Instead of maintaining a star or snowflake relational schema, denormalize data and take advantages for nested and repeated fields.

o There is less concern nowadays for storage savings from normalized data. It is always worth to increase in storage costs over the performance gains from denormalized data.

o Data coordination is required for joins (communication bandwidth) while denormalize directs the data to individual slots to make execution in parallel.

o Avoid denormalization in case if you have to start a schema with frequently changing dimensions.

- **Using nested and repeated fields:** BigQuery does not necessarily need flat denormalization; we can nest and repeated fields to maintain relationships:

  o **Nesting data (ARRAY):**

    ▪ In order to represent foreign entities inline, nesting data plays an important role.

    ▪ When querying nested data, the *dot* syntax is used for reference leaf fields.

    ▪ Nested data is represented as the STRUT type in standard SQL.

  o **Repeated data (ARRAY):**

    ▪ Creating a field of type RECORD with the mode set to REPEATED.

    ▪ Shuffling is not necessary for repeated data.

    ▪ An ARRAY is a representation of repeated data.

Google Data Studio

Data Studio is Google's reporting reply to all the users who want to create impressive visualization on top of different data sources and go beyond the data and dashboards of Google Analytics. The data widgets in Data Studio are prominent for their variation, customization choices, live data, and interactive controls (such as column sorting and table pagination). Data sources could be a variety of products which include Google products (Analytics, AdWords, Search Console, Sheets, YouTube, and more), database connectors, and file upload and community connectors to popular marketing services.

With Google Data studio, one can go from data to insight to wisdom via great visualization supported by the GCP cloud service. It is a comprehensive suite of data analytics tools from Google and which has couple of built-in functionalities like flexibility, scalability, collaboration, and advanced analytics. Data Studio not only is BI workloads backed by the power and scale of BigQuery, but it is also accelerated by BigQuery BI Engine, an in-memory analysis service for fast, interactive visual analytics.

Data Studio handles the authentication, access rights, and structuring of the data in an organized manner. Once a data source is connected to Data Studio, underlying dimensions and metrics are easily available for calculations, transformations, and visualizations.

With Data Studio, one can turn data into compelling visuals with out-of-the-box, community-built, or their own custom visualizations. The Data Studio service console is not readily available within the GCP console like other services; however, users can open the data studio console via its own web URL. Once ready for delivery, include them into dashboards, reports, or data stories and get blazing fast insights when they're connected to both BigQuery, Google's MPP analytics data warehouse, and to BigQuery BI Engine, an in-memory analysis service with sub-second query response, high concurrency, and smart performance tuning. Data Studio reports can be easily shared with anyone within and outside the organization, depending on the report configuration. It also comes with the report scheduling option where recipients can receive the report in their inbox at a particular scheduled interval.

The following are the features of Data Studio:

- Visualized data through highly configurable charts and tables.
- Easily connects to a variety of data sources.
- Shares dashboards with the team and or with the external world.
- Speeds up report development within built sample reports.
- **Usability:** Data Studio was designed to support so many easy-to-use features, which seasoned analytics teams are sure to enjoy them.

Building the Google Data Studio report

In order to create your first Data Studio report, you need to be connected to the source and Google provides the opportunity to connect to sample data sources. The sample Google Analytics data is part of the Google Merchandise Store. Working with Google's sample data is a great way to get acclimated to Data Studio. The following screenshot shows the sample datasets:

Figure 5.11: Sample public dataset

Now, let's see how to build charts and graphs using the Merchandise Store Data. This is explained in the following section in detail.

Connecting Google Analytics Account to Google Data Studio

Firstly, add new data sources to the account from right-side of reports. To set up a new data source, follow the given steps:

1. Go to the blue + icon to enable a new data connection as shown in the following screenshot:

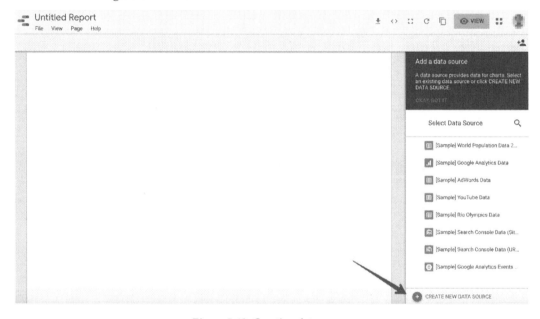

Figure 5.12: Creating data source

2. Then, select the required data source which is Google Analytics data connector for this example:

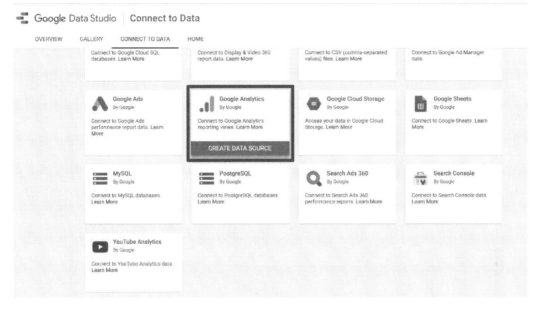

Figure 5.13: *List of available data sources*

3. Next, Data Studio needs to be authorized to access the Google Analytics account.

4. Once it is authorized, then choose the account property and view (*Master, Test, Raw Data*) he dataset which user want to connect to Google Data Studio:

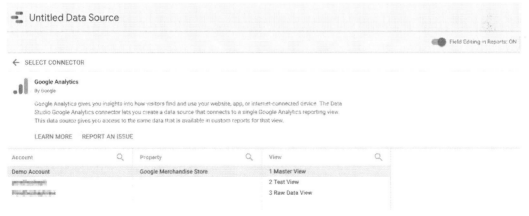

Figure 5.14: *Google Analytics dataset*

5. Once the source is connected to Google analytics, fields need to be added from the account to the sample report.

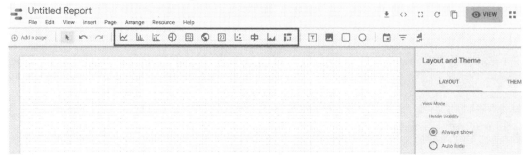

Figure 5.15: Field Mapping in Data Studio

Google Data Studio accesses data via the Google Analytics API. Hence, before Data Studio does an import, it will show a list of all the metrics and dimensions which are available. The option of disabling any of these fields is available before users create their report. Not only disable but as required users can also access and edit these fields from their reporting screen.

Let's start playing and creating new visualizations via the given steps:

1. **Building visualizations in Google Data Studio and attaching data to reports:**

    Addition of visualizations to the Google Data Studio report is very simple. It is easy to add visuals from the menu located above the reporting area as shown in the following screenshot:

Figure 5.16: Data Visualization Options

There is multiple graph supported some of them are Time series graph, bar chart, pie chart, table, geo map, scorecard, scatter chart, area chart, bullet chart, area map, or pivot table. While adding visualization, simply select the one from the list to use, and draw it into the report as shown in the following screenshot:

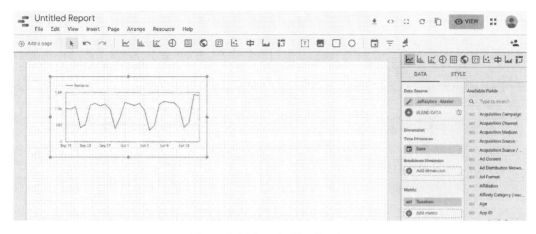

Figure 5.17: Sample Visualization

2. **Connecting visualizations to data:**

   Two data points are required which are *Metric* and *Dimension* for Visualizations (except for scorecards and bullet charts).

   After drawing visualizations, data/style which is located on the right-hand side of the screen (as shown in the preceding screenshot) can be used to develop the report. This menu is where most of the time is spend working in Google Data Studio.

3. **Change your metrics and dimensions:**

   The following screenshot describes about adding metrics and dimension to the report:

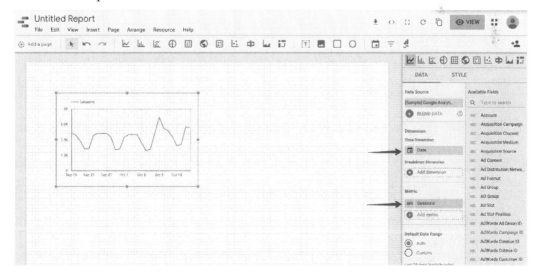

Figure 5.18: Adding Dimension and Metrics

4. **Add filters:**

The following screenshot explains about adding the filter to the Data studio report:

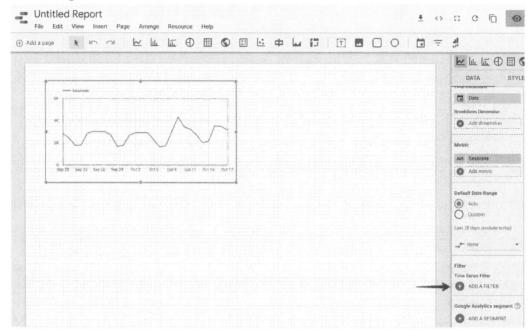

Figure 5.19: Adding filter to Report

5. **Change the chart types which is being used:**

There are different types of charts available within the Data studio console and can be modified based on the requirement as shown in the following screenshot:

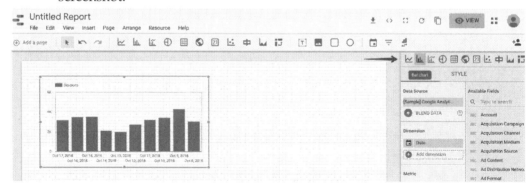

Figure 5.20: Updating Chart Type

6. **Adjust date range:**

   Date range can be adjusted based on the requirement as shown in the following screenshot:

   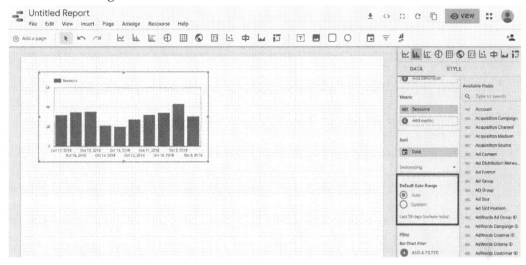

   Figure 5.21: *Updating Data Range*

7. **Change data source:**

   Data source can be changed for the complete report as shown in the following screenshot:

   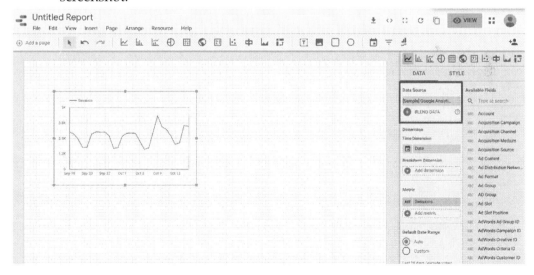

   Figure 5.22: *Changing Data Source*

8. **Style visualizations:**

    Users can add and update the default style of the visualization by going to next tab of data as shown in the following screenshot:

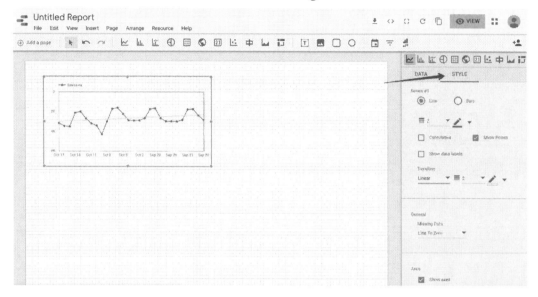

Figure 5.23: Style within Visualization

Some more features and specifications to be considered about Data Studio reports are listed below.

9. **Data Studio support view only relationship with data sources:**

    Data Studio has a view only relationship with data sources, which means that the changes made in reports won't have any effect on data collection systems. So, click around and play with the data in reports as much as you want without impacting anything.

10. **Sharing access to reports:**

    Because users can't damage their data in Google Data Studio; it doesn't mean they will give others the edit access to their reports.

11. **Edit access:**

    Data Studio comes with two levels of access, edit and view. Anyone who has been provided with edit access has free reign when it comes to working in reports. They can manipulate any visualization which is displayed in reports. They can also adjust data sources and see all included data elements. However, it is advisable to limit edit access to known team members.

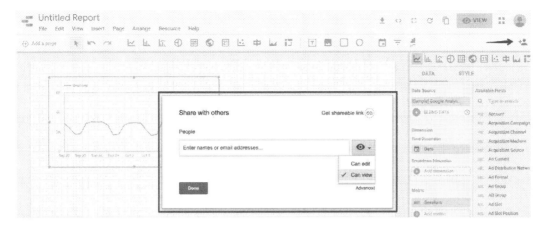

Figure 5.24: *Data Studio report sharing*

12. View access in Google Data Studio:

View access in Google Data Studio only allows others to see the front-end of report. This is the access level that is generally provided to clients or people outside team.

If a user wants to allow their clients or team members to manipulate the data in their reports, consider using date pickers and filters. These tools provide some basic filtering options, without allowing others to access the back-end or your report.

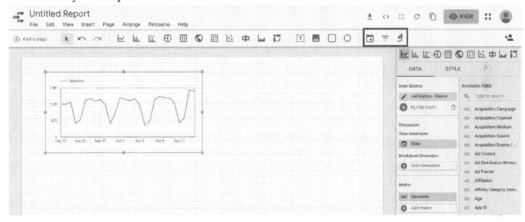

Figure 5.25: *View Access of Report*

13. Embed your report on the web:

Google Data Studio is very flexible and allows you to share interactive reports publicly on website. This can be done via embedding the report to the web. In order to embed the report, include the following embed code for report:

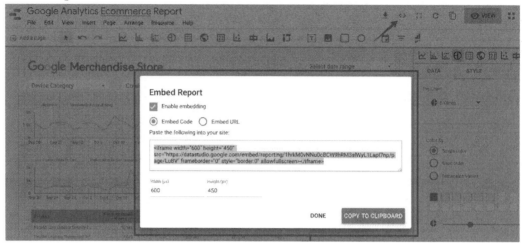

Figure 5.26: Embedding Data Studio Report

And paste the code into the CMS editor or HTML page:

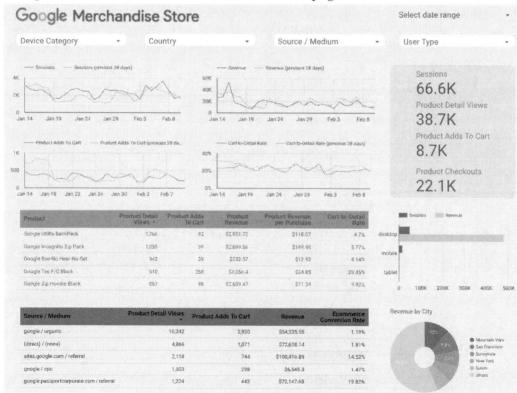

Figure 5.27: Embedded Report

Conclusion

In this chapter, we discussed about the BigQuery architecture and its usage in detail. There are some features in BigQuery which makes it unique for online analytical processing. Partitioning and quota are two important aspects which need to be considered while using BigQuery. BigQuery also supports reading data directly from external source systems. Google Data Studio is a visualization technique provided by GCP to develop reports. There are different types of graphs and data sources supported in Google Data Studio.

Questions

1. What is columnar storage of data and what are its advantages?
2. Explain the different types of partitioning in BigQuery. How does it relate to cost saving?
3. What are federated queries? Which external sources are supported in BigQuery?
4. What are quota limits for different types of operations in BigQuery?
5. What are different types of visualizations supported in Google Data Studio?

Machine Learning with GCP

Objective

This chapter will be covering the basics of machine learning, types of machine learning, Google Cloud ML, and TensorFlow constructs.

Structure

This chapter will start with the basic concepts of machine learning and the types of machine learning, as stated below:

- Supervised learning
- Steps in supervised learning
- Linear regression in TensorFlow
- The Estimator API
- Unsupervised
    - o K-mean clustering 2D points
    - o Working with image (image classification)
- Cloud ML API (vision, translate, speech)

Machine learning and types of machine learning

Machine learning (ML) systems automatically learn and enhance from experience machine learning, based on programming, which accesses the data and uses it to learn for prediction.

> *Learning is any process by which a system improves performance from experience*
>
> *Herbert Simon*

The following diagram depicts a high-level representation of machine learning:

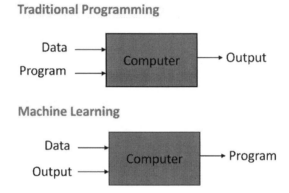

Figure 6.1: Depicting machine learning

Machine learning can be broadly classified into:

- Supervised learning
- Unsupervised learning

Supervised learning

Supervised means that the *machine* (system) learns with the help of something, typically a labeled training. A training data (dataset) is the basis on which the system learns how to infer. An example of this process is to show the *system* a set of images of cats, dogs with the corresponding labels of the image (the label says whether the image is of cat or a dog) and let the system decipher the features of a cat and a dog.

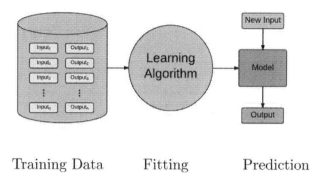

Training Data   Fitting   Prediction

Figure 6.2: *Supervised machine learning*

The following are the steps in supervised learning:

1. Confirm the type of training examples and prepare the training dataset.
2. Perform the data pre-processing (normalization, scaling, binning, outlier management, correlation between features, and more).
3. Gather the training dataset. The training dataset should leverage real-world use cases. Thus, a group of input objects is gathered, and the corresponding outputs are gathered either from human consultants, or from measurements.
4. Perform feature engineering and determine if the feature object is transformed in to feature vector that contains a range of options that are descriptive of the object. Feature should not be overlarge due to the curse of dimensionality.
5. Apply the machine learning algorithm on the gathered training set.
6. Perform cross validation and dimensional reduction (if any) on the dataset and rerun the model.
7. Evaluate the accuracy of the machine learning model and hyper-tune the model.

The following are the supervised learning techniques:

- Linear regression
- Classification logistic regression
- Decision tree
- Bagging and random forest
- Boosting (Adaboost/GBM/XgBoost)
- Cross validation
- Support vector machine

TensorFlow and machine learning

TensorFlow is an open source software package for numerical computation, using data flow graphs. This was very tactfully open sourced by Google. This is a generic numerical computation library, so there is nothing which says that we can only use it for machine learning or neural network applications. It models these combinations as dataflow graphs. The idea of presenting the operations on the data in the form of a directed, acyclic graph is an old and established one.

The advantage of TensorFlow is that, for one, it is distributed and as we have already seen, the ability to run a complex competition in a cluster of machines, on multiple CPU/GPU's use, is increasingly important as the assets get too big to fit in memory on a single machine.

The second important advantage of TensorFlow is that it lies at the heart of an entire suite of software tools. In addition to a bunch of powerful libraries available within TensorFlow, there is also a board, which is a visualization tool that we can access with the browser and other associated mechanism.

The following are the uses of TensorFlow:

- Research and development of the new ML algorithm
- Taking models from training to production
- Large scale, distributed models
- Models for mobile and embedded systems

The following are the strengths of TensorFlow:

- Easy to use, stable Python API
- Runs on large and small systems
- Efficient and performant
- Great support form Google
- Additional tools like tensor board and TensorFlow serving

Computation in neural network, in our model using directed acyclic graph. This is an abstraction, which is used in other technologies.

The below diagram represents a graph with nodes, which represents the computations that the edges between those nodes are a data item and those data items are called **tensors**:

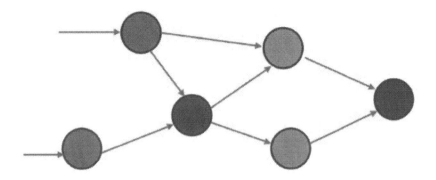

Figure 6.3: *Representation of data tem/tensor*

The reason why the TensorFlow is so popular these days is because, it has become the tool of choice for building complicated neural networks. Neural networks rely on the same underlying abstraction, which is interconnected nodes which represent operations to be guided or can get items and edges between those nodes. These nodes represent the items and prediction graph or basic graph which is exactly mirrors of the setup of a neural network. Remember that neural networks consist of neurons which are basic operands and these neurons are wired up in complexities and flow easily and allows them to create nodes. A tensor is an array with several indices (like in numpy). An order is the number of indices and the shape is the range:

```
import numpy as np
T1 =no.asarray([1,2,3]) # tensor of Order 1 aka Vector
T1
Output: array([1,2,3])
T2 =np.asarray([[1,2,3],[4,5,6]]) # tensor of Order 2 aka Matrix
T2
Output: array([[1,2,3],[4,5,6]])
T3 =np.zeroes ((10,2,3)) # tensor of order 3 (Volume like objects)
Print(T1.shape)
Print(T2.shape)
Print(T3.shape)

Output:
(3)
(2,3)
(10,2,3)
```

Linear regression with TensorFlow

We now have a decent sense of TensorFlow mechanics, of how programs are set up and implemented on. Let's understand the basic building block - the neuron, and the role that neurons play as learning units. The neural network corpus of images and perceives that these are images of fish or mammals being in a sense of learning a function. These function which tells us how those images link to their output level and that function is to learn using these layers in the neural network. This is what the feature selection and classification algorithm is all about.

But the intent of all these layers in the neural network is the same - to reverse engineer the relationship between the output and the input. An ML algorithm can learn from data. This is a standard definition of machine learning. This brings us to the definition of learning algorithms:

> *A computer program is said to learn from experience E, with respect to some class of tasks T, and performance measure P. If its performance at tasks in T is as measured by P, improves with experience E.*

There are a bunch of standard tasks in machine learning - classification, regression, clustering and rule the action have already had some exposure to three of these classification and regression as well as clustering, where K is the nearest algorithm.

Now, to tell whether an algorithm is getting better or not, we also need a performance measure; and performance measures are specific to the individual tasks. It might be the residual variance, or it might be a metric known as cross entropy, for using logistic rather than linear regression.

All of these are performance measures, which tell us how well our learning algorithm is improving, much like how a human export a learning algorithm that improves with experience, and that experience is in terms of the training process. It is in terms of exposure to several the liberal instances. That is a corpus.

So, putting all of this together, a learning algorithm learns from experience, which means that it improves performance and tasks as measured by some of the formants measure up. This is the heart of a learning algorithm, and this is the reason for leaking the insides of a model during the cleaning process.

It is relatively straightforward to understand how an algorithm, like the linear progression loan, is given a large number of data points. This kind of does tweak the experience. It will tweak the values of its constants, both, at the slope and the Intersect of the regression line, and if we treat this in ways which decrease the loss function, i.e. increase the performance, this process of learning is easy to quantify and understand for simple algorithms. However, it can be a challenging to understand how deep learning algorithms actually learn. In a nutshell, deep learning algorithms learn by tweaking the features, which depends on weights of their neurons and using a couple of examples. The simplest possible example, which is a regression using a single neuron and then a slightly more in-world example involving XOR learning. The XOR function requires three neurons arranged in 2 layers.

We shall see how such a neural network and the low, and the XOR, function via the training process. Before we plunge into that, let's once again reiterate the exact relationship between the neurons and neural network layers in a computational graph and represent the groups of neurons, which perform similar functions. Each layer is going to consist of neurons, which are then interconnected with neurons in other layers in possibly very complex ways.

And as we have discussed, the deep learning arises because there are many layers of the neurons arranged in the directed computation graphs, which we discussed in the context of TensorFlow. The relationships between the data is that the more complex the graph, the more the number of relationships it can learn.

For instance, simple functions, such as linear regression, can be learned using a really simple graph with just one layer. That means that one neuron will suffice, as we can see, to learn and even with slightly more complex functions, such as the XOR function, 2 layers and three neurons.

Clearly, we can learn many more complex functions by adding more layers and more neurons connected in increasingly complex ways. The connections between these neurons and how they learn that complex function, becomes opaque to us very quickly. Neural networks become black boxes very quickly, but that doesn't really matter if they learn a complex function.

Training in linear regression TensorFlow

Let us suppose that if we have two features, x and y, and we need to predict the value. Once the data is plotted, a positive relationship between independent feature, x and the dependent feature y can been seen, as showcased below:

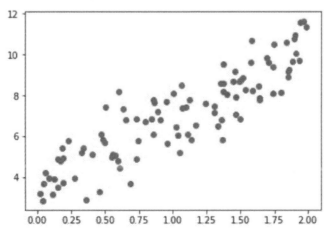

Figure 6.4: Variables without linear regression

It can be observed from the preceding diagram that if *x=1*, *y* will approximately be equal to *5* and if *x=2*, then y will be around *8.3*. This is not a very accurate way and is prone to error; generally, when a dataset has hundreds or thousands of points.

A linear regression is based on an equation. The feature *y* is described by one or many covariates. For example, there is only one dependent feature. In order to write this in an equation, it will be:

$$y = \beta + \alpha X + \epsilon$$

Where:

β is the bias. That is, *if x=0, y=* β .

α is the weight associated to *x*.

ϵ is the residual or the error of the model. It comprises of something that the model cannot learn from the data.

Think of fitting the model and find the following solution for:

β = 3.7

α = 2.68

Once those numbers in the equation are substituted, and it becomes:

$$y= 3.7 + 2.68x$$

Based on above equation, now there is a better way to find the values for *y*. That is, replace *x* with any predefined value to predict *y* accordingly. In the following diagram, the value of *x* is replaced in the equation with all the values in the dataset to plot the result:

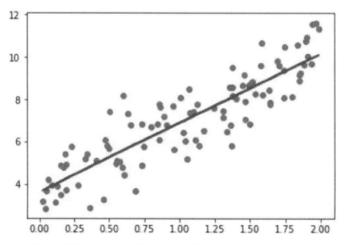

Figure 6.5: *Representation of variables using linear regression*

The red line indicates the fitted value, which is the value of y for each value of x. Now it is not required to see the value of x to predict y, for each x there is a y, which belongs to the red line. This can also help to predict the values of x higher than 2.

It is easy to extend the linear regression to more covariates, by adding more features to the model. The difference between the traditional analysis and linear regression is that the linear regression shows how y will react for each feature of x taken independently.

TensorFlow has three different ways to import the data:

- With Pandas
- With Numpy
- Only TF

> **Note:** All the above approaches provide the same results.

The user will now learn how to use the high-level API to build, train and evaluate a linear regression model. While using the low-level API, the following point needs to be defined by hand:

- Loss function
- **Optimize:** gradient descent
- Matrices multiplication
- Graph and tensor

Let us start with linear regression use cases for insurance companies, which they are considering for decision making with the below example.

Problem statement: Is there a connection between the number of fires and thefts in a neighborhood? If there is, can it be found? In alternate words, the problem is to find a function f, so that if X is the number of fires and Y is the number of thefts, then: Y = f(X)?

Given the relationship, if the number of fires in a particular area is present, it can help in predicting the number of thefts in that area. The dataset used for this example is collected by the U.S. *Commission on Civil Rights*, courtesy of *Cengage Learning*.

```
Dataset Details: Name: Fire and Theft in Delhi X = fires per 2000 housing units
```

```
Y = thefts per 2000 population within the same Zip code in the Delhi metro area
```

```
Total number of Zip code areas: 52
```

First, the relationship between the number of fires and thefts is linear: Y = mX + c

Below is the program code:

```
import numpy as np
```

```
import matplotlib.pyplot as plt
import tensorflow as tf import xlrd
DATA_FILE = "testdata/fire_theft.xls"

# Step 1: Reading data from the .xls file
book = xlrd.open_workbook(DATA_FILE, encoding_override="utf-8")
sheet = book.sheet_by_index(0)
data = np.asarray([sheet.row_values(i) for i in range(1, sheet.nrows)])
n_samples = sheet.nrows - 1

# Step 2: create placeholders for input X (number of fire) and label Y
(number of theft)
X = tf.placeholder(tf.float32, name="X")
Y = tf.placeholder(tf.float32, name="Y")

# Step 3: create weight and bias, initialized to 0
w = tf.Variable(0.0, name="weights")
b = tf.Variable(0.0, name="bias")

# Step 4: construct a model to predict Y (number of theft) from the number
of fires
Y_predicted = X * w + b

# Step 5: use the square error as the loss function
loss = tf.square(Y - Y_predicted, name="loss")

# Step 6: using gradient descent with the learning rate of 0.01 to
minimize loss
optimizer    =    tf.train.GradientDescentOptimizer(learning_rate=0.001).
minimize(loss)
with tf.Session() as sess:
# Step 7: initialize the necessary variables, in this case, w and b
sess.run(tf.global_variables_initializer())

# Step 8: train the model for i in range(100): # run 100 epochs for x, y
in data: # Session runs train_op to minimize loss
```

```
sess.run(optimizer, feed_dict={X: x, Y:y})

# Step 9: output the values of w and b
w_value, b_value = sess.run([w, b])
```

For **100** epochs, we got the average square loss to be **1372.77** with w = **1.62071** and
b = **16.9162.** The loss is quite big:

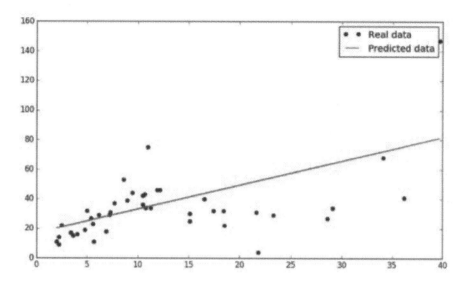

Figure 6.6: Graph showing real vs. predicted data

As per the above diagram, this may not be a good fit. Now, let's apply the quadratic
function Y = wXX + uX + b. We only need to add another feature, b, and change
the formula for Y_predicted.

```
# Step 3: create variables: weights_1, weights_2, bias. All are initialized
to 0
w = tf.Variable(0.0, name="weights_1")
u = tf.Variable(0.0, name="weights_2")
b = tf.Variable(0.0, name="bias")


# Step 4: predict Y (number of theft) from the number of fires
Y_predicted = X * X * w + X * u + b


# Step 5: Profit!
```

Run `10` epochs, square loss to be `797.335975976` with `w, u, b = [0.071343
0.010234 0.0]`, which is not the best fit:

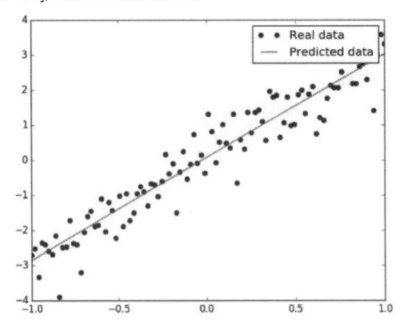

Figure 6.7: Graph for real vs. predicted data

In the above code, the gradient descent optimizer method is being used and we
can set the keyword trainable to `False`, when we declare a feature; and if we don't
want to train, it is the global step - a common feature, which will be seen in many
TensorFlow models to keep a track of how many times the model has been executed:

```
global_step = tf.Variable(0, trainable=False, dtype=tf.int32) learning_
rate = 0.01 * 0.99 ** tf.cast(global_step, tf.float32)
```

```
increment_step = global_step.assign_add(1)
```

```
optimizer = tf.GradientDescentOptimizer(learning_rate)
```

```
# learning rate can be a tensor
```

Optimizer takes the gradients of specific variables. Gradients can also be optimized,
which was calculated by the optimizer via the below program:

```
tf.Variable(initial_value=None, trainable=True, collections=None,
validate_shape=True, caching_device=None, name=None, variable_def=None,
dtype=None, expected_shape=None, import_scope=None)
```

```
# create an optimizer.
```

```
optimizer = GradientDescentOptimizer(learning_rate=0.1)
```

```
# compute the gradients for a list of variables.
```

```
grads_and_vars = opt.compute_gradients(loss, <list of variables>)
# grads_and_vars is a list of tuples (gradient, variable).  Do whatever
you # need to the 'gradient' part, for example, subtract each of them by 1.
subtracted_grads_and_vars = [(gv[0] - 1.0, gv[1]) for gv in grads_and_vars]
# ask the optimizer to apply the subtracted gradients.
optimizer.apply_gradients(subtracted_grads_and_vars)
```

The above set of code can be used to optimize the gradient.

The Estimator API

Estimators are a high-level way to perform a linear task or in logistic regression. The basic idea of how estimate does all the work will explain why estimators are a high-level API.

The tf.estimator is a high-level TensorFlow API. Estimators handle the following steps:

- Training
- Evaluation
- Prediction
- Export for serving

Either an existing, inbuilt estimator can be used, or it can also be customized in the estimator's class. The following is a sample code snippet:

```
import tensorflow as tf
import pandas as pd
download and prase the iris dataset
train_path = tf.keras.utils.get_file(
        "iris_training.csv", "https://storage.googleapis.com/download.
tensorflow.org/data/iris_training.csv")
test_path = tf.keras.utils.get_file(
    "iris_test.csv", "https://storage.googleapis.com/download.tensorflow.
org/data/iris_test.csv")

train = pd.read_csv(train_path, names=CSV_COLUMN_NAMES, header=0)
test = pd.read_csv(test_path, names=CSV_COLUMN_NAMES, header=0)
train.head()
train_y = train.pop('Species')
test_y = test.pop('Species')
```

```
# The label column has now been removed from the features.
train.head()
```

The following are the Estimators steps:

1. Create a function for training, evaluation, prediction, it will return tf.data. Dataset object:

```
def input_evaluation_set():
    features = {'SepalLength': np.array([6.4, 5.0]),
                'SepalWidth':  np.array([2.8, 2.3]),
                'PetalLength': np.array([5.6, 3.3]),
                'PetalWidth':  np.array([2.2, 1.0])}
    labels = np.array([2, 1])
    return features, labels
```

2. Define the model's feature columns:

```
my_feature_columns = []
for key in train.keys():
        my_feature_columns.append(tf.feature_column.numeric_
column(key=key))
```

3. Instantiate an Estimator. The Iris problem is a classic classification problem. TensorFlow provides various in-built classifiers:

- `tf.estimator.DNNClassifier` for multi-class classification.
- `tf.estimator.DNNLinearCombinedClassifier` for wide and deep models.
- `tf.estimator.LinearClassifier` for linear models.

4. The best choice for the Iris problem is the tf.estimator.DNNClassifier. Here's how this estimator can be instantiated:

```
# Build a DNN with 2 hidden layers with 30 and 10 hidden nodes each.
classifier = tf.estimator.DNNClassifier(
    feature_columns=my_feature_columns,
    # Two hidden layers of 10 nodes each.
    hidden_units=[30, 10],
    # The model must choose between 3 classes.
    n_classes=3)
```

5. Initiate the following steps, once you instantiate the object:
    -   Train the model.
    -   Evaluate the trained model.
    -   Use the trained model to make predictions.

Unsupervised machine learning

Unsupervised learning is the process of grouping data into similar categories. An example of this is to input into the *system* a set of images of dogs and cats, without mentioning which image belongs to which category, and letting the system group the two types of images into different buckets depending on the similarity of images.

Clustering helps in grouping our data points in some way. The benefits of grouping variables can be:

-   For a business user to understand the various types of users among the customers.
-   Make business decisions at a cluster (group) level, rather than at a granular level.
-   Help improve the accuracy of predictions – as different groups exhibit different behaviors, and hence, a separate model of each group.

The cluster evaluation:

-   **Intra-cluster cohesion (compactness):** Cohesion measures how close the data points in a cluster are to the cluster centroid. **Sum of squared error (SSE)** is a commonly used measure.
-   **Inter-cluster separation (isolation):** Separation means that different cluster centroids should be far away from one another.

The clustering techniques are as follows:

-   **Hierarchical:** Agglomerative (bottom-up) or divisive (top-down)
-   **Partitional:** All clusters at once
-   **Bayesian:** Generate a posteriori distribution over the collection of all partitions of the data

The objective of the clustering exercise is as follows:

-   All points belonging to the same group are as close to each other as possible
-   Each groups center is far away from the other group's center.

K-means clustering:

1. Consider the data points D to be $\{x1, x2, …, xn\}$, where $xi = (xi1, xi2, …, xir)$ is a vector in $X\ Rr$, and r is the number of dimensions.

2. The K-means algorithm partitions the specified data into k clusters. Each cluster has a cluster center, called centroid, where k is specified by the user.

K-means algorithm:

Once k is given, the K-means algorithm operates as follows:

1. Select k (random) data points to be the initial centroids, cluster centers.
2. Allocate each data point to the closest centroid.
3. Re-compute the centroids using the current cluster memberships.
4. When a convergence criterion is not satisfied, repeat steps 2 and 3.

K-means stopping criteria:

- No re-assignments of data points to different clusters
- No change or shift of centroids, or
- Minimum decrease in the sum of squared error (SSE)

The following are the steps for creating a cluster model:

1. Generate random data points and assign them to the 2D tensor constant:

```
points = tf.constant(np.random.uniform(0, 10, (points_n, 2)))
centroids = tf.Variable(tf.slice(tf.random_shuffle(points), [0, 0],
[clusters_n, -1]))
```

2. Elaborate the points and centroids into three dimensions, which enables us to use the broadcasting feature of the subtraction operation:

```
points_expanded = tf.expand_dims(points, 0)
centroids_expanded = tf.expand_dims(centroids, 1)
```

3. Verify distances between the points and centroids, and determine the cluster assignments:

```
distances = tf.reduce_sum(tf.square(tf.subtract(points_expanded,
centroids_expanded)), 2)
assignments = tf.argmin(distances, 0)
```

4. Let's update the centroids variable with the new values:

```
means = []
for c in range(clusters_n):
    means.append(tf.reduce_mean(
        tf.gather(points,
                tf.reshape(
                    tf.where(
```

```
            tf.equal(assignments, c)
        ),[1,-1])
    ),reduction_indices=[1]))

new_centroids = tf.concat(means, 0)

update_centroids = tf.assign(centroids, new_centroids)
```

5. Visualize the build clusters

```
with tf.Session() as sess:

    sess.run(init)

    for step in xrange(iteration_n):

        [_, centroid_values, points_values, assignment_values] =
sess.run([update_centroids, centroids, points, assignments])

print("centroids", centroid_values)

plt.scatter(points_values[:, 0], points_values[:, 1], c=assignment_
values, s=50, alpha=0.5)

plt.plot(centroid_values[:,  0],  centroid_values[:,  1],  'kx',
markersize=15)

plt.show()
```

We will get the following output:

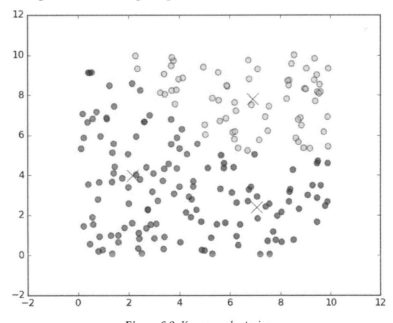

Figure 6.8: K-means clustering

K-means clustering (with MNIST image dataset):

```
import numpy as np
import tensorflow as tf
from random import randint
from collections import Counter
from tensorflow.examples.tutorials.mnist import input_data

mnist = input_data.read_data_sets("MNIST_data/")
X, y, k = mnist.test.images, mnist.test.labels, 10

# select random points as a starting position. You can do better by
randomly selecting k points.
start_pos = tf.Variable(X[np.random.randint(X.shape[0], size=k),:],
dtype=tf.float32)
centroids = tf.Variable(start_pos.initialized_value(), 'S', dtype=tf.
float32)

# populate points
points         = tf.Variable(X, 'X', dtype=tf.float32)
ones_like      = tf.ones((points.get_shape()[0], 1))
prev_assignments = tf.Variable(tf.zeros((points.get_shape()[0], ),
dtype=tf.int64))

# find the distance between all points:
p1 = tf.matmul(
    tf.expand_dims(tf.reduce_sum(tf.square(points), 1), 1),
    tf.ones(shape=(1, k))
)
p2 = tf.transpose(tf.matmul(
    tf.reshape(tf.reduce_sum(tf.square(centroids), 1), shape=[-1, 1]),
    ones_like,
    transpose_b=True
))
distance = tf.sqrt(tf.add(p1, p2) - 2 * tf.matmul(points, centroids,
transpose_b=True))
```

```
# assign each point to the closest centroid
point_to_centroid_assignment = tf.argmin(distance, axis=1)

# recalculate the centers
total = tf.unsorted_segment_sum(points, point_to_centroid_assignment, k)
count = tf.unsorted_segment_sum(ones_like, point_to_centroid_assignment, k)
means = total / count

# continue, if there is any difference between the current and the
previous assignment
is_continue = tf.reduce_any(tf.not_equal(point_to_centroid_assignment,
prev_assignments))

with tf.control_dependencies([is_continue]):
   loop = tf.group(centroids.assign(means), prev_assignments.assign(point_
to_centroid_assignment))

sess = tf.Session()
sess.run(tf.global_variables_initializer())

# do many iterations. Hopefully, you will stop because of has_changed is False
has_changed, cnt = True, 0
while has_changed and cnt < 300:
    cnt += 1
    has_changed, _ = sess.run([is_continue, loop])

# see how the data is assigned
res = sess.run(point_to_centroid_assignment)

Verify Good Cluster:
nums_in_clusters = [[] for i in xrange(10)]
for cluster, real_num in zip(list(res), list(y)):
    nums_in_clusters[cluster].append(real_num)

for i in xrange(10):
    print Counter(nums_in_clusters[i]).most_common(3)
```

```
Output:
[(0, 638), (4, 17), (2, 11)]
[(1, 541), (3, 53), (2, 51)]
[(1, 388), (2, 115), (7, 56)]
[(4, 450), (9, 433), (7, 280)]
[(6, 634), (9, 400), (4, 302)]
[(6, 649), (4, 27), (0, 14)]
[(4, 269), (6, 244), (0, 161)]
[(8, 646), (5, 164), (3, 125)]
[(2, 598), (3, 34), (7, 14)]
[(2, 612), (5, 290), (8, 110)]
```

Cloud ML API (vision, translate, speech)

Google provides various tools and inbuilt machine learning packages to reduce the complex machine learning implementation. In this chapter, we will discuss some of the inbuilt Google cloud tools and API packages.

AutoML

AutoML inbuilt package which we can use for build and deploy the machine learning models on structured data at enormously increased speed and scale. The following figure explains the Machine learning lifecycle at a high level.

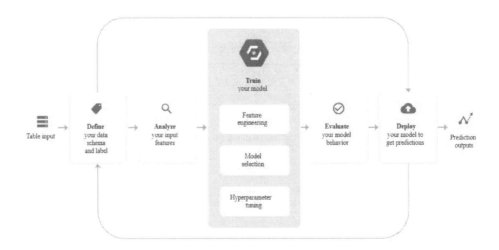

Figure 6.9: Machine Learning Lifecycle

The following are the pre-requisites:

1. In the GCP Console, on the project selector page, select or create a GCP project.

2. Make sure that the billing is activated for your GCP project.

3. Activate the Cloud AutoML, Storage, and Big Query APIs.

4. Set the `GOOGLE_APPLICATION_CREDENTIALS` environment variable on the path to the service account key file that is downloaded when a service account has been created.

5. Grant the `AutoML | AutoML` Editor role to your service account.

The following are the steps for AutoML:

1. Prepare the dataset.

2. Import the table data from a CSV file into the dataset or Big Query. Go to the **AutoML** Tables page in the GCP Console to start the process of generating the dataset. Then, go to **Datasets**, and select **New dataset**. Specify the name of the dataset and click on **Create** dataset.

3. Identify the features in the imported data.

4. **Train a model:** After the model is successfully trained, the following report is generated in the console:

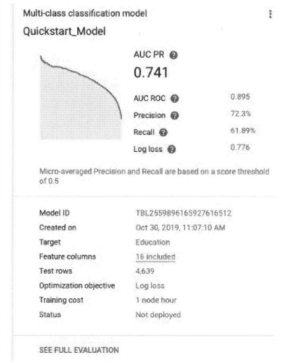

Figure 6.10: Model report

5. Evaluating model: We can view and analyze all the regression model and classification model metrics in the GCP console.

AutoML provides the following metrics:

- **AUC PR:** The area under the **precision-recall (PR)** curve. Higher value | Good Model.

- **AUC ROC:** The area under the receiver operating characteristic (ROC) curve. Range (0 to 1) Higher value | Good Model.

- **Accuracy:** Verify or determine the best model to identify the relationship between features.

- **Log loss:** The cross-entropy between the model predictions and the target values. This ranges from zero to infinity, where a lower value indicates a higher-quality model.

- **F1 score:** To check the balance between precision and recall, and check the imbalance in class distribution.

- **Precision:** The fraction of classification predictions produced by the model that were correct.

- **Recall:** The fraction of rows with this label that the model correctly predicted. Also known as *True positive rate*.

- **False positive rate:** The fraction of rows predicted by the model to be the target label but aren't (false positive).

- Confusion Matrix

- Feature Importance

  o **Make online predictions:** Online prediction of the model in the GCP Console and if model is not yet deployed, it can be deployed by clicking on `Deploy model.`

> **Note: If we have not planned to request for more online predictions, we can un-deploy your model to avoid deployment charges by clicking on Undeploy model.**

  o Make batch prediction:
     1. Using Big Query
     2. Using the CSV file in the cloud storage

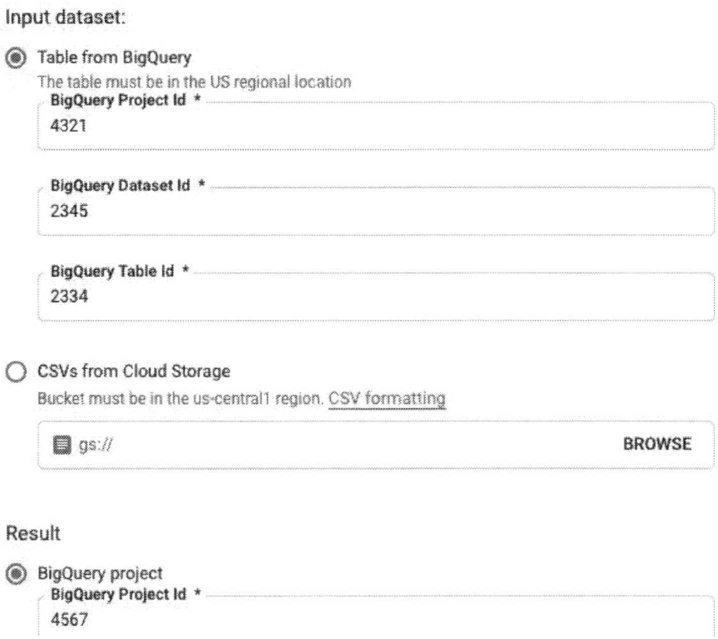

Input dataset:

◉ Table from BigQuery
The table must be in the US regional location

BigQuery Project Id *
4321

BigQuery Dataset Id *
2345

BigQuery Table Id *
2334

◯ CSVs from Cloud Storage
Bucket must be in the us-central1 region. CSV formatting

▤ gs://   BROWSE

Result

◉ BigQuery project
BigQuery Project Id *
4567

Figure 6.11: *BigQuery input dataset.*

Below is the AutoML API List:

- **REST resource** (`v1p1beta.projects.locations`):

Get	`GET /v1p1beta/{name}`: Obtains information about a location.
`getIamPolicy`	`GET /v1p1beta/{resource}:getIamPolicy`: Obtains the access control policy for a resource.

- **REST resource** (`v1p1beta.projects.locations.datasets`):

Create	`POST /v1p1beta/{parent}/datasets`: Creates a dataset.
Delete	`DELETE /v1p1beta/{name}`: Deletes a dataset and all its content.
exportData	`POST /v1p1beta/{name}`: exportData: Exports the dataset's data to the provided output location.
get	`GET /v1p1beta/{name}`: Obtains a dataset.
getIamPolicy	`GET /v1p1beta/{resource}:getIamPolicy`: Gets the access control policy for a resource.
importData	`POST /v1p1beta/{name}:importData`: Imports data into a dataset.
list	`GET /v1p1beta/{parent}/datasets`: Lists datasets in a project.
patch	`PATCH /v1p1beta/{dataset.name}`: Updates a dataset.

| setIamPolicy | POST   /v1p1beta/{resource}:setIamPolicy: Sets the access control policy on the specified resource. |
| delete | DELETE /v1p1beta/{name}: Removes a dataset and all its content. |

- **REST resource** (v1p1beta.projects.locations.datasets.tableSpecs):

| get | GET /v1p1beta/{name}: Gets a table spec. |
| list | GET /v1p1beta/{parent}/tableSpecs: Lists table specs in a dataset |

- **REST resource** (v1p1beta.projects.locations.datasets.tableSpecs.columnSpecs):

get	GET /v1p1beta/{name}: Obtains a column spec.
list	GET /v1p1beta/{parent}/columnSpecs: Lists column specs in a table spec.
patch	PATCH /v1p1beta/{columnSpec.name}: Updates a column spec.

- **REST resource** (v1p1beta.projects.locations.models):

batchPredict	POST /v1p1beta/{name}: batchPredict: Performs a batch prediction.
create	POST /v1p1beta/{parent}/models: Creates a model.
delete	DELETE /v1p1beta/{name}: Removes a model.
deploy	POST /v1p1beta/{name}:deploy: Deploys a model.
export	POST /v1p1beta/{name}:export: Exports a trained, export-able, model to a user defined Google Cloud Storage location.
export Evaluated Examples	POST /v1p1beta/{name}:exportEvaluatedExamples: Exports examples on which the model was evaluated
batchPredict	POST /v1p1beta/{name}: batchPredict: Performs a batch prediction.

- **REST resource** (v1p1beta.projects.locations.models.modelEvaluations):

get	GET /v1p1beta/{name}: Obtains a model evaluation.
list	GET /v1p1beta/{parent}/modelEvaluations: Lists the model evaluations.
get	GET /v1p1beta/{name}: Finds a model evaluation.

Note: It takes several hours to complete the training of a model. The progress of training the model can be seen in the GCP Console.

Google could also provide various client libraries This library not only provides functionality for API-specific library implementations, but also provides the types and methods that we can use directly, when using any Cloud API during the machine learning model design, evaluation, and more.

Vision AI

For analyzing and clustering of image based on specific requirement, we can get the insight that is hiding in the images via Vision AI API. These inbuilt Vision API models quickly cluster the images into multiple clusters of individual objects, faces, and words. We can also integrate the vision AI API with AutoML API to get the optimal solution.

Goggle Vision AI provides various options to integrate the model into the application:

- AutoML Vision-Image Classification
- AutoML Vision –Object Detection
- AutoML Vision Edge –Image Classification

The following are the pre-requisites:

1. Setup the project in the GCP Console.
2. In the GCP Console, on the project selector page, select or create a GCP project.
3. Activate the Cloud AutoML and Storage APIs.
4. Set the environment variable.
5. Add in a service account.
6. Allow the AutoML service account to access the Google Cloud project resource

The following are the steps:

1. Create a Cloud Storage:
   ```
   gsutil mb -p project-id -c regional -l us-central1 gs://project-id-vcm/
   ```
2. Move the sample image into the storage
   ```
   gsutil -m cp -R gs://cloud-ml-data/img/flower_photos/ gs://${BUCKET}/img/
   ```
3. Prepare the CSV file.
4. Go to the AutoML vision UI for creating the dataset and training the model.
5. Train the model, and once training is completed, the model will automatically get deployed.
6. Click on **Evaluate** and get the *F1*, *Precision*, and *Recall scores.*
7. Make a prediction.

> **Note: To avoid unnecessary GCP charges, use the GCP Console to delete the project if it is not needed.**

The following table shows the Cloud AutoML Vision API list:

Get	`GET /v1beta1/{name}`: Obtains information about a location.
getIamPolicy	`GET /v1beta1/{resource}:getIamPolicy`: Obtains the access control policy for a resource.
List	`GET /v1beta1/{name}/locations`: Lists information about the supported locations for this service.
setIamPolicy	`POST /v1beta1/{resource}:setIamPolicy`: Sets the access control policy on the specified resource.
testIam Permissions	`POST /v1beta1/{resource}:testIamPermissions`: Get the Identity permission details
Create	`POST /v1beta1/{parent}/datasets`: Creates a dataset.
Delete	`DELETE /v1beta1/{name}`: Removes a dataset and all its content.
exportData	`POST /v1beta1/{name}:exportData`: Exports the dataset's data to the provided output location.
Get	`GET /v1beta1/{name}`: Obtains a dataset.
getIamPolicy	`GET /v1beta1/{resource}:getIamPolicy`: Gets the access control policy for a resource.
importData	`POST /v1beta1/{name}:importData`: Imports data into a dataset.
List	`GET /v1beta1/{parent}/datasets`: Lists datasets in a project.
Patch	`PATCH /v1beta1/{dataset.name}`: Updates a dataset.
setIamPolicy	`POST /v1beta1/{resource}:setIamPolicy`: Sets the access control policy on the specified resource.
batchPredict	`POST /v1beta1/{name}:batchPredict`: Performs a batch prediction.
Create	`POST /v1beta1/{parent}/models`: Creates a model.
Delete	`DELETE /v1beta1/{name}`: Removes a model.
Deploy	`POST /v1beta1/{name}:deploy`: Deploys a model.
Export	`POST /v1beta1/{name}:export`: Exports a trained, export-able, model to a user specified Google Cloud Storage location.
exportEvaluated Examples	`POST /v1beta1/{name}:exportEvaluatedExamples`: Exports examples on which the model was evaluated.
Undeploy	`POST /v1beta1/{name}:undeploy`: Undeploys a model.
Cancel	`POST /v1beta1/{name}:cancel`: Begins asynchronous cancellation on a long-running operation.

Delete	DELETE /v1beta1/{name}: Removes a long-running operation.
Get	GET /v1beta1/{name}: Gets the latest state of a long-running operation.
List	GET /v1beta1/{name}/operations: Lists operations that match the specified filter in the request.
Wait	POST /v1beta1/{name}:wait: Waits for the defined long-running operation until it is finishes, or reaches at most a specified timeout, returning the latest state.

Video AI

Video Intelligence API's inbuilt models extract the metadata, recognize key nouns, and interpret the video content. It can be integrated with AutoML to get the optimal solution.

- AutoML Video Intelligence
- Video Intelligence API

AutoML Video Intelligence

AutoML Video Intelligence is a graphical console that is used to train and customize the model.

The following are the pre-requisites:

1. Go to the GCP console and AutoML Video UI, and click on Activate API.
2. After the API has been Activated, click Get Started.

The following are the steps:

1. Create dataset.
2. Provide the Cloud Storage URI, it contains the training data.
3. Import the data.
4. Access the list of videos in the dataset by going to the **Videos** tab for the dataset.
5. Train the model.

6. The following screenshot showcases the evaluation of the model and gets the *F1*, *Precision*, and *Recall* scores.

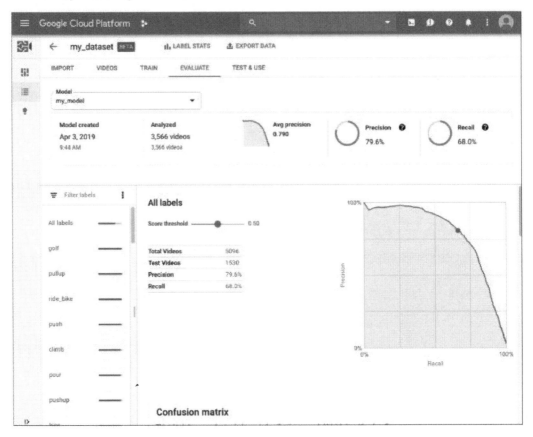

Figure 6.12: Evaluation of Model

7. Classify a video.

8. Go to the **Test & Use** tab for the model

9. Click **Test** to test the model, type gs://automl-video-demo-data/hmdb_split1_test_gs_predict.csv.

10. Under **Test** your model, select a directory within the Cloud Storage bucket to receive the annotation results.

11. Click **Get Predictions.**

12. Go to the **Recent prediction** tab and see the result.

Cloud Video Intelligence API

Cloud Video Intelligence API has inbuilt ML models that automatically identify the objects, places, and actions in the stored and streaming video.

The following are the pre-requisites:

1. Go to the GCP Project.
2. Activate the Cloud Video Intelligence API.
3. Setup Authentication.
4. Set the environment variable.
5. Install and initialize the Cloud SDK.

The following are the steps:

1. Execute the `gcloud` command line tool to call the `detect-labels` command:

    `gcloud ml video detect-labels gs://cloud-ml-sandbox/video/california.mp4`

2. The request returns the annotation results.

REST resource:

get	GET /v1beta1/{name}: Obtains information about a location.
getIamPolicy	GET /v1beta1/{resource}:getIamPolicy: Obtains the access control policy for a resource.
list	GET /v1beta1/{name}/locations: Lists information regarding the supported locations for this service.
setIamPolicy	POST /v1beta1/{resource}:setIamPolicy: Sets the access control policy on the specified resource.
testIam Permissions	POST /v1beta1/{resource}:testIamPermissions: Returns the permissions that a caller has on the specified resource.
create	POST /v1beta1/{parent}/datasets: Creates a dataset.
delete	DELETE /v1beta1/{name}: Removes a dataset and all its content.
exportData	POST /v1beta1/{name}:exportData: Exports the dataset's data to the provided output location.
create	POST /v1beta1/{parent}/datasets: Creates a dataset.
delete	DELETE /v1beta1/{name}: Removes a dataset and all its content.
exportData	POST /v1beta1/{name}:exportData: Exports the dataset's data to the provided output location.
get	GET /v1beta1/{name}: Obtains a dataset.
importData	POST /v1beta1/{name}:importData: Imports data into a dataset.
create	POST /v1beta1/{parent}/models: Makes a model.
delete	DELETE /v1beta1/{name}: Removes a model.
deploy	POST /v1beta1/{name}:deploy: Deploys a model.
get	GET /v1beta1/{name}: Obtains a model.
list	GET /v1beta1/{parent}/models: Lists models.

predict	POST /v1beta1/{name}:predict: Not available for AutoML Video Intelligence.
setIamPolicy	POST /v1beta1/{resource}:setIamPolicy: Sets the access control policy on the specified resource.
undeploy	POST /v1beta1/{name}:undeploy: Removes a deployed model.
create	POST /v1beta1/{parent}/models: Creates a model.
delete	DELETE /v1beta1/{name}: Removes a model.
cancel	POST /v1beta1/{name}:cancel: Begins asynchronous cancellation on a long-running operation.
delete	DELETE /v1beta1/{name}: Removes a long-running operation.
wait	POST /v1beta1/{name}:wait: Waits for the specified long-running operation until it is done or reaches at most a specified timeout, returning the latest state.
get	GET /v1beta1/{name}: Gets a model evaluation.
list	GET /v1beta1/{parent}/modelEvaluations: Lists model evaluations.

Speech to text API

Cloud Speech-to-text API converts audio to text by applying the deep learning models in an easy-to-use API. We can integrate the speech-to-text APIs in call centers and Auto translator requirements. It will provide a real-time translator and convertor. The API identifies 120 languages to support. We can activate the voice command-and-control, transcribe audio from call centers, and more.

The following are some of the use cases:

- Automatic speech recognition
- Global vocabulary
- Real-time processing or prerecorded audio support

We need to send an audio and receive a text transcription from the speech-to-text API service. Different ways of implementation:

- Client libraries
- gccloud tools
- Command line

Using client libraries

Speech-to-Text API receives audio data, which then sends back a text transcription of that audio file as an output.

The following are the pre-requisites:

1. Set up a GCP Console project
2. Create or select a project.
3. Activate the Google Speech-to-text API for that project.
4. Generate a service account and download a private key
5. Set the environment variable `GOOGLE_APPLICATION_CREDENTIALS` to the file path of the JSON file. This file includes your service account key.
6. Install the cloud SDK.
7. Install the client library.
8. Create your own request (audio):

```java
// Imports the Google Cloud client library
import com.google.cloud.speech.v1.RecognitionAudio;
import com.google.cloud.speech.v1.RecognitionConfig;
import com.google.cloud.speech.v1.RecognitionConfig.AudioEncoding;
import com.google.cloud.speech.v1.RecognizeResponse;
import com.google.cloud.speech.v1.SpeechClient;
import com.google.cloud.speech.v1.SpeechRecognitionAlternative;
import com.google.cloud.speech.v1.SpeechRecognitionResult;
import com.google.protobuf.ByteString;
import java.nio.file.Files;
import java.nio.file.Path;
import java.nio.file.Paths;
import java.util.List;

public class QuickstartSample {

  /**
   * Demonstrates using the Speech API to transcribe an audio file.
   */
  public static void main(String... args) throws Exception {
    // Instantiates a client
    try (SpeechClient speechClient = SpeechClient.create()) {

      // The path to the audio file to transcribe
      String fileName = "./resources/audio.raw";
```

```java
        // Reads the audio file into memory
        Path path = Paths.get(fileName);
        byte[] data = Files.readAllBytes(path);
        ByteString audioBytes = ByteString.copyFrom(data);

        // Builds the sync recognize request
        RecognitionConfig config = RecognitionConfig.newBuilder()
            .setEncoding(AudioEncoding.LINEAR16)
            .setSampleRateHertz(16000)
            .setLanguageCode("en-US")
            .build();
        RecognitionAudio audio = RecognitionAudio.newBuilder()
            .setContent(audioBytes)
            .build();

        // Performs speech recognition on the audio file
        RecognizeResponse response = speechClient.recognize(config,
audio);
        List<SpeechRecognitionResult> results = response.
getResultsList();

        for (SpeechRecognitionResult result : results) {
            // There can be several alternative transcripts for a
given chunk of speech. Just use the
            // first (most likely) one here.
            SpeechRecognitionAlternative alternative = result.
getAlternativesList().get(0);
            System.out.printf("Transcription: %s%n", alternative.
getTranscript());
        }
    }
  }
}
```

Using gccloud tool

Similarly, we can send the audio request via the gccloud command:

1. Open command line and run below:

    ```
    gcloud ml speech recognize 'gs://cloud-samples-tests/speech/xxx.
    flac' \
        --language-code='en-US'
    ```

2. After the request is sent successfully, the server returns a response in the JSON format:

    ```
    {
      "results": [
        {
          "alternatives": [
            {
              "confidence": 0.9840146,
              "transcript": "how old is the Brooklyn Bridge"
            }
          ]
        }
      ]
    ```

References for REST API:

Get	GET /v1/operations/{name=**}: Obtains the latest state of a long-running operation.
List	GET /v1/operations: Lists operations that match the specified filter in the request.
Get	GET /v1/{name=projects/*/locations/*/operations/*}: Obtains the latest state of a long-running operation.
List	GET /v1/{name=projects/*/locations/*}/operations: Lists operations that match the defined filter in the request.
Longrunning recognize	POST /v1/speech:longrunningrecognize: Executes asynchronous speech recognition: receives the results via the google.longrunning.Operations interface.
Recognize	POST /v1/speech:recognize: Executes synchronous speech recognition: receives the results after all the audio has been sent and processed.

Get	GET /v1p1beta1/operations/{name=**}: Obtains the latest state of a long-running operation.
list	GET /v1p1beta1/operations: Lists operations that match the defined filter in the request.
get	GET /v1p1beta1/{name=projects/*/locations/*/operations/*}: Obtains the latest state of a long-running operation.
list	GET /v1p1beta1/{name=projects/*/locations/*}/operations: Lists operations that match the specified filter in the request.
longrunning recognize	POST /v1p1beta1/speech:longrunningrecognize: Performs asynchronous speech recognition: receives the results via the google.longrunning.Operations interface.
recognize	POST /v1p1beta1/speech:recognize: Executes synchronous speech recognition: receives the results after all the audio has been sent and processed.

Text-to-Speech API

This text-to-speech API is a plug and play API. An interactive experience can be created with the help of the Text-to-speech API and can also integrate in various applications with 180 voices in multiple languages. It supports plug and play with the enterprise applications and IoT along with mobile devices, which includes exclusive access to the WaveNet technology.

The following are the different ways of implementation:

- Client libraries
- Command line

Using client libraries

The following are the pre-requisites:

1. Set up a GCP Console project.
2. Create or select a project.
3. Activate the Google Text-to-Speech API for that project.
4. Create a service account.
5. Download a private key
6. Set the environment variable, GOOGLE_APPLICATION_CREDENTIALS to the file path of the JSON file. This file includes your service account key.
7. Install the cloud SDK.
8. Install the client library** (based on the preferred language – JAVA/C#/NodeJS/Python):

```xml
<dependency>
  <groupId>com.google.cloud</groupId>
  <artifactId>google-cloud-texttospeech</artifactId>
  <version>0.101.0-beta</version>
</dependency>
<dependency>
  <groupId>net.sourceforge.argparse4j</groupId>
  <artifactId>argparse4j</artifactId>
  <version>0.8.1</version>
</dependency>
```

9. Create audio data.

10. Now we can use text-to-speech to create an audio file of human speech and send the request to the Cloud's text-to-speech API:

```java
// Imports the Google Cloud client library
import com.google.cloud.texttospeech.v1.AudioConfig;
import com.google.cloud.texttospeech.v1.AudioEncoding;
import com.google.cloud.texttospeech.v1.SsmlVoiceGender;
import com.google.cloud.texttospeech.v1.SynthesisInput;
import com.google.cloud.texttospeech.v1.SynthesizeSpeechResponse;
import com.google.cloud.texttospeech.v1.TextToSpeechClient;
import com.google.cloud.texttospeech.v1.VoiceSelectionParams;
import com.google.protobuf.ByteString;
import java.io.FileOutputStream;
import java.io.OutputStream;

/**
 * Google Cloud TextToSpeech API sample application.
 * Example usage: mvn package exec:java
 *                     -Dexec.mainClass='com.example.texttospeech.
QuickstartSample'
 */
public class QuickstartSample {

  /**
```

```java
 * Demonstrates using the Text-to-Speech API.
 */
public static void main(String... args) throws Exception {
  // Instantiates a client
  try (TextToSpeechClient textToSpeechClient = TextToSpeechClient.create()) {
      // Set the text input to be synthesized
      SynthesisInput input = SynthesisInput.newBuilder()
          .setText("Hello, World!")
          .build();

      // Build the voice request, select the language code ("en-US") and the ssml voice gender
      // ("neutral")
      VoiceSelectionParams voice = VoiceSelectionParams.newBuilder()
          .setLanguageCode("en-US")
          .setSsmlGender(SsmlVoiceGender.NEUTRAL)
          .build();

      // Select the type of audio file you want returned
      AudioConfig audioConfig = AudioConfig.newBuilder()
          .setAudioEncoding(AudioEncoding.MP3)
          .build();

      // Perform the text-to-speech request on the text input with the selected voice parameters and
      // audio file type
      SynthesizeSpeechResponse response = textToSpeechClient.synthesizeSpeech(input, voice,
          audioConfig);

      // Get the audio contents from the response
      ByteString audioContents = response.getAudioContent();

      // Write the response to the output file.
```

```
    try (OutputStream out = new FileOutputStream("output.mp3")) {
        out.write(audioContents.toByteArray());
        System.out.println("Audio content written to file \"output.
mp3\"");
    }
  }
 }
}
```

Reference for API:

Synthesize	POST /v1beta1/text:synthesize: Synthesizes speech synchronously: gets the results after all the text input has been processed.
List	GET /v1beta1/voices: Returns a list of the voice supported for synthesis.

Dialogue Flow

Dialogue flow is an end-to-end development suite for a Chatbot or conversational interfaces. It uses machine learning and provides human readable and real time interactions experience with your users on websites, mobile apps, messaging platforms, and IoT devices.

The following are the Dialogue Flow features:

- Using Google in-built natural language processing API's
- Integrated analytics dashboard
- Automatic spelling and grammar check

The following are the use cases:

- Chatbots
- Conversational IVR
- Automated phone service
- Integration with IoT devices

The following diagram showcases the flow of conversation in the Dialog Flow:

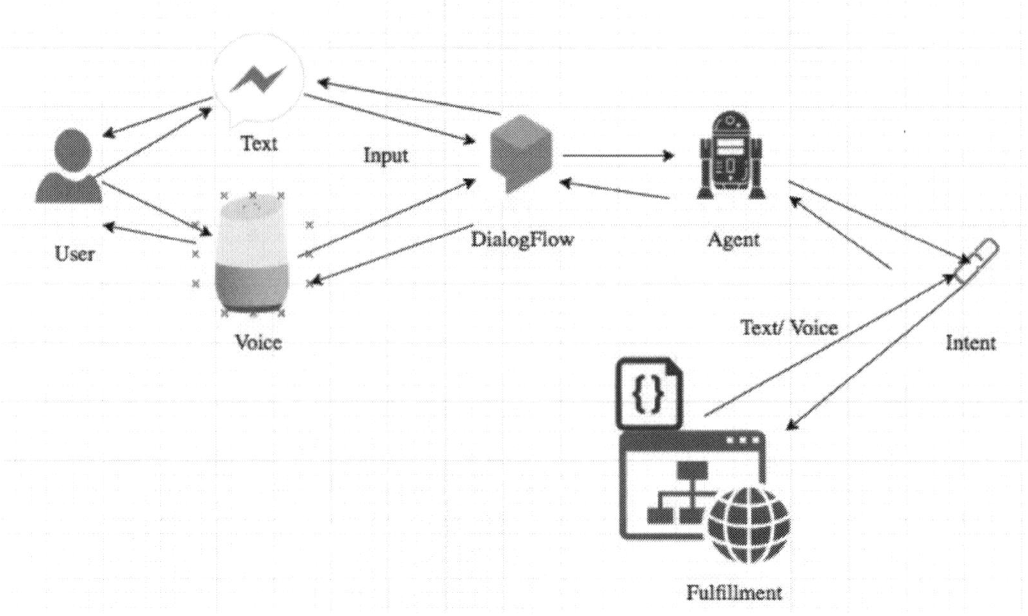

Figure 6.13: Flow of Dialogue Flow

The following are the fundamentals of the Dialogue Flow:

1. Introduction of Dialogue flow console.
2. How to create Agents?
3. How to use intents to map user input?
4. How to use entities to extract useful information?
5. How to use events to extract the intents?
6. How to use fulfillments to setup your agent to service?
7. How to integrate the agent with messaging and NLP platforms?
8. How to use the Dialogue Flow API Integration?

Dialogue Flow Console introduction

We can use the Dialogue Flow Console to create, build, and test agents. Dialog Flow Console is different from the Google Cloud Platform (GCP) Console. We can use the Dialog Flow Console to customize agents, but we can also use the dialog flow API to build agents for more complex scenarios:

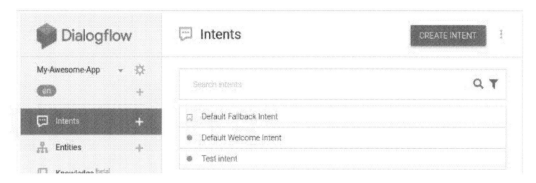

Figure 6.14: Dialogue Flow Console

Agents

A Dialog Flow agent is a simulated agent. It interacts dialogues with end-users. It is a natural language insight module that understands the tones of human language. The Dialog Flow decodes the end-user text or audio during a conversation to structure data so that any apps and services can understand.

The following are the steps to create Agents:

1. Launch the Dialog Flow Console.
2. Click on **Create Agent**.
3. Put the agent's name, default language, time zone and GCP project, and then finally click on the **Create** button.

Intents

Intent classifies the end-user's intention for one dialogue input. For each agent, we can describe many intents. The Dialog Flow matches the end-user's input expression to the optimal intent in the agent. Equivalent intent is also known as intent classification. The following figure showcases the different types of Intent.

Figure 6.15: Dialogue flow Intent Classification

How to use intents to map the user input?

The Dialog Flow console or intent API can be used to building intent.

The following are the steps for creating intent:

1. Go to the Dialog Flow console.
2. Select an Agent.
3. Click the **Add** button next to Intents, in the left sidebar menu.
4. Enter Intent details.
5. Click on **Save**.

The following are the steps for the training phrases:

1. Go to the Dialog Flow Console.
2. Select an agent.
3. Select Intents.
4. Go to the `Training phrases` section.
5. Click on the `Add user expression`.
6. Type training phrases and press the *Enter key* after each. The following image is one of the screenshots for the training Phrases.

Note: We can set the intents priority also.

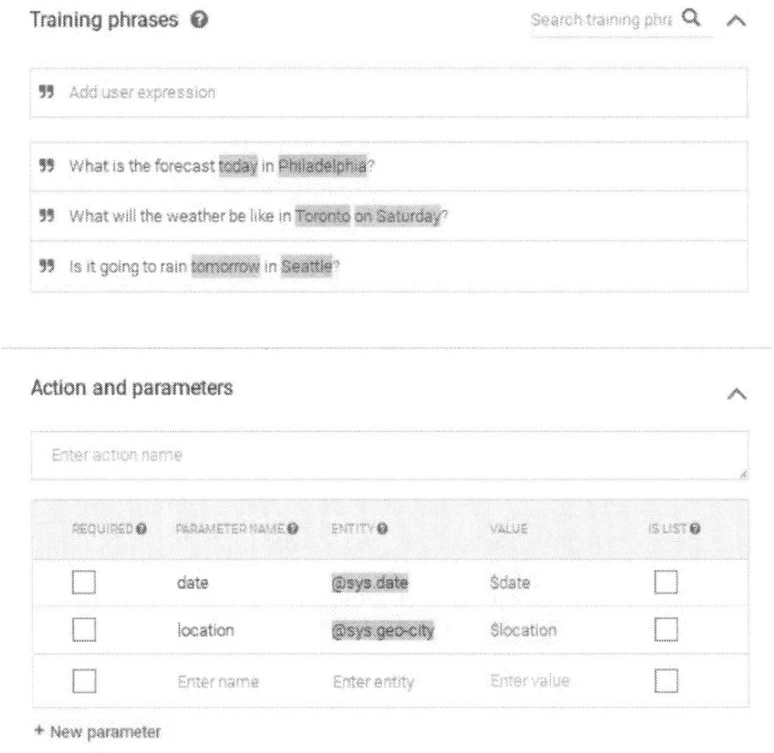

Figure 6.16: Intents Training Phrases

Entities

Each Intent parameter has a type called the entities type. The Dialog Flow offers inbuilt system entities. For example, dedicated entities for dates, times, colors, email addresses, and more. We can also create our own, customized entities for matching the custom data.

The following steps are performed for creating Entities:

1. Go to the Dialog Flow Console.
2. Click on **Entities** and select **Create entities**.
3. Enter the name of the entity.
4. Add more entities.
5. Click **Save**. The following image is a sample Entity's screenshot.

Figure 6.17: Sample Entities

Events

Events allow triggering the intents based on specific Event/task that have occurred/ performed, instead of direct user input. The Dialog Flow supports events from several platforms (like Google Assistant, Slack, and more) based on the actions that the users take on those platforms. We can also create our own tailor-made events that can be invoked via fulfillment

To add an event, follow the below mentioned steps:

1. Go to the Dialog Flow Console.
2. Click on **Intent** and go to **Event**.
3. Enter the name of the event.
4. Click on *Enter*.
5. Click on **Save**.

Fulfillments

Fulfillment is required for the connection between a service and an Agent. Connecting service permits to take actions based on end-user expressions and deliver dynamic responses back to the end-user.

For example, when the end-user wants to book a doctor's appointment on Monday, the service can validate the database and reply to the end-user with availability information for Monday. If the intent requires a specific action, then we can enable fulfillment for the intent.

The following diagram showcases the processing flow for fulfillment.

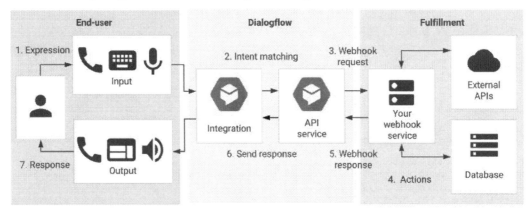

Figure 6.18: *Processing flow for fulfillment*

The end-user input speaks an expression and the Dialogue Flow matches the intent. Once the matching is done, the web hook service will trigger for the next action for

DB update or an external API's calls. Webhook sends a web hook response to the dialogue flow, and the Dialog Flow directs the response to the end-user.

The following is a Webhook sample request:

```
POST https://my-service.com/action

Headers:
//user defined headers
Content-type: application/json

POST body:
{
    "responseId": "ea3d77e8-ae27-41a4-9e1d-174bd461b68c",
   "session": "projects/your-agents-project-id/agent/sessions/88d13aa8-
2999-4f71-b233-39cbf3a824a0",
     "queryResult": {
       "queryText": "user's original query to your agent",
       "parameters": {
         "param": "param value"
       },
       "allRequiredParamsPresent": true,
        "fulfillmentText": "Text defined in Dialogflow's console for the
intent that was matched",
       "fulfillmentMessages": [
         {
           "text": {
             "text": [
                 "Text defined in Dialogflow's console for the intent that
was matched"
             ]
           }
         }
       ],
       "outputContexts": [
         {
       "name": "projects/your-agents-project-id/agent/sessions/88d13aa8-
2999-4f71-b233-39cbf3a824a0/contexts/generic",
```

```
        "lifespanCount": 5,
        "parameters": {
          "param": "param value"
        }
      }
    ],
    "intent": {
    "name": "projects/your-agents-project-id/agent/intents/29bcd7f8-
f717-4261-a8fd-2d3e451b8af8",
      "displayName": "Matched Intent Name"
    },
    "intentDetectionConfidence": 1,
    "diagnosticInfo": {},
    "languageCode": "en"
  },
  "originalDetectIntentRequest": {}
}
```

The following is a Webhook response:

```
  {
    "fulfillmentText": "This is a text response",
    "fulfillmentMessages": [
      {
        "card": {
          "title": "card title",
          "subtitle": "card text",
          "imageUri": "https://assistant.google.com/static/images/
molecule/Molecule-Formation-stop.png",
          "buttons": [
            {
              "text": "button text",
              "postback": "https://assistant.google.com/"
            }
          ]
```

```
        }
      }
    ],
    "source": "example.com",
    "payload": {
      "google": {
        "expectUserResponse": true,
        "richResponse": {
          "items": [
            {
              "simpleResponse": {
                "textToSpeech": "this is a simple response"
              }
            }
          ]
        }
      },
      "facebook": {
        "text": "Hello, Facebook!"
      },
      "slack": {
        "text": "This is a text response for Slack."
      }
    },
    "outputContexts": [
      {
        "name": "projects/${PROJECT_ID}/agent/sessions/${SESSION_ID}/
contexts/context name",
        "lifespanCount": 5,
        "parameters": {
          "param": "param value"
        }
      }
```

```
    ],
    "followupEventInput": {
      "name": "event name",
      "languageCode": "en-US",
      "parameters": {
        "param": "param value"
      }
    }
}
```

Integration

Dialogue Flow provides various collaboration platforms like Google Assistant, slack, Facebook Messenger, and many more. We can build the agent with many integration options. Many in-built lists of API/client libraries are available for integrating the all dialogue flow features (Agent, Intents, event, fulfillments, and more).

Dialogue flow provides client libraries for various programming languages (C#, NodeJS, Java, Python, and more)

Conclusion

There are different types of machine learning algorithms, which are readily exposed via the API in GCP. In this chapter, we started with the basic explanation of Machine learning technology and covered the Google supported Machine learning API that can be used for traditional machine learning use cases, which are not very customized.

Questions

1. What are the types of supervised and unsupervised learning algorithms?
2. TensorFlow and its components.
3. Dialogue flow and its components.
4. Explain in detail about Vision API and Translator API.

CHAPTER 7
Sample Use Cases and Example

Introduction

In this chapter, the actual solutioning of the GCP data services has been elaborated and explained with real-time examples.

Structure

There are three case studies about the implementation and solutioning that are covered as a part of this chapter:

- Setting up a mobile gaming analytics platform - a reference architecture
- Managing and processing logs at scale, by leveraging the Cloud Dataflow
- Product recommendations using machine learning on Compute Engine

Objective

The main objective of this chapter is to explain the industry wide implementation of different use cases of analytics like log processing, machine learning recommendation engine by leveraging **Google Cloud Platform (GCP)** services. These use cases explain the practical implementation, which enables the end user to get a different perspective on the GCP services usage, based on different scenarios.

In the earlier chapters, most of the GCP data analytics services has been covered. The following diagram provides an overall view of each service, based on their usage in the entire data analytics life cycle. All these services are classified in the **Capture, Process, Store, Analyze**, and **Use** phase of the data analytics cycle:

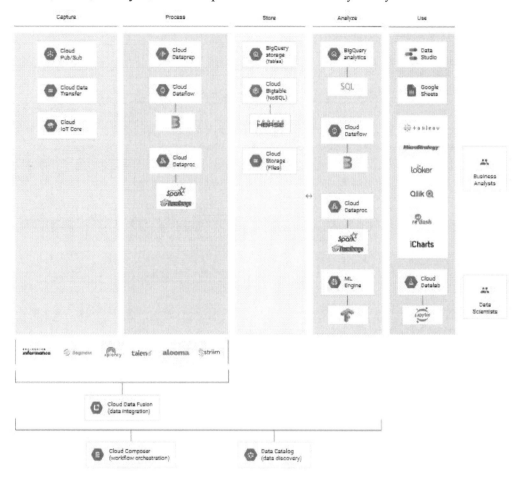

Figure 7.1: Google Cloud Platform Data Analytics Services

Setting up a mobile gaming analytics platform - a reference architecture

Mobile game applications tend to create a huge volume of player-telemetry and game-event data. This data, when analyzed, has a huge potential to deliver intelligence into player performance and their engagement with the game. The nature of mobile games is such that, there are a huge number of client devices, intermittent and slow internet connections, battery, and power management concerns, which means that the player telemetry and game event analytics face very different and unique challenges to deal with. The reference architecture, which is explained in this chapter, delivers a high-level method to collect, store, and analyze a huge volume of player-telemetry data on GCP.

Specifically, it will allow us to learn about the two main architecture designs for analyzing mobile game events:

- Real-time processing of individual events using a streaming processing mechanism.
- Bulk processing of aggregated events by utilizing a batch processing pattern.

The following diagram illustrates the processing pipelines for both patterns, and some optional elements to further explore, visualize, and share the output:

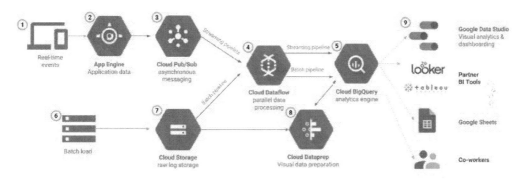

Figure 7.2: *Game telemetry reference architecture*

The reference architecture is highly available and permits to scale, as the data volumes grow. Please note that this architecture is composed solely of fully managed services for data-analytics pipelines, eliminating the requirement to run virtual machines or to manage operating systems. This is especially true if the game server handles the user authentication through an App Engine. The rest of this chapter will explain in further details and will walk you through this architecture, step-by-step.

Real-time event processing using streaming pattern

This section explains about the architecture pattern that ingests processes and analyses a huge number of events concurrently from multiple sources. The processing of the event takes place as the events in the game evolve, permitting response and enabling the insights in real-time.

Various mobile games produce a huge number of event messages. Certain events are triggered by the player, some of them by the time of day and so on. As a result, the data sets are unbounded, and it is difficult to know how many events to process in advance. Hence, the right approach is to process the data using a streaming execution engine. Imagine that the mobile app is a role-playing game that permits players to fight evil forces by attempting quests to defeat danger monsters. A typical event message consists of a unique identifier for the player, an event time stamp, metrics indicating the quest, the player's current health, and so on, which when generated, keeps a track of the progress of the player. A sample event will look like The following example, displaying an end-of-battle event message along with an event identifier of `letsdefeat`:

```
{
   "eventTime":"2017-09-22T10:26:24.345273548+08:00",

   "userId":"gamer@test.com",

   "sessionId":"b6ff4441-0c30-9add-374c-c54032def236",

   "eventId":" letsdefeat ",

…

   "attackRoll":43,

   "damageRoll":26

}
```

This example featured a battle-related event, but the event messages can be any kind of data that is relevant to business, for example, in-game purchase events.

Since it is difficult to predict what questions can be asked about the data in the future, it is a good strategy to log as many data points as possible. This offers the need of additional context for future data queries. For example, more insightful could be the fact that a player got an in-game purchase costing 50 cents, or that they bought a potent magic spell against the boss in quest 15 and that the player was killed by that monster six times continuously in the 30 minutes preceding the purchase. Capturing rich events data enables detailed insight into exactly what's going on in a game.

Message source: mobile or game server

Regardless of the fields in event messages, it must be decided whether to send the event messages directly from the end-user device running the mobile app to the Cloud - Pub/Sub ingestion layer, or it needs to go through the game server. The main advantage of going via the game server is that the authentication and validation is handled by the application. There could be some drawback, and that is the extra server processing capacity that will be needed to handle the load of the event messages generating from the mobile devices.

Some caution needs to be taken while sending messages directly from mobile phones to the Cloud - Pub/Sub, which requires to manually handle the authentication and key management for the client applications. This could be a non-trivial exercise.

If this method is considered, then one option is to deploy a new service account with each generation of the mobile application and a different Cloud - Pub/Sub topic to be linked with each. This will also permit rotation of the keys over time. For additional assurance, a signature can be included, which can be certified by the Cloud Dataflow. The following diagram depicts the real-time processing of events from the game clients and the game servers:

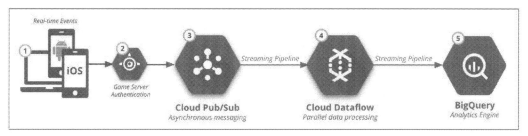

Figure 7.3: Real-time processing of events from game clients and game servers

Regardless of the source of the data, the backend architecture remains largely the same. As shown in *Figure 7.3*, there are five main parts:

1. Real-time event messages are sent by many sources, for example, millions of mobile apps.
2. Authentication is handled by the game server.
3. Cloud Pub/Sub ingests and temporarily stores these messages.
4. Cloud Dataflow transforms the JSON event into structured, schema-based data.
5. That data is loaded into the BigQuery analytics engine.

Cloud Pub/Sub: As explained in the earlier chapter , the Cloud Pub/Sub helps in ingesting events at scale. In order to manage this load, scalable service is required, which can receive and temporarily storing these event messages. Since each individual event is quite small, the total number of messages is more of a matter than the normal storage requirement. Another important requirement for this ingestion service is to permit for the various output methods. This means that the events should be consumable by several destinations. Finally, there should be an option between the service acting as a queue, where each destination polls to fetch new messages, and a push method, that sends events proactively from the moment they are received.

Fortunately, the Cloud Pub/Sub service delivers all the required functionalities. *Figure 7.4,* shows the proposed ingestion layer, which is capable of processing millions of messages per second and saving them for up to 7 days on persistent storage. Cloud Pub/Sub works on a publish/subscribe pattern, where it can have one or more publishers sending messages to one or more topics. There can also be multiple subscribers for each topic:

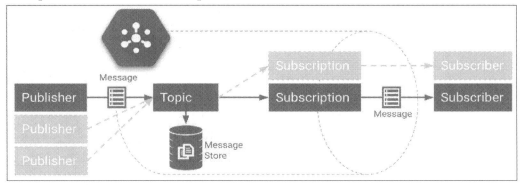

Figure 7.4: Cloud Pub/Sub publishes subscribe model along with persistent storage

The number of topics can be chosen along with the grouping of each. Because there is a direct relationship among the number of topics and the number of Cloud Dataflow pipelines that has been created, it is better to group the logically connected events. For example, a publisher can be an individual mobile device or a game server, with multiple publishers for a single topic. All that is needed is the capability to authenticate and send a correctly formatted message over HTTPS.

Once a message is sent in this scenario, a player telemetry event is received by the Cloud Pub/Sub service, it is durably stored in the **Message Store** till the time every Topic, Subscription has retrieved that message.

Cloud Dataflow streaming pipeline

Cloud Dataflow offers a high-level language to define the data processing pipelines in an easy way. These pipelines can be executed using the Cloud Dataflow managed service. The Cloud Dataflow pipeline operates in streaming mode and gets messages from the Cloud Pub/Sub topic as they come, via a subscription. Cloud Dataflow then performs any required processing, before pushing them into a BigQuery table.

This processing can take the form of simple, element-wise operations, like making all the usernames lower case or joining the elements with the other data sources; for example, joining a table of usernames to player statistics as showcased below.

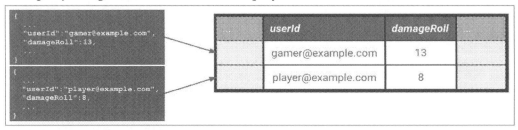

Figure 7.5: Transforming JSON messages into BigQuery table format

Cloud Dataflow can perform any type of data processing tasks, moreover as a real-time validation of the input data. One of the sample use case could be fraud detection, for example, highlighting a player with the most hit-points outside the valid range. One more use case could be data cleansing to make sure that the event message is properly formed and fits in the BigQuery schema.

The example in *Figure 7.5* shows the initial JSON message generating from the game server and transforms it into a BigQuery schema. The key issue is that it doesn't need to manage any servers or virtual machines to implement this action; the Cloud Dataflow will take care of starting, running, and stopping compute resources to process the pipeline in parallel. An identical code can be used for every streaming and batch processing.

The open-source Cloud Dataflow SDK offers pipeline execution, which is generally independent from the Cloud Dataflow program's execution. The Cloud Dataflow program constructs the pipeline, and the code has been written, which generates a series of steps to be executed by a pipeline runner. The pipeline runner is also a Cloud Dataflow managed service on GCP. There are third-party runner services like Spark and Flink, the pipeline runner that executes the steps directly among the local environment, which is helpful for development and testing purposes.

Cloud Dataflow ensures that each component is processed exactly once, and also enabling it for time windowing and triggers options to aggregate events based on the particular time they occurred (event time) as against the time they are sent to Cloud Dataflow (processing time). Some messages are additionally delayed from the source because of the mobile internet connection problems or batteries running out. However, it can still be grouped along by the user session eventually. This type of windowing functionality is built in and is available in the Cloud Dataflow.

Alternatively, if events contain a unique session field, sort of a **universally unique symbol (UUID),** it will be ready to use this key to group the connected events, as well. The most acceptable choice will depend upon the specific scenario.

BigQuery: BigQuery is a fully managed data warehouse for large-scale data analytics. BigQuery comprises of two important components: a storage system that has persistence of data with geographic redundancy and high availability. On top of that, it is the analytics engine that permits to run SQL-like queries against massive datasets. BigQuery organizes its data into Datasets, which will comprise multiple tables. BigQuery wants a schema to be outlined for each table, and therefore the main job of the Cloud Dataflow within the previous section was to construct the JSON-formatted raw event data into a BigQuery schema configuration, utilizing the built-in BigQuery connector.

Once the data is loaded into a BigQuery table, it can be queried via the interactive SQL queries against it to extract valuable intelligence. BigQuery is made for a very large scale and permits to run aggregation queries against petabyte-scale datasets with quick response times. This is often nice for interactive analysis.

Data visualization tools

Google Data Studio permits forming and sharing interactive dashboards that access a good type of data sources, along with BigQuery. BigQuery also integrates with several popular third-party BI and visualization tools, like Tableau and QlikView. In case the users are acquainted with Jupyter (formerly IPython) notebooks, the Cloud Datalab service provides built-in connectivity to BigQuery. With this, it allows the running of the BigQuery queries directly from Google Sheets and Microsoft stand out.

Bulk process using batch pattern

The other major pattern is the regular process of enormous, bounded, data sets, which is not required to be processed in real-time. The use case of the batch pipelines is typically for generating reports or combined with the real-time sources for best-of-both worlds. When reliable historical data combined with the latest data are available in through the real-time stream pipelines it makes powerful insights. The following figure showcases the batch processing of events and logs.

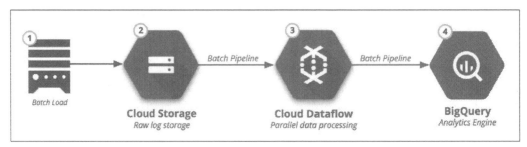

Figure 7.6: Batch processing of events and logs from game servers

Cloud Storage is the suggested storage for large files. Cloud Storage has properties like durability, high availability and cost-effective for object storage service. But there are some questions that need to be discovered like How to get the data into Cloud Storage in the first place. The answer to this question depends on data sources. This topic is covered in detail in the later sections. There are three different data source scenarios: on-premises, other cloud providers and GCP. Let's understand each scenario in detail:

- **Scenario 1: Transmitting files from on-premises servers**

    Log files can be securely transferred from the on-premises data center using a number of different methods. The most popular and easy way is to utilize the open source `gsutil` command line utility to arrange recurring file transfers.

The `gsutil` command offers multiple valuable features, including multi-threaded parallel uploads when many files need to be uploaded, automatic synchronization of a local directory, resumable uploads for large files, and for very large files, it can be broken into smaller parts of the file and upload it in parallel. These features reduce the upload time and use as much of the network connection as possible.

In case of insufficient internet bandwidth to accomplish timely uploads, it can connect directly to the GCP using direct peering or carrier peering. Alternatively, if physical media file need to be sent, there is a third-party service called Offline Media Import / Export that will receive the media and upload it on the user's behalf.

- **Scenario 2: Moving files from other cloud providers**

  In some scenarios, a couple of log files may be stored with other cloud providers. Perhaps the game server is running there and outputs the logs to a storage service on that cloud provider. Or a default storage target service has been used. **Amazon CloudFront** (a Content Delivery Network service), for example, keeps its logs in an Amazon S3 bucket. Luckily, pushing data from Amazon S3 to Cloud Storage is uncomplicated.

  Moving large quantities of files on a daily basis from Amazon S3 to Cloud Storage, can utilize the Storage Transfer Service to transfer files from various sources, including Amazon S3 and HTTP/HTTPs services. It is easy to set up frequently recurring transfers. The Storage Transfer Service supports the multiple advanced options. This service gets the benefits of the large network bandwidth between major cloud providers and uses advanced bandwidth optimization techniques to accomplish very high transfer speeds.

  The guideline is to use this service for 1 TB to 10 TB or more per transfer, since it could save the operational overhead of running the gsutil tool, stated in Scenario 1, on multiple servers. For smaller transfers, or where it needs to move data several times per day, it is easy to utilize the gsutil tool described in *Scenario 1: Transmitting files from on-premises servers.*

- **Scenario 3: Data is already in GCP**

  In some cases, the data is stored in the Cloud Storage by default. For example, the data which is getting generated from the Google Play Store, including reviews, financial reports, installs and crash of applications, and **application not responding (ANR)** reports, are present in a Cloud Storage bucket within the Google Play Developer account. In these scenarios, maintain the data in the original bucket that it was exported to unless there are reasons to transfer them to another bucket.

Asynchronous transfer service pattern

A long term and scalable method need to be implemented for an asynchronous transfer service pattern, where one or more queues are used and messaging to kick off the transfers is based on events or triggers. For example, in case a new log file is written to disk or the source file store, a message is posted to the queue and the workers then initiate the job of effectively transferring that object to Cloud Storage, and deleting the message from the queue only when successfully finished.

Alternative batch pattern: Direct loading from Cloud Storage to BigQuery

It may be good to explore whether it is necessary to use the Cloud Dataflow between Cloud Storage and BigQuery. Directly loading the files from JSON files in the Cloud Storage by providing a schema and starting a load job, can be possible. Or this allows direct query to CSV, JSON, or Cloud Datastore backup files in a Cloud Storage bucket. This may be an adequate solution to get started, but keep in mind the advantages of using the Cloud Dataflow:

- **Transform the data before committing to storage:** For example, Data can be aggregated before loading it into BigQuery, grouping different types of data in separate tables. This can help reduce the BigQuery costs by minimizing the number of rows query against complete data in the table. In a real-time scenario, the Cloud Dataflow can be used to compute leader boards within individual sessions or cohorts, like guilds and teams.

- **Interchangeably use streaming and batch data pipelines written in Cloud Dataflow:** For example, change the data source and data sink from Cloud Pub/Sub to Cloud Storage, and a similar code will work in both scenarios.

- **Be more flexible in terms of database schema:** For example, if additional fields were added to events over time, it is good to add the additional raw JSON data to a catch-all field in the schema and use the BigQuery JSON query functionality to query inside that field. This will allow querying over multiple BigQuery tables, even though the source event would strictly require different schemas. This is displayed in *Figure 7.7*:

	userId	damageRoll	additionalJsonField
	gamer@example.com	13	{"newKey":"yes", "anotherKey":45}
	player@example.com	8	{"newKey":"no", "anotherKey":4, "justAdded": 59}

Figure 7.7: Additional column to capture new event fields in raw JSON

Operational factors for the reference architectures

Once the establishment and pipeline creation are done, it is crucial to monitor the performance and any exceptions that may occur. The Cloud Dataflow Monitoring User Interface provides a graphical view of the data pipeline jobs as well as the important metrics. *Figure 7.8* is a sample screenshot of this in:

Figure 7.8: Built-in Cloud Dataflow monitoring console

The Cloud Dataflow console gives information on the pipeline execution graph along with the current performance statistics, such as the number of messages being processed at each step, the estimated system lag and data watermark.the Cloud

Dataflow is combined with the Stackdriver Logging service to get more detailed information, which is showcased as an example in *Figure 7.9:*

Figure 7.9: Stackdriver Logging is integrated with Cloud Dataflow

Managing and processing logs at scale by leveraging the Cloud Dataflow

Google Cloud Platform (GCP) provides the scalable infrastructure that is needed to handle large and diverse log-analysis operations. This section shows how to enable the GCP to develop analytical pipelines that process log entries from various sources. Log data is combined in ways that help in retrieving meaningful information and persist insights developed from the data, which can be utilized for analysis, review and reporting.

Overview

As an application grows more complex and vital, deriving insights from the data captured in the logs becomes more challenging. Logs are generated from a large number of sources, so that it can be hard to collate them and retrieve for valuable information. Building, operating, and maintaining one's own infrastructure to study these log data at scale can involve extensive expertise in running distributed systems and storage. A dedicated infrastructure like this often requires a one-time capital expense, resulting in fixed capacity, which makes it hard to scale beyond the original investment. These limitations can influence the business because they lead to go-slows in generating meaningful and actionable insights from the collected data.

The solution showcased below shows how to move past the limitations described above, by using the GCP products, as demonstrated in the following diagram:

Figure 7.10: *Application Log Data Processing*

In this solution, a number of sample microservices run on **Google Kubernetes Engine (GKE)** to implement a website. Stackdriver Logging gathers the logs from these services and keeps them in Cloud Storage buckets. The Cloud Dataflow processes those logs by extracting the metadata and computing the basic aggregations. The Cloud Dataflow pipeline is considered to process the log data daily, to generate aggregate metrics for multiple key metrics like the server response times, based on the logs for each day. Further, the output from Cloud Dataflow is pushed into BigQuery tables, where it can be processed to provide business intelligence. This solution also explains how a pipeline can be changed to execute in streaming mode, for low-latency, asynchronous log processing.

This section delivers a sample Cloud Dataflow pipeline, a sample web application, configuration information, and the phases to execute the sample.

Let's jump to the Cloud Dataflow pipeline. Once enough traffic is permitted to reach the services, start with the dataflow pipeline. For this use case, consider that the Cloud Dataflow pipeline is run in batch mode. The pipeline.sh shell script manually initiates the pipeline:

```
cd ../dataflow
```
```
./pipeline.sh $PROJECT_ID $DATASET_NAME $BUCKET_NAME run
```

Understanding the Cloud Dataflow pipeline

Cloud Dataflow can be used for different types of data processing tasks. The Cloud Dataflow SDK provides a unified data model that can signify a data set of any size, containing an unbounded or infinite data set from a nonstop updating data source; it is ideal for working with the log data in this solution. The Cloud Dataflow managed service can run both, batch and streaming jobs. This means utilizing a single codebase for asynchronous or synchronous, real-time, event-driven data processing.

The Cloud Dataflow SDK offers simple data representations through a particular collection class named PCollection. The SDK provides built-in and customized data transforms through the PTransform class. In Cloud Dataflow, transforms correspond to the processing logic of a pipeline. Transforms can be applied for a range of processing operations such as joining data, computing values mathematically, filtering data output, or converting data from one format to another.

The following diagram represents the pipeline operations for the log data stored in Cloud Storage:

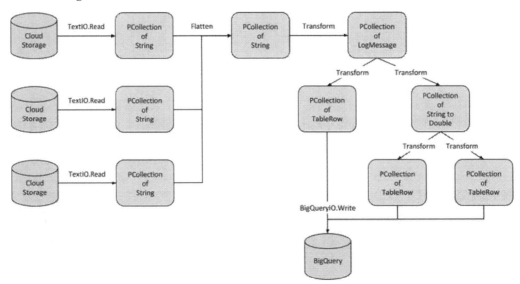

Figure 7.11: *Pipeline Operation to Process and Store Log Data*

Although the figure seems complex, Cloud Dataflow makes it easy to build and use the pipeline. The following sections describe the specific operations at each stage of the pipeline.

Receiving the data

The pipeline begins by consuming the input from the Cloud Storage buckets, which contain the logs from the three microservices in this example. Each set of the logs turn into a PCollection of String elements, where each element relates to a single LogEntry object. In the following code snippet, homeLogs, browseLogs, and locateLogs are of the type PCollection<String>:

```
homeLogs = p.apply("homeLogsTextRead", TextIO.read().from(options.
getHomeLogSource()));

browseLogs = p.apply("browseLogsTextRead", TextIO.read().from(options.
getBrowseLogSource()));

locateLogs = p.apply("locateLogsTextRead", TextIO.read().from(options.
getLocateLogSource()));
```

In order to deal with the challenges of a constantly updating data set, the Dataflow SDK utilizes a technique called 'windowing'. Windowing operates by logically subdividing the data in a `PCollection` with respect to the timestamps of its individual elements. Because the source type is `TextIO` in this case, all the objects are firstly read into a single global window, which is the default behavior.

Collecting the data into objects

The next step merges the individual microservice `PCollections` into a single `PCollection`, using the flatten process:

```
PCollection<String> allLogs = PCollectionList
    .of(homeLogs)
    .and(browseLogs)
    .and(locateLogs)
    .apply(Flatten.<String>pCollections());
```

This operation is valuable, since each source `PCollection` consists of the same data type and uses the same, global windowing strategy. Although the sources and structure of each log is the same in solution, this approach could be extended into one where the source and structure are distinct.

With a single `PCollection` generated, now process the individual String elements by using a custom transform that performs several steps on the log entry. Here are the steps demonstrated in the following diagram:

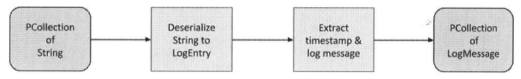

Figure 7.12: Custom Processing of Log Message

Deserialize the JSON string into a Stackdriver Logging `LogEntry` Java object. Extract the timestamp from the `LogEntry` metadata. Extract the following individual fields from the log message by utilizing regular expressions: timestamp, `responseTime`, `httpStatusCode`, `httpMethod`, source IP address, and destination endpoint. Use these fields to make a timestamped LogMessage custom object. Output the `LogMessage` objects, into a new `PCollection`.

The following code performs the steps:

```
PCollection<LogMessage> allLogMessages = allLogs
    .apply("allLogsToLogMessage", ParDo.of(new
EmitLogMessageFn(outputWithTimestamp, options.getLogRegexPattern())));
```

Aggregating the data by days

The goal is to process the elements on a daily basis, to produce aggregated metrics based on logs for each day. To accomplish this, aggregation needs a windowing function that can bifurcate the data by day, which is possible because each `LogMessage` in the `PCollection` has a timestamp. After the Cloud Dataflow partitions, the `PCollection` along daily boundaries, operations that support windowed `PCollections`, will honor the windowing scheme:

```
PCollection<LogMessage> allLogMessagesDaily = allLogMessages

    .apply("allLogMessageToDaily", Window.<LogMessage>into(FixedWindows.
of(Duration.standardDays(1))));
```

With a single, windowed `PCollection`, now calculate the aggregate daily metrics around all the three multi-day log sources by executing a single Cloud Dataflow job:

```
PCollection<KV<String,Double>> destMaxRespTime = destResponse
TimeCollection

  .apply(Max.<String>doublesPerKey());

 // .apply(Combine.<String,Double,Double>perKey(new Max.doublesPerKey()));


PCollection<KV<String,Double>> destMeanRespTime = destResponseTime
Collection

  .apply(Mean.<String,Double>perKey());
```

First, a transform uses the `LogMessage` objects as an input and then outputs a `PCollection` of key-value pairs that map the destination endpoints as keys to the response time values, as showcased in the following diagram:

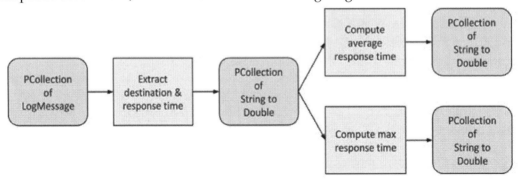

Figure 7.13: PCollection of Key Value Pair

Using that `PCollection`, two aggregate metrics can be calculated, which are - maximum response time per destination and average response time per destination. Because the `PCollection` is still partitioned by day, the output of each computation will signify a single day's log data. This indicates that the two final `PCollection`, which contain the maximum response time per destination per day and one contains the average response time per destination per day.

Loading the data into BigQuery

The last step in the pipeline outputs the resultant `PCollection` to BigQuery for downstream analysis and data warehousing.

First, the pipeline transforms the `PCollection` that contains the `LogMessage` objects for all log sources into a `PCollection` of BigQuery `TableRow` objects. This step is needed in order to utilize the built-in support in the Cloud Dataflow to use BigQuery as a sink for a pipeline:

```
PCollection<TableRow> logsAsTableRows = allLogMessagesDaily
  .apply("logMessageToTableRow", ParDo.of(new LogMessageTableRowFn()));
```

BigQuery tables need defined schemas. For this example, the schemas are defined in `LogAnalyticsPipelineOptions.java` by utilizing a default-value annotation. For example, the schema for the maximum-response-time table is defined as below:

```
@Default.String("destination:STRING,aggResponseTime:FLOAT")
```

An operation on the `PCollection` that consists of the aggregated response-time values, transforms them into `PCollection` of `TableRow` objects, utilizing the appropriate schemas and creating the tables, in case if they are not present:

```
logsAsTableRows.apply("allLogsToBigQuery", BigQueryIO.writeTableRows()
  .to(options.getAllLogsTableName())
  .withSchema(allLogsTableSchema)
  .withWriteDisposition(BigQueryIO.Write.WriteDisposition.WRITE_APPEND)
    .withCreateDisposition(BigQueryIO.Write.CreateDisposition.CREATE_IF_
NEEDED));
```

This solution continuously appends new data to the already present data. This is a proper selection, since this pipeline runs in a periodic manner to analyze new log data. However, it can be possible to truncate the existing table data or only write to the table if it is empty, if one of those options makes more common sense in a distinct scenario.

Querying the data from BigQuery

The BigQuery console enables to run queries against the output data and integrate seamlessly to third-party business intelligence tools such as Tableau and QlikView for additional analysis:

1. Go to the GCP Console and click on BigQuery.
2. Select the project processing-logs-at-high-scale and click the dataset `processing_logs_using_dataflow`.

3. Select `all_logs_table`, and in the data pane, select **Preview**, to view a sample of the data in the all logs table.

4. In the **Query editor**, put the below query:

SELECT * FROM `processing_logs_using_dataflow.max_response_time_table`

ORDER BY aggResponseTime DESC

LIMIT 1000;

5. In order to execute the query, click on **Run**. The following screenshot showcases the sample output from the Big Query Console.

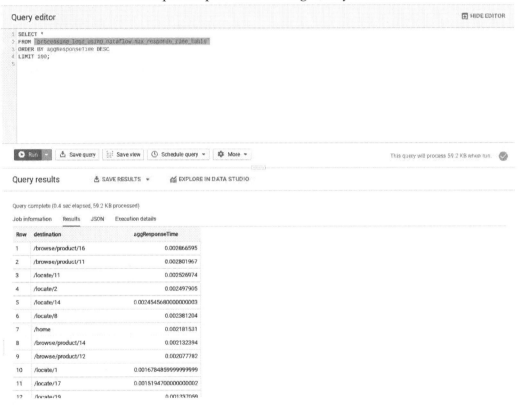

Figure 7.14: Big Query Output

Using a streaming pipeline

The sample includes support for executing the pipeline in one of the modes, which could be batch or streaming mode. There are very simple steps to change the pipeline from batch to streaming. First, the Stackdriver Logging setup exports the logging information to Cloud Pub/Sub instead of Cloud Storage. The following step is to switch the input sources in the Cloud Dataflow pipeline from Cloud Storage to Cloud Pub/Sub topic subscriptions. Each input source requires one subscription:

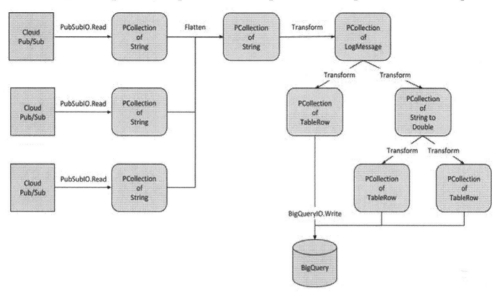

Figure 7.15: *Real Time Processing of Log Message*

SDK commands, which are in use in `logging.sh.`, can be seen

The `PCollection` objects created from the Cloud Pub/Sub input data, use an unbounded global window. However, the individual entries already include the timestamps. This indicates that it may not be necessary to pull out the timestamp data from the Stackdriver Logging `LogEntry` object; by just extracting the log timestamps to create the custom `LogMessage` objects as shown below:

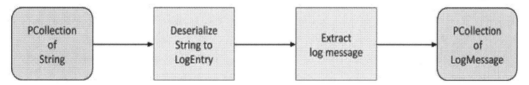

Figure 7.16: *Log Message Processing*

Other than the above-mentioned changes, the rest of the pipeline is intact as-is, which includes downstream flatten, transformation, aggregation, and output operations.

Monitoring the pipeline

When a Cloud Dataflow job is executed, the GCP Console can be leveraged to monitor the progress and view information of every stage in the pipeline.

The below screenshot illustrates the GCP Console while executing a sample pipeline:

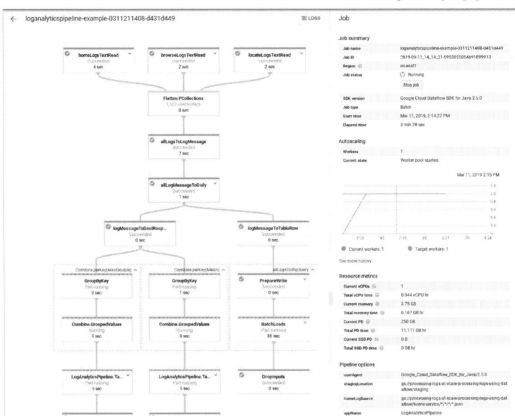

Figure 7.17: Dataflow Pipeline Monitoring

Cleaning up

There are two ways to clean up the resources, which are mentioned below.

Delete the project

Deleting a project has the following effects:

- **Everything in the project is deleted:** If an existing project is used for this example, while deleting it, any other works related to this project will be deleted.

- **Custom project IDs are lost:** While creating this project, a custom project ID is created, which can be used in the future. In order to preserve the URLs that use the project ID, such as an appspot.com URL, delete the required resources within the project, instead of deleting the whole project.

1. Login to GCP Console page and then Navigate to the **Manage resources** page in the GCP Console.

2. In the project list, select the project that needs to be deleted and then select **Delete** to delete the project.

3. In the popup screen, enter the project ID, and then click **Shut down** in order to delete the project.

Removing all the components

Some environment variables are used ,which are still set to the values used in the setup:

1. Remove the BigQuery dataset:

   ```
   bq rm $DATASET_NAME
   ```

2. Disable the Cloud Logging exports. This step removes the exports and the specific Cloud Storage bucket:

   ```
   cd ../services
   
   ./logging.sh $PROJECT_ID $BUCKET_NAME batch down
   ```

3. Erase the Compute Engine cluster, which is used to execute the example web applications:

   ```
   /cluster.sh $PROJECT_ID $CLUSTER_NAME down
   ```

Product recommendations using machine learning on Compute Engine

GCP is extensively used to develop a scalable, efficient and effective service for providing relevant product recommendations to users in an online store.

In the current world, competition in online-selling sites is at a peak and has never been as intense as it is today. Customers pay more money across all their providers, but they spend less per retailer. The average size of a single cart has reduced, partly because the competition is simply one click away. Providing relevant recommendations to potential customers can play a major role in converting the shoppers to buyers and growing up the average order size.

After going through this section, it is easy to set up an environment that supports a basic recommendation engine that can expand and improve, based on the needs of a particular workload. Setting up a recommendation engine on GCP delivers additional flexibility and scalability in the complete solutions.

In this implementation, it has been shown how a real estate rental company can compute appropriate recommendations and introduce them to the customers who are accessing a website.

Scenario

John is searching for a house to rent for his vacation. He has a profile on a vacation rentals portal and has previously rented and rated multiple holiday packages. John is looking for recommendations based on his likings and tastes. The system should already know John's tastes. He looks to like the type of house, based on his rating page. The system also should be capable of recommending somewhat similar, as showcased below.

Figure 7.18: Recommendation Output

Solution overview

In order to deliver these recommendations, whether in real-time, while customer's access and browse or through email later, multiple events need to happen. First, since there is some little known information about the users on his tastes and preferences, base recommendations might be on the item attributes alone. But the system requires to be able to learn from the users, gathering data about their tastes and preferences. Over time and with enough data, ML algorithms can be used to perform useful analysis and deliver meaningful recommendations. More users' inputs can also enhance the results, making sure the system is retrained periodically. This explanation deals with a recommendations system that already has enough data to benefit from the ML algorithms.

A recommendation engine usually processes data over the below mentioned four phases:

Figure 7.19: Recommendation Engine Phases

The architecture of a system like this can be symbolized by the following diagram:

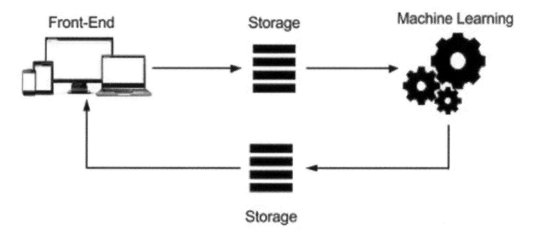

Figure 7.20: *Architecture Diagram*

Each step can be customized to meet the requirements. The system comprises of:

1. A scalable front-end system, to collect and record user interactions.

2. Permanent data storage that can be retrieved by a machine learning platform. Data loading into this storage can consist of multiple steps, such as import-export and transformation of the data.

3. A robust machine learning platform that can evaluate the existing content to generate relevant recommendations.

4. Storage that can be used by the frontend, in real-time or later, based on the suitability needs for recommendations.

Choosing the components

This implementation utilizes App Engine, Cloud SQL, and Apache Spark running on App Engine, using Cloud Dataproc, to accomplish a good compromise between speed, simplicity, cost control, and accuracy.

App Engine is capable of handling tens of thousands of queries per second, with minimum management required. Whether it is making the website or saving the data to a backend storage, App Engine enables writing and deploying code to the production environment in a few seconds.

Cloud SQL also proposes effortlessness of deployment. Cloud SQL has the ability to scale up to 32-core virtual machines, with up to 208 GB of RAM and can expand the storage on demand to 10 TB with 30 IOPS per GB and thousands of concurrent connections. These measurements are enough for the example in this implementation and for a huge number of real-world recommendation engines. Cloud SQL also offers the benefit of being directly read from Spark.

Spark poses a greater performance than a standard Hadoop setup. Spark is generally 10 to 100 times faster than the standard Hadoop. With Spark MLlib, analysis of hundreds of millions of ratings in minutes can be done, which enhances the agility of the recommendations, allowing the administrator to execute the algorithm more frequently. Spark consumes the memory for computing as far as possible to reduce the round trips to the disk. Spark also makes sure to reduce I/O. This explanation uses the Compute Engine to host the analysis infrastructure. Compute Engine facilitates and enables price optimization of the analysis to as low as possible via its per-second, on-demand pricing.

The following figure maps to the earlier architecture diagram, but illustrates the technology at use for each stage:

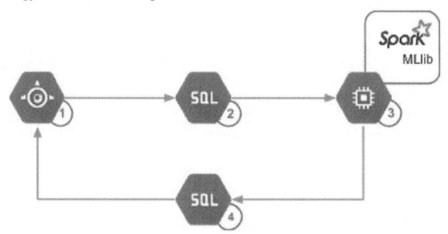

Figure 7.21: *Usage of Google Cloud Services*

Collecting the data

A recommendation engine has the ability to gather data around the users based on their implicit *behavior* or their *explicit* input.

Behavior data is simple to collect, because of keeping logs of the user activities. This data collection is also straightforward because it doesn't need any extra action from the user, since they are already using the application. Demerits of this approach are that it is difficult to analyze. For example, taking out the interesting logs from the less-interesting ones can be bulky.

Input data can be tougher to gather, since the users need to perform extra actions, like writing a review. Users do not like to perform these activities to provide the necessary data for various reasons. But when it comes to identifying user preferences, such results are quite precise.

Storing the data

The more data available for the algorithms, the clearer the recommendations will be. This indicates that since lots of data is captured, any recommendations project can rapidly convert into a big data project.

Type of storage of the data is depends on the type of data that is being used to create the recommendations. A NoSQL database, a standard SQL database, or even some kind of object storage can be considered for use. Each of these choices is viable, depending on whether we are gathering user input or behavior and on elements such as ease of implementation, the volume of data that the storage can manage, alignment with the other environment and portability.

When keeping user ratings or events, a scalable and managed database reduces the volume of the operational tasks needed and enables to concentrating on the recommendation. Cloud SQL serves both the requirements, and also makes it simple to load the data directly from Spark.

The following example code illustrates the schemas of the Cloud SQL tables. The `Accommodation` table signifies the rental property and the Rating table signifies a user's rating for a particular property:

```
CREATE TABLE Accommodation
(
  id varchar(255),
  title varchar(255),
  location varchar(255),
  price int,
  rooms int,
  rating float,
  type varchar(255),
  PRIMARY KEY (ID)
);


CREATE TABLE Rating
(
  userId varchar(255),
  accoId varchar(255),
  rating int,
  PRIMARY KEY(accoId, userId),
```

```
    FOREIGN KEY (accoId)
      REFERENCES Accommodation(id)
);
```

Spark can consume data from multiple sources; some of them are Hadoop HDFS or Cloud Storage. In this example, the data is received directly from Cloud SQL by consuming the Spark **Java Database Connectivity (JDBC)** connector. Since Spark jobs execute parallelly, the connector must be residing on each cluster instances.

Generating the insights from data

An understanding of the application is required in order to design the insight and analytics. Couple of these requirements include, firstly the timeliness of a recommendation, which means that how speedily does the application need to show the recommendations. Secondly, the approach to filter the required data, which means that the application will base its recommendation on the user's preferences alone, pivot the data based on what other users believe, or pivot on which products logically fit together?

- **Understanding timeliness implementation:** The first use case to consider in analyzing the data is how quickly it needs to present the recommendations to the end user. If it requires introducing the recommendations immediately when the user is seeing a product, it will require a more agile analysis compared to dispatching an email to the customer that comprises recommendations at some later point of time or date.

  o Data gets processed when it gets generated in Real-time systems. This type of approach generally involves tools that can process and analyze the streams of events. To provide in-the-moment recommendation, a real-time system will be required.

  o To perform Batch analysis, data needs to be processed periodically. This method implies that sufficient data needs to be generated for the analysis to be relevant, for example daily sales volume. A batch system can enable sending an e-mail at a later point of time or date.

  o Near-real-time analysis helps to gather data quickly so that analytics can be refreshed every few minutes or seconds. A near-real-time system will be helpful for offering recommendations through the same browsing session.

A recommendation can be a part of any of these three timeliness classifications but, for an online sales tool, think about something between near-real-time and batch processing, depending on the volume of application traffic and user input. The platform generating the analysis could work directly, based on a database, where the data is saved or on a dump saved periodically in persistent storage.

- **Filtering the data:** The most important component of developing a recommendation *engine* is filtering. The most common methods include:
  - o **Content-based:** A standard, recommended product has related attributes to what the user views or likes.
  - o **Cluster:** Recommended products can be clubbed together; it does not depend on what other users have done.
  - o **Collaborative:** Other users, who like the same products the user views or likes, also loved a recommended product.

While GCP has the ability to support any of these methods, this solution focuses on collaborative filtering, which is implemented by using Apache Spark.

Collaborative filtering enables making the product attributes abstract and create predictions based on user tastes. The output of this filtering assumes that two different users, who liked the same products in the past, will probably like the same ones now.

Data can be represented for ratings or interactions as a set of matrices, with products and users as dimensions. Collaborative filtering attempts to predict the missing cells in the matrix showcased below for a particular user-product pair. The two matrices mentioned below are related, but the second is generated from the first by substituting the existing ratings with the number one and missing ratings with the number zero. The resultant matrix is a truth table, showcased below, where a number one represents a contact by users with a product:

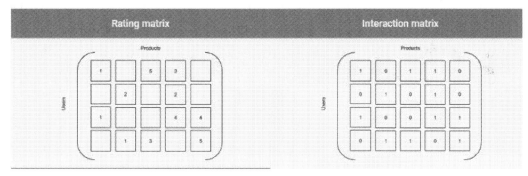

Figure 7.22: Resultant Matrix Truth Table

There are two separate approaches to apply collaborative filtering:

- First one is that memory-based filtering computes similarities between products or users.
- Second one is that model-based filtering attempts to learn the underlying pattern that explains how users' rate or interact with items.

This example leverages the model-based approach, where users have rated items.

Analysis features for this implementation can be availed via PySpark, which offers a Python interface to the Spark programming language. There are multiple options available, which includes Scala or Java.

Training the models

Spark MLlib employs the **Alternating Least Squares (ALS)** algorithm to train the models. Multiple combinations of the below parameters are used from the list to make the best agreement between variance and bias:

- **Rank:** The number of unknown elements that led a user to give a rating. These could consist of factors like age, gender, or location. The greater the rank, the better the recommendation will be, to a certain extent. Starting with 5 and increasing by 5 till the recommendation improvement rate slows down, memory and CPU permitting, is a nice approach.

- **Lambda:** A regularization parameter to avoid overfitting, signified by high variance, and low bias. Variance symbolizes how much the predictions vary at a given point, over various runs, compared to the theoretically correct value for that particular point. Bias signifies about how far away the generated predictions are from the true value, which are being predicted. Overfitting occurs when the model performs well on training data with known noise, but the performance goes down with the actual testing data. The greater the lambda, the lower the overfitting; but the greater the bias. Values of 0.01, 1 and 10 are decent values to test.

The following diagram showcases the connection between variance and bias. The bullseye represents the value that the algorithm is trying to predict:

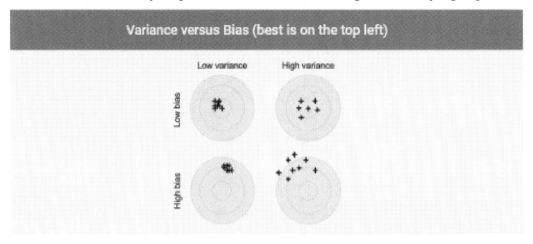

Figure 7.23: Comparison of Variance vs. Bias

- **Iteration:** The number of times the training will execute. In this example, 5, 10, and 20 iterations are executed for a variety of patterns of rank and lambda.

The below code snippet demonstrates how to start an ALS model training run in Spar:

```
from pyspark.mllib.recommendation import ALS
model = ALS.train(training, rank = 10, iterations = 5, lambda_=0.01)
```

Finding the right model

The collaborative filtering utilizing the ALS algorithm is built on three distinct sets of data:

- **Training set:** This set consists of the data with a known output. This set would look like a perfect result. In this example, it consists of the user ratings.
- **Validating set:** This set consists of the data that will improve training of the model to choose the best combination of parameters in order to pick the best model.
- **Testing set:** This set consists of the data that will be utilized to evaluate the performance of the best trained model. This would be equivalent to executing the analysis in a real-world example.

In order to come up with the best model, the **root-mean-square error (RMSE)** needs to be calculated, which is based on the model that was calculated, the validation set, and its size. The smaller the RMSE, the better the model.

Delivering the recommendations

To make the results available to the user immediately and easily, it needs to be inserted into a database that can be queried as and when required, on demand. Again, Cloud SQL is a fantastic choice here. From Spark 1.4, the results can be written off the prediction, directly to the database from PySpark.

The schema of the Recommendation table looks like the below mentioned example:

```
CREATE TABLE Recommendation
(
  userId varchar(255),
  accoId varchar(255),
  prediction float,
  PRIMARY KEY(userId, accoId),
  FOREIGN KEY (accoId)
    REFERENCES Accommodation(id)
);
```

Code walkthrough

The following section describes the walks through the code to train the models.

Fetching the data from Cloud SQL

The Spark SQL context enables seamless connection to a Cloud SQL instance via the JDBC connector. The loaded data is in the DataFrame format.

```
jdbcUrl    = 'jdbc:mysql://%s:3306/%s?user=%s&password=%s' % (CLOUDSQL_
INSTANCE_IP, CLOUDSQL_DB_NAME, CLOUDSQL_USER, CLOUDSQL_PWD)

dfAccos = sqlContext.read.jdbc(url=jdbcUrl, table=TABLE_ITEMS)

dfRates = sqlContext.read.jdbc(url=jdbcUrl, table=TABLE_RATINGS)
```

Translate the DataFrame to RDD and generate the various datasets

Spark utilizes a concept called a **Resilient Distributed Dataset (RDD)**, which enables working on the elements parallelly. RDDs are read-only collections generated from persistent storage. Since they can be handled and managed in memory, they are suitable for iterative processing.

As explained earlier, to get the best model to make prediction, datasets need to be broken into three distinct sets. The below-mentioned code utilizes a helper function that randomly divides the non-overlapping values with a 60/20/20 percentage basis:

```
rddTraining, rddValidating, rddTesting = dfRates.rdd.randomSplit([6,2,2])
```

Please note that it is vital to create the Rating table with the columns as per the order: `accoId, userId, rating`. ALS needs to work with specified product-user pairs to make its prediction. In case if this is not the scenario, then either alter the database, or use a call to map on the RDD to arrange the columns in the correct way.

Train models based on various parameters

As explained earlier. when utilizing the ALS method, the system requires to work with the rank, regularization, and iteration parameters to come up with the best model. The ratings exist, so the outcomes of the train function must be compared to the validation set. We need to be make sure that the user's tastes are also in the training set. The below-mentioned code is for training the model.

```
for cRank, cRegul, cIter in itertools.product(ranks, reguls, iters):

    model = ALS.train(rddTraining, cRank, cIter, float(cRegul))
    dist = howFarAreWe(model, rddValidating, nbValidating)
```

```
if dist < finalDist:
    print("Best so far:%f" % dist)
    finalModel = model
    finalRank  = cRank
    finalRegul = cRegul
    finalIter  = cIter
    finalDist  = dist
```

Please note that the howFarAreWe function utilizes the model to forecast the ratings on the validation dataset by means of the user-product pairs only:

```
def howFarAreWe(model, against, sizeAgainst):
    # Ignore the rating column
    againstNoRatings = against.map(lambda x: (int(x[0]), int(x[1])) )

    # Keep the rating to compare against
    againstWiRatings = against.map(lambda x: ((int(x[0]),int(x[1])),
int(x[2])) )

    # Make a prediction and map it for later comparison
    # The map has to be ((user,product), rating) not ((product,user), rating)
    predictions = model.predictAll(againstNoRatings).map(lambda p: (
(p[0],p[1]), p[2]) )

    # Returns the pairs (prediction, rating)
    predictionsAndRatings = predictions.join(againstWiRatings).values()

    # Returns the variance
    return sqrt(predictionsAndRatings.map(lambda s: (s[0] - s[1]) **
2).reduce(add) / float(sizeAgainst))
```

Calculating top predictions for the user

Now that a model that can provide a satisfactory prediction is present, it can be used to find out what the user is likely to be interested in, based on their tastes and ratings by others with related tastes. In this step, the matrix- mapping that was described earlier, can been seen. The below-mentioned code is for building the model.

```
# Build our model with the best found values
# Rating, Rank, Iteration, Regulation
model = ALS.train(rddTraining, BEST_RANK, BEST_ITERATION, BEST_REGULATION)
# Calculate all predictions
predictions = model.predictAll(pairsPotential).map(lambda p: (str(p[0]),
str(p[1]), float(p[2])))

# Take the top 5 ones
topPredictions = predictions.takeOrdered(5, key=lambda x: -x[2])

print(topPredictions)
schema = StructType([StructField("userId", StringType(), True),
StructField("accoId", StringType(), True), StructField("prediction",
FloatType(), True)])

dfToSave = sqlContext.createDataFrame(topPredictions, schema)

dfToSave.write.jdbc(url=jdbcUrl, table=TABLE_RECOMMENDATIONS,
mode='overwrite')
```

Saving the top predictions

Since a list of all the predictions is available now, the top 10 can be saved in Cloud SQL so that the system can suggest some recommendations to the user. For example, the best time to utilize these predictions might be when the user logs on to the site.

```
dfToSave = sqlContext.createDataFrame(topPredictions, schema)

dfToSave.write.jdbc(url=jdbcUrl, table=TABLE_RECOMMENDATIONS,
mode='overwrite')
```

Executing the solution

The final SQL code receives the top recommendation from the database and presents it on John's welcome page.

The query, when executed in the GCP Console or a MySQL client, returns a result like the following example:

```
+----+------------------------+-------+----------------+
| id | title                  | type  | prediction     |
+----+------------------------+-------+----------------+
| 66 | Beautiful Private Villa | house | 4.69887483663 |
| 49 | Big Private Villa      | house | 4.68217603492 |
| 76 | Pleasant Calm Villa    | house | 4.65072189683 |
| 61 | Large Calm Place       | house | 4.58421728982 |
| 99 | Pleasant Quiet Place   | house | 4.45886076547 |
+----+------------------------+-------+----------------+
```

Figure 7.24: MySQL Output

In the website, the same query can improve the welcome page and enhance the likelihood of the conversion of a visitor to a customer:

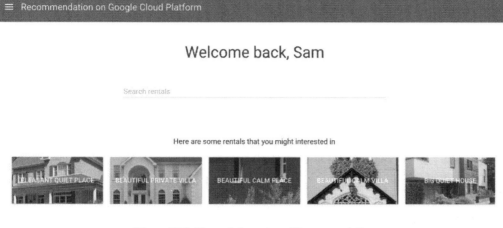

Figure 7.25: *Upgraded version of Recommendation*

This seems to be quite in line with what Sam likes, based on what the system already knew about Sam, as discussed in the scenario description.

Conclusion

In this chapter, the actual industry wise implementation of the GCP data analytics components have been explained. Real-time data streaming to process logs, Machine Learning implementation and Game Logs processing with GCP services has been explained in detail. We can conclude that GCP provides powerful and scalable data analytics services, which can be used to perform end-to-end implementation.

Questions

1. What are the different steps involved during the machine learning process?

2. What are the different ways to ingest, store and generate insights on the mobile games data?

3. Explain best and efficient ways to process real-time generated logs from an application.

Made in the USA
Coppell, TX
11 February 2020